Financial Exclusion and the Poverty Trap

The persistence of poverty hurts us all, and attacking poverty is a major policy objective everywhere. In Britain, the main political parties have an anti-poverty mandate and in particular an agreed commitment to eliminate child poverty by 2020, but there is controversy over how this should be done. This book addresses one of the main causes of poverty, *financial exclusion* – the inability to access finance from the high-street banks. People on low or irregular incomes typically have to resort to loan sharks, 'doorstep lenders' and other informal credit sources, a predicament which makes escape from the poverty trap doubly difficult.

Over the last fifteen years, a strategy for escaping from the poverty trap has been implemented, known in the UK as *community development financial institutions* (CDFIs): typically non-profit lending institutions focussed on the financially excluded, and seeking to learn from the achievements of microfinance around the world. Focussing on the period 2007–09, during which the UK went into a global recession, this book investigates how CDFIs work and how well they have helped low-income people and businesses to weather that recession. Based on a study of eight CDFIs in four UK cities, we ask: what ideas for overcoming financial exclusion have worked well, and which have worked badly? What can we learn from the experience of these CDFIs which can help reduce poverty in this country and globally?

We assess the impact of CDFIs using a range of indicators (including income, assets, education, health) and ask what changes in policy both by CDFIs and government agencies (for example, benefits agencies) might be able to increase impact. Some of the key lessons are: CDFIs need to work with appropriate partners to build up savings capacity in their clients; the community environment is vital in determining who escapes from the poverty trap; and CDFIs can never function properly unless they learn how to control their overdue debts.

This book will be vital reading for those concerned with social policy, microfinance and anti-poverty policies in industrialised countries and around the world.

Pamela Lenton is Lecturer in Economics at the University of Sheffield, UK.

Paul Mosley is Professor of Economics at the University of Sheffield, UK.

Routledge advances in social economics
Edited by John B. Davis
Marquette University

This series presents new advances and developments in social economics thinking on a variety of subjects that concern the link between social values and economics. Need, justice and equity, gender, cooperation, work poverty, the environment, class, institutions, public policy and methodology are some of the most important themes. Among the orientations of the authors are social economist, institutionalist, humanist, solidarist, cooperatist, radical and Marxist, feminist, post-Keynesian, behaviouralist and environmentalist. The series offers new contributions from today's most foremost thinkers on the social character of the economy.

Publishes in conjunction with the Association of Social Economics.
Previous books published in the series include:

1 **Social Economics**
   Premises, findings and policies
   Edited by Edward J. O'Boyle

2 **The Environmental Consequences of Growth**
   Steady-state economics as an alternative to ecological decline
   Douglas Booth

3 **The Human Firm**
   A socio-economic analysis of its behaviour and potential in a new economic age
   John Tomer

4 **Economics for the Common Good**
   Two centuries of economic thought in the humanist tradition
   Mark A. Lutz

5 **Working Time**
   International trends, theory and policy perspectives
   Edited by Lonnie Golden and Deborah M. Figart

6 **The Social Economics of Health Care**
John Davis

7 **Reclaiming Evolution**
A Marxist institutionalist dialogue on social change
William M. Dugger and Howard J. Sherman

8 **The Theory of the Individual in Economics**
Identity and value
John Davis

9 **Boundaries of Clan and Color**
Transnational comparisons of inter-group disparity
Edited by William Darity Jnr. and Ashwini Deshpande

10 **Living Wage Movements**
Global perspectives
Edited by Deborah M. Figart

11 **Ethics and the Market**
Insights from social economics
Edited by Betsy Jane Clary, Wilfred Dolfsma and Deborah M. Figart

12 **Political Economy of Consumer Behaviour**
Contesting consumption
Bruce Pietrykowski

13 **Socio-Economic Mobility and Low-Status Minorities**
Slow roads to progress
Jacob Meerman

14 **Global Social Economy**
Development, work and policy
Edited by John B. Davis

15 **The Economics of Social Responsibility**
The world of social enterprises
Edited by Carlo Borzaga and Leonardo Becchetti

16 **Elements of an Evolutionary Theory of Welfare**
Assessing welfare when preferences change
Martin Binder

17 **Financial Exclusion and the Poverty Trap**
Overcoming deprivation in the inner city
Pamela Lenton and Paul Mosley

Financial Exclusion and the Poverty Trap

Overcoming deprivation in the inner city

Pamela Lenton and Paul Mosley

Routledge
Taylor & Francis Group

LONDON AND NEW YORK

First published 2012
by Routledge
2 Park Square, Milton Park, Abingdon, Oxon OX14 4RN

Simultaneously published in the USA and Canada
by Routledge
711 Third Avenue, New York, NY 10017

Routledge is an imprint of the Taylor & Francis Group, an informa business

British Library Cataloguing in Publication Data
A catalogue record for this book is available from the British Library

Library of Congress Cataloging-in-Publication Data
Mosley, Paul.
Financial exclusion and the poverty trap : overcoming deprivation in the
inner city / by Paul Mosley and Pamela Lenton.
  p. cm.
Includes bibliographical references and index.
  1. Community development, Urban–Great Britain. 2. Community
development corporations–Great Britain. 3. Urban policy–Great Britain.
4. Urban poor–Great Britain. I. Lenton, Pamela, 1959– II. Title.
HN400.C6M674 2011
362.5′525–dc22
                                                     2011013970

ISBN: 978-0-415-46039-2 (hbk)
ISBN: 978-0-203-80237-3 (ebk)

Typeset in Times
by Wearset Ltd, Boldon, Tyne and Wear

Printed and bound in Great Britain by
TJI Digital, Padstow, Cornwall

Contents

List of figures ix

List of tables x

List of case studies xii

Preface xiii

1 Introduction 1

Background 1

*The emergence and transformation of community development
    finance organisations 6*

2 Scope and method 17

3 Financial performance of CDFIs 25

Outreach 25

Case-study organisations 28

CDFI architecture and the determinants of outreach 35

Summary of argument 46

4 CDFI clients: impacts on individuals 47

Approach 47

Business-lending clients 48

Personal-lending clients 63

*Impacts on business and personal-lending clients
    compared 66*

Determinants of the process of exit from poverty 71

*Conclusion: is a 'win–win' technology available for
    CDFIs? 87*

5   CDFI clients: community-level impacts   89

Approach 89
Investment in social networks: case studies 92
The formation of social capital networks and trust: explanatory
*   hypotheses 106*
Microfinance and community-building in ethnic-minority
*   communities 111*
Conclusion 128

6   Fiscal impacts   131

Introduction 131
Policy towards CDFIs and welfare benefits, and their
*   interrelationship 132*
Impact of the welfare system on CDFIs 141
Implications and conclusions 149

7   Where next?   153

The impact of CDFIs: summary of argument 153
What CDFIs need to do 154
What other institutions need to (and are able to) do:
*   the institutional and policy context 155*

Appendix: transitions into and out of poverty, 2007–09   163

Notes   184
Bibliography   199
Index   209

Figures

1.1 Poverty in the UK: share of the population with below half
average income, 1960–2009   5
2.1 Major areas of financial exclusion (2004), with survey areas
superimposed   18
2.2 The conventional model of the impact chain   22
2.3a Glasgow: locations of Scotcash and DSL clients   22
2.3b Location of Derby Loans clients   23
2.3c Location of Moneyline Yorkshire clients   24
3.1 Distinctive capabilities, costs and financial performance   28
3.2 Cost functions for four CDFIs, 1995–2009   40
4.1 Business-lending CDFIs: impact (2007–09) in relation to initial
income (2007)   52
4.2 Response to shocks as a determinant of client trajectories   54
4.3 Business-lending and consumer-lending CDFIs as contributors
to ladders out of poverty   71
4.4 Glasgow: mapping of CDFI clients and doorstep lenders in
relation to zones of multiple deprivation   74
4.5 Scatterplots of saving in relation to income   79
5.1 The possible two-way relationship between microfinance clients
and social networks   92
5.2 Social capital creation through CDFIs in Glasgow   100
5.3 Birmingham 2007–09: CDFI lending to BMEs in relation to
deprivation indicators   114
6.1 The crowding-out and pinning-in effects in business and
consumer CDFIs   138
6.2 Scatters of working tax credit in relation to change in income,
2007–09   143

Tables

1.1	Some 'pioneer' CDFIs of the 1990s	8
1.2	Descriptives of CDFIs, 2003–09	14
2.1	Sample sizes	20
2.2	Targeting accuracy for CDFI loans: sample data	21
3.1	Outreach of CDFIs and possible determinants	36
3.2	Case-study organisations: loan delinquency and possible causes	43
3.3	Estimates of financial viability/subsidy dependence ratios, 2009	45
4.1	Sample descriptives	49
4.2	Business CDFIs: upward and downward income transitions, 2007–10	51
4.3	Business CDFIs: analysis of income transitions	53
4.4	Consumer-lending CDFIs: income dynamics and possible causes, 2007–10	64
4.5	Consumer and business CDFIs: health, health-seeking behaviour and other non-income dimensions of well-being, 2007–10	65
4.6	Estimated CDFI impact on income (2007–09): summary table	67
4.7	The samples: poverty dynamics 2007–09	68
4.8	Poverty transitions analysed by possible cause	76
4.9	The determinants of exit from poverty	82
4.10	Likelihood of escape from poverty: Heckman probit estimates and marginal effects	86
5.1	Instances of social capital creation and possible causal factors	108
5.2	Volunteering, trust and community-building	112
5.3	CDFI members: membership of social groups among ethnic minorities and the sample as a whole, 2009	116
5.4	Ethnic-minority microfinance and community-building in Birmingham and the Black Country	122
5.5	Ethnic minority cases: social capital development and its possible causes	127
6.1	Amendments to the benefits system and their rationale, late 1990s to 2010	134
6.2	Likely interlinkages between CDFIs and state welfare benefits	140
6.3	Business and consumer-lending operations: estimated fiscal impacts	142

6.4   Sample institutions: value of benefits per capita, CDFI clients,
      2007 and 2009   144
6.5   Poverty trends 2007–09, in relation to CDFI loan and uptake of
      specific benefits   147
6.6   Working tax credit in a model of exit from poverty   150
7.1   Supporting institutions and the efficiency of CDFIs   161

Case studies

1	Loan advice in Scotcash	33
2a	Take-off	59
2b	Discovering a niche and hanging on	60
2c	Overcommitment and failure	62
3	Savings mobilisation in ELM	75
4	Social capital-building and survival at the subsistence level	94
5	TIGERS (DSL7) and MacVicar (DSL8)	97
6	An ethnic-minority entrepreneur	104
7	The Osmaston Information Centre	105
8	Construction of mentoring networks	119
9	The roscas (rotating savings and credit associations) of Sparkbrook	125

Preface

The origins of this book go back to the early 2000s, at which time governments and voluntary agencies in industrial countries were searching for new ways of organising social protection and welfare. Among the options in the frame was the possibility of adapting in some way the achievements of microfinance in the developing world to the very different environment of industrial countries. In Britain, the search for a way forward against social and specifically financial exclusion was being carried forward with great energy by a new Labour government committed to reversal of the upward trend in poverty, and specifically to halving child poverty within ten years.

Having studied the operations of microfinance at first hand in developing countries during the 1990s, one of us (Mosley) became fascinated by the question of what it might be able to contribute to the resolution of UK inner-city problems, starting with a pilot study of microfinance institutions in his home city of Sheffield, financed by the Nuffield Foundation. It was always our hope to extend this study into something bigger that might enable us to properly measure the social impact of these institutions and, in 2005, it was the Esmee Fairbairn Foundation, with support from Barclays Bank and the Small Business Service of the Department of Trade and Industry (now BIS), who very kindly made this possible by making a grant of about £50,000 to us (and a parallel grant to Karl Dayson of the University of Salford) which enabled us to study the working of community development finance institutions in Glasgow, Sheffield, Derby and Birmingham over a two-year period.

This book is the result, and definitely the nicest part of the process of writing it is to be able to thank the many people who helped us do so. First amongst these is Nicola Pollock, the director of grant-making at the Esmee Fairbairn Foundation, and her co-sponsors, William Derban at Barclays and Ian Drummond at DTI. In Glasgow, Sharon Macpherson of Glasgow City Council and Helen Jackson of the Glasgow Housing Association provided a supplementary grant which enabled us to expand the Glasgow sample and conduct intensive interviews with clients. All of these people made the enterprise possible and provided numerous valuable comments and ideas.

It was always our hope to involve the managers of community development finance institutions in the process of assessing, and hopefully increasing, their impact; and one of the most rewarding aspects of the research has been the relationships we have built up with practitioners. I must first mention Eunice Lancaster, the general manager of DSL (Developing Strathclyde Ltd) in Glasgow, Fiona Greaves, formerly manager of Sheffield Enterprise and now chair of the board of Sheffield Credit Union and Moneyline Yorkshire, and Niamh Goggin, the founder-manager of Aspire Micro Loans in Belfast, who helped us launch our Nuffield pilot inquiry in the early 2000s and stayed with us through the current adventure. The other microfinance managers who came on board subsequently – Leah Cameron of Scotcash, Glasgow, Andrew Baker and Melanie Andrew (now Elliott) of Derby Loans (now Midlands Community Finance) and Steve Walker of ART, Birmingham – have been no less tolerant of the multiple demands of our enquiries, conducted in sometimes crowded offices with, altogether, some 600 clients and control-group members and their sometimes slightly less tolerant children. They not only put up with us but gave us ideas which hugely improved the final product. Beyond these people who submitted to our questionnaire surveys, we would like to thank the managers of other community finance institutions whom we interviewed, and in particular Diane Burridge, Ian Clough and Helen Charlesworth of East Lancashire Moneyline (ELM), Simon Frost of South Coast Moneyline, Owen McKenzie of 3Bs, Birmingham, Stuart MacCallum of the Glasgow Credit Union and Jim Garrity of Pollok Credit Union, Glasgow. The contribution of the banks, credit unions, business advisers, and money advisers and sponsors who support the operations of the lenders is also crucial, and amongst these we would like to pay especial tribute to Rob Mackay and Anne Mills of the Citizens' Advice Bureau (currently on secondment to Scotcash); Will Nisbet and Alan Porteous of Glasgow North and Glasgow East Regeneration Agencies; Peter Armstrong, Eric Thompson, Jane Bulloss and Jacqueline Hallewell of Sheffield Credit Union; Alec Shelton of Derby City Partnership and John Parnham of Derby City Council; Monica Coke of Advantage West Midlands; and Nas Hussain of Birmingham Enterprise.

To gather our data, we interviewed our sample of clients typically at least twice and sometimes repeatedly, and often in relation to sensitive issues such as indebtedness, business finances, household income and expenditure, the operations of loan sharks and doorstep lenders, and the impact of the recession more generally. That we were able to carry this demanding project through speaks volumes for the patience, the sensitivity and the thoroughness shown by a team of some fifty interviewers. We would particularly like to thank the supervisors of those teams – Linsay Waddell in Glasgow, Toindepi Toindepi in Derby and Patricia Anderson and Jane Hughes in Sheffield – for the care and enthusiasm they put into their work. We also appreciate the efforts of Katy Jenkins who was research assistant to the project for a year and launched the interviewers into the field, and some of the interviewers themselves deserve special mentions – Anne-Marie Smith and Alison Kennedy in Glasgow, Jennifer Dowling, Chris Malins and Francesca Mosley in Sheffield, and Emma Boswell and Andrew Hall in Derby. And of course nothing would have been possible without our almost 600 interviewees. Some of these – Paul Udenze in Birmingham, Sallie Powell,

Don Parker and Ian Maxfield in Derby, and Karen Barr, Kim Duff, John Gibson, Jim MacVicar and Patricia Watson in Glasgow – figure in our case studies, and we are especially grateful to them for the extended insight they have given us into how microfinance impacted on their businesses and, in several cases, inspired them into social entrepreneurship in their own right.

In addition, we have received advice, ideas and commentary on our drafts from a number of co-researchers. First amongst these we should mention Javed Hussain, who has advised us since the beginning on those parts of our research which concern ethnic minorities and who should be regarded as co-author of the section of Chapter 5 which concerns this theme. In addition we would like to thank Mustafa Caglayan and Liddy Goyder of the University of Sheffield, Karl Dayson of Salford University – who as mentioned above has executed his own independent survey of CDFIs in other cities within the Esmee Fairbairn project – and Cameron Donaldson and Rachel Baker of Glasgow Caledonian University, all of whom have commented on parts or the whole of our draft. Finally, we very much appreciate the cheerfulness and forbearance of Louisa Earls of Routledge, who patiently waited past a number of deadlines. Without the support of all these the book could not have existed. We hope that they feel that what they have now got was worth waiting for; but, we stress, all responsibility for any errors rests with the authors alone.

Pamela Lenton and Paul Mosley
December 2010

1 Introduction

This book is about poverty, and about one of its main causes – *financial exclusion*, the inability of many low-income people to build up their capital through access to fair-priced financial services. It asks why financial exclusion occurs, and discusses what can be done to get rid of it in the context of four British cities.

Background

As far back as 1942, a British government committed itself to the elimination of poverty. William Beveridge, the civil servant asked by the government to draft a plan which would achieve this, presented a report entitled *Social Insurance and Allied Services*, which was intended to provide everyone with a basic income on which they could decently live. But, he emphasised, the ending of poverty, in the sense of an income which falls below a decent level,[1] 'is only one of five giants on the road of reconstruction, and in some ways the easiest to attack. The others are Disease, Ignorance, Squalor and Idleness'.[2] The other giants, indeed, were also attacked with vigour in the wake of the Beveridge report – through the National Health Service, through the 1944 Education Act which for the first time provided free secondary education, through a massive post-war rehousing programme and through a return, for the first time since 1914, to full employment. And the principal giant, income poverty, was very nearly slain within a decade. Having run at average levels in excess of 30 per cent of the adult population throughout the inter-war period,[3] income poverty was estimated by the great pioneer investigator Seebohm Rowntree to have fallen below 5 per cent by 1950.[4] Here, and in other industrialised countries, the 'Welfare State', as it quickly became known, offered a promise, sixty years ago, of social protection for everyone for as far ahead as anyone wished to look.

As we now know, things turned out differently. Two of the giants, unemployment and poverty itself, reared their heads again at the beginning of the 1980s (see Figure 1.1, below), as a consequence of governments discovering all round the world that two of the foundations on which Beveridge had built, full employment with stable prices, were not in the long run compatible. With unemployment and inflation both growing rapidly, the Beveridge principles were helpless, and the decision taken both in Britain and in other industrialised countries was to put the objective of stable prices first. In the process, governments discovered that poverty was a more complex thing than it had been visualised in the 1940s and 1950s. One reason for this was the problem of the 'cycle of deprivation' or of the persistence of poverty: some people, in spite of the best efforts of the welfare state, remained caught in a poverty trap by the interaction of a multiplicity of factors – family break-up, multiple children, eviction from insecure tenure, low education, ill health, high prices of consumer goods, an inability to save or borrow to finance these purchases, an inability to get back into work. Several of these impacts were not chronicled by Beveridge, and some of them, having once locked the sufferer into chronic poverty, were then passed on to the next generation. Indeed poverty might occur, not just in spite of, but *because* of the best efforts of the welfare state. One illustration of this problem was a new welfare benefit, Family Income Supplement, introduced in 1971, which was taxed and means tested, so that for every pound earned typically at least eighty-five pence, and sometimes more than the original £1, were debited in lost entitlements. 'It is now a fact', lamented Frank Field and David Piachaud in an article in the *New Statesman* that same year, 'that for millions of low paid workers very substantial pay increases have the absurd effect of increasing only marginally their family's new income and in some cases actually make the family worse off'.[5] In this way the welfare benefits which had been the key element in originally enabling families to escape from poverty could now be seen as an element in the poverty trap itself – indeed, Field and Piachaud have a claim to have invented the term, although it is now often used, and we shall use it, in a much wider sense than their concept of a disease which the doctor unintentionally makes worse.[6] Rather, our main concern in this book is to see what financial inclusion initiatives can do against persistent poverty in all its forms.

In addition to Beveridge's five giants, two other key influences which contributed to keeping people in the poverty trap were *social* and *financial* exclusion. During the Conservative administration of Margaret Thatcher from 1979 to 1990 most indicators of income poverty rose, due to a sustained increase in unemployment (to a level of three million, or 12 per cent of the labour force, by 1986),[7] a sustained reduction in the real value of welfare benefits and a change in the behaviour of banks – which in pursuit of their own viability closed a number of their branches in less remunerative, in other words poorer, neighbourhoods. Beyond this, banks typically refused to make loans to people who were unemployed or on benefits, and indeed often would not lend to anyone, employed or not, within defined postcodes.[8] Thus, across large zones which often corresponded exactly to the council estates established by the first great flowering of the comprehensive welfare state in the 1940s and 1950s, those many low-income people who suffered from unmanageable levels of debt also found that little help in dealing with this predicament was available to them from conventional financial institutions. This is financial exclusion, and it links in an obvious way with social exclusion, which is the inability of poor people to participate in the social processes which determine people's life chances (Askonas and Stewart 2000: 9,

Lister 2004). The question which we now confront is: apart from the eroding welfare state, what alternatives were available within the private or voluntary (or public) sector to combat social and financial exclusion? The answer to this question will take us to the main theme of this book.

Two of the most significant alternatives available in principle to those caught in the poverty trap of the 1980s were *mutual organisations* (and especially credit unions) and *sub-prime financial organisations* (and especially home credit or 'doorstep lending' organisations). Both of these groups are an important part of the backdrop to the innovative financial institutions considered later in this book, and need some description here.

Credit unions are mutual financial organisations which lend and at the same time take savings deposits. They are legally obliged to define as members a group of people who share a 'common bond', often in the workplace or in the local community. They have existed since at least the eighteenth century, and during the century-and-a-half between the industrial revolution and the arrival of the Beveridge welfare state constituted an important part of the process by which working-class households built up a capital reserve to protect them against shocks[9] and insure the household's basic subsistence (Hollis and Sweetman 1998; King and Tomkins 2003; Maltby 2009). Within credit unions, loans are made (at a legal maximum interest rate of 12 per cent, raised to 24 per cent in 2005) only to those who have previously accumulated collateral in the form of savings, and this requirement excludes many people, since the poorest often see themselves as unable to save on a regular basis.[10] Traditionally the role of credit unions has been seen as supporting household consumption and savings, and increasingly they are now used for acquisition of consumer durables, but they rarely lend for small business development. A more detailed discussion of credit unions, and a mapping of their role within our case-study areas, is given in Chapter 3.

Sub-prime financial organisations are, formally, those financial organisations not licensed by the Financial Services Authority to operate as banks, and therefore forced to raise resources from higher-cost sources than prime-rated financial markets. Often sub-prime financial organisations are willing to lend to riskier clients than high-street banks, and in particular to uncollateralised low-income individuals. A detailed account of sub-prime financial organisations has been provided by, amongst others, Kempson and Whyley (1999), Brooker and Whyley (2005), Collard and Kempson (2005) and several contributions to the Financial Inclusion Task Force, such as Finney and Kempson (2009) and Experian (2009). Sub-prime financial organisations, like credit unions, offer short-term loans for the purchase of consumer goods, but unlike credit unions do not ask for savings or any other form of security; in many ways, as we shall see, they substitute by intensive loan collection methods, just like microfinance institutions in developing countries, for the building-up of savings capacity amongst the poor. In some cases – such as *pawnbrokers*, who offer loans secured against jewellery or other collateral – these institutions have been established since pre-industrial times. Also existing since time immemorial and still thriving are *loan sharks* – unlicensed individuals offering unsecured loans at extremely high rates of interest to insecure people such as refugees and asylum seekers, who use violence and threats of it to enforce repayment.[11] However, the most interesting category of sub-prime lenders is neither of these, but a group of legitimate and highly profitable commercial companies which have adapted themselves to the predicament of low-income borrowers by collecting loan repayments from borrowers not in the lender's office, but in the borrower's own house. These home credit companies, informally known as 'doorstep lenders' and also known as licensed moneylenders and weekly collected credit companies, are an oligopoly: the largest of them, National Provident, has over two million customers, and has almost half the market to itself, with three other companies, Cattles, London and Scottish Bank and S & U, accounting for another 20 per cent.[12] Benefiting from their extremely strong bargaining position vis-à-vis poor clients and not being able to take collateral from them, they charge interest rates which amply reflect the risks of non-repayment and the costs of going to the doorstep to pick repayments up, and usually run well into three figures.[13] Annual percentage rates on doorstep loans can be anywhere between 100 and 500 per cent (Kempson and Whyley 1999), though Palmer and Conaty (2002) cite examples where people were paying more than 1,000 per cent interest; the cost of credit emerging from our own surveys (Chapter 4) averages out across our survey cities at around 190 per cent. These loans often include hidden charges, insurance premiums and the like, which are not necessarily obvious, especially to those with low levels of financial literacy. On the evidence of our interviews, most of these loans are used for covering the costs of everyday living and basic essentials (Palmer and Conaty 2002), rather than for luxury items.

The appeal of such massively expensive credit is, simply, uniqueness within the areas where it is supplied, compounded by ignorance about the cost and considerable skill in sales and client management on the part of loan collectors. The initial approach, in the Stocksbridge area north of Sheffield, typically comes in the form of a £50 voucher slipped through the door or available in the supermarket, which is then paid back in thirty-two instalments at £2.50 per week – an annual percentage rate of 399 per cent. This is the only form of credit seen to be available by those living on benefits – certainly to buy consumer durables, but sometimes even to pay for food. As illustrated by the following anecdote from the Meadowell estate in Newcastle, if you are living on benefits and most of your income is already pre-empted by debt repayments, your time horizons are extremely short:

> Pat, who had worked in a hospital before having children, was struggling to make income support stretch to cover her food, fuel bills and nappies. Before she had paid off her first loan [from National Provident],[14] a salesman from another credit company, Shopacheck, came to the door offering more vouchers. She took them and another loan to help clear the first. 'I knew I was getting into debt but I needed it for the kids, just to survive that day.'[15]

Often the pressure to borrow, to the point of stealing, to afford the loan repayments comes through peer pressure via the children. As another Newcastle client mentioned,

> I've had Provys [loans from National Provident] in the past and got so desperate I'd break into the meter on the TV to steal the money. You want your kids to be equal otherwise they'll be targets. The kids say, 'You've got snide trainers, you're a tramp.'[16]

In spite of the high rates of interest which they charge, doorstep lenders and their agents are seen as sympathetic partners by many of their clients who are unaware of the cost which they are paying for credit, who are unaware of any alternative methods of getting credit, and who appreciate the time their collectors are willing to put into chatting to them about their problems and, indeed, postponing instalments without additional charge in the event of financial misfortunes encountered by the client (Brooker and Whyley 2005: Leyshon *et al.* 2006). If default or delay on repayment occurs on such a loan, then so far from being met with harassment it is courteously and helpfully rescheduled: the opportunity to extend the term of the loan is welcomed by doorstep lenders as a means of widening the market, and indeed is part of the process by which they are kept within the poverty trap. An enormous extension of the coverage of doorstep lenders occurred during the 1980s recession, and has occurred again during the current (2007–11) global crisis.

Against this background, let us pick up the story of poverty through the 1990s, and what resources and institutions were available to defend against it. Figure 1.1 provides a summary statistical picture of the time-pattern of headcount poverty,

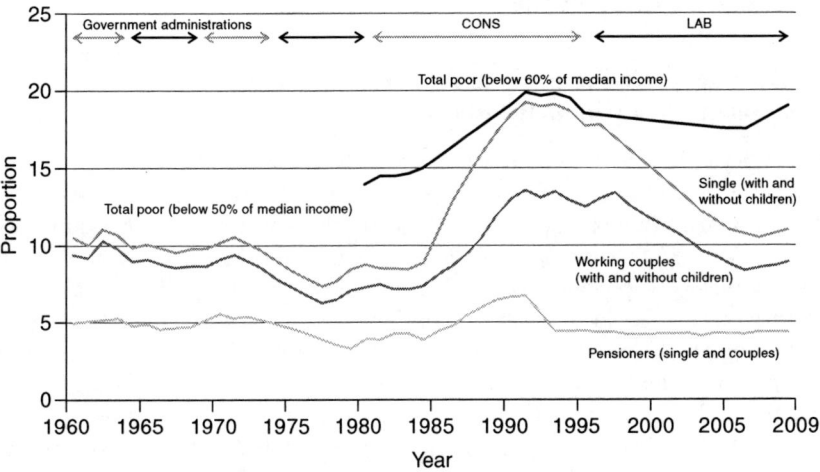

Figure 1.1 Poverty in the UK: share of the population with below half average income, 1960–2009.

measured as half of mean income and separately assessed for different groups of households (working single people, working couples and pensioners, with and without children, and pensioners) from 1960 right through to the present.

As Figure 1.1 shows, total poverty in the sense of those below half median income[17] began to rise in 1977, well before the onset of the recession and the advent of a Conservative administration in 1979–80, and after a pause in the early 1980s it rose continuously until by 1992 it stood at 19 per cent of the population, or about two-and-a-half times its 1977 level, and, as best we can make the comparison, far above the proportion of the population calculated by Rowntree in York to be poor at the beginning of the 1950s.[18] The real value of welfare benefits, as measured by the level of poverty among pensioners, also worsened sharply, from about 3 per cent to 7 per cent of the population over the same period. Many of those hurt in this way were the long-term poor and their dependants, initially made unemployed by the sharp cuts in declining industries such as steel, coal, textiles and heavy engineering in the 1980s and not able to shift into alternative jobs. Focussing on the financial dimension of their poverty, about one-tenth of the population, most of whom were poor, had no bank account and no means of borrowing. Credit unions in principle offered some relief for this predicament, but only a minor one because the poorest could not satisfy the requirement to save, and informal lenders also provided 'relief', but only in the superficial sense that they enabled the financially included to pay for some consumption requirements that they could not otherwise pay for. In every other sense of the word, they provided not relief but oppression, as they deepened the trap consisting of the interlinkage between debt dependency, low consumption standards and asset poverty. Although much better represented in areas of deprivation, the doorstep lenders were not helping the poor to capitalise themselves but doing the precise opposite. What other options were available for attacking the financial exclusion problem?

The emergence and transformation of community development financial institutions

During the 1990s, the idea emerged of trying to deal with long-term unemployment by assisting the unemployed to start and run their own businesses. An illustrative list of institutions applying this approach, which came to be known as *community development finance institutions* (CDFIs), is in Table 1.1. In Britain, CDFIs developed spontaneously and independently within individual cities or conurbations to meet local needs, and initially were not part of any movement or national organisation. Except in the case of the Wellpark Enterprise Centre in Glasgow, the initiating spark was in the voluntary rather than the state sector, outwith the formal apparatus of the welfare state; however, grants from government, and in the case of ASPIRE (Belfast) and DSL (Glasgow) from supranational organisations as well, were in all cases an important part of their financing base.[19] Politically, the motive underlying these initiatives was the desire to do something about long-term unemployment at a local level, usually, as in all the cases in Table 1.1, through encouraging self-employment in small- and medium-sized enterprises. What was new about this way of operating was that the supported organisations and their beneficiaries, although initially grant-dependent, expected to evolve into financially self-supporting entities. Rather than poverty being tackled by providing a flow of welfare benefits, as in the Beveridge model, it was now also being tackled by providing, via subsidy from the agencies listed in the fourth column of Table 1.1, a capital asset (equipment for the start up or maintenance of a small business), the returns on which would finance movement across the poverty line for the entrepreneur and/or his/her employees. As will be readily seen, if this model could be made to work and to expand, it could potentially transform the welfare state, by enabling it to pay for itself. Certainly, CDFIs are pioneering entities: the first institutions to seek to contribute to the social protection of the most vulnerable in a financially self-sustaining manner. But whether they can expect to change the face of welfare in this way by scaling themselves up, in Britain or anywhere else, is quite another matter. To understand whether and how this may be an achievable objective is the main purpose of this book.

How did these pioneer organisations hope to serve the poorest and at the same time cover their costs? The answers to this question are quite various and individualistic, but one important inspiration in most of the cases listed above was the innovation known as *microfinance*.

Microfinance is simply the provision of financial services – loans, savings, insurance and so on – on a small-scale basis. It began in a number of developing countries in the late 1970s – its parentage is disputed between Latin America and South Asia – and has grown to become one of the main poverty-reduction instruments on the globe, especially for women who in most cases have proved to be more successful and enthusiastic clients than men.[20] Its central insight is that poor people, even if they are too poor to have any assets which can be taken as security, nonetheless can be highly efficient and even profitable clients of financial institutions, if they are given the right incentives. One possible incentive consists of organising savers and borrowers in groups close to their residence, or place of work, and then stipulating that nobody within a group may have a loan unless all members of it are paying back their loans on time. This is known as the *peer-monitoring* approach, since it prompts all clients of a financial institution to pressure one another to repay loans, and it won for its originator, Professor Muhammad Yunus of the Bangladesh Grameen Bank, the Nobel Peace Prize of 2006. However, this is not the only possible model, and incentives to repay can be perfectly successfully applied within a context of individual saving and borrowing. A useful discussion of the different ways in which microfinance operates, and of the massive literature related to its effectiveness, is provided in Armendariz and Morduch (2005), in Hermes and Lensink (2007) and in Morduch and Italey (2002).

In making all the necessary design decisions required to establish this new financing mode, the institutions listed in Table 1.1 were forced to improvise. Several industrialised countries experimented in the 1990s with the group-lending model, in the US and Europe as well as in Britain, but of all the

Table 1.1 Some 'pioneer' CDFIs of the 1990s

Institution	Founded	Geographical base	Source of finance	Catchment and organisational basis
Developing Strathclyde Ltd (DSL)[1]	1993	Glasgow conurbation	European Union; Glasgow City Council; Scottish Enterprise Glasgow; some private industrialists and Local Economic Development Companies	Small businesses; individual lending, but with obligatory mentoring from local economic development companies
Wellpark Enterprise Centre	1995 (microfinance programme)	Glasgow	Glasgow City Council; Scottish Enterprise; European Regional Development Fund	Women entrepreneurs; group lending and mentoring
Aston Reinvestment Trust (ART)	1994	Birmingham and Black Country		Small- (and increasingly also medium-sized) businesses
Doncaster Business Advice Centre (DONBAC)	1995	Doncaster and South Yorkshire	Government and private restructuring funds for coal and engineering industries	Small- and medium-scale manufacturing enterprises
Sheffield Enterprise Agency (SENTA)	1997	Sheffield	Sheffield Chamber of Commerce	Small enterprises mostly in service sector
ASPIRE	1999	Northern Ireland, mainly Belfast area	US funds provided in support of Northern Ireland peace initiative	Small and medium enterprises in services and manufacturing
Women's Employment, Enterprise and Training Unit (WEETU)	1987	Norwich	Barclays/European Social Fund	Unemployed and low-waged women, both working and on benefits

Source: Prospectuses of institutions listed in first column.

Note
1 The CDFIs in italics feature in the surveys later in the book.

institutions listed in Table 1.1, only WEETU continues with a group-lending approach, and all the others now offer individual loans only.[21] Moreover, all of the 1990s pioneer institutions listed in Table 1.1 offered micro-loans only to initiate, or to build, small *businesses*. This is perfectly consistent with the practice of microfinance institutions in developing countries, and also with the ideology of enterprise as the driver of economic growth which characterised the Conservative governments of the 1980s and 1990s. However, it is completely alien to the practice of the only institutions which had previously 'lent into poverty' in Britain – the credit unions and the doorstep lenders, which typically lend short term for the purchase of consumer goods or simply to relieve debt problems. In this sense, it represents a highly innovative break with previous practice.

During the period of Conservative administration in the early and mid 1990s, the experimental financial institutions listed in Table 1.1 received significant financial support from branches of the UK government, especially local government; however, they were not the subject of any central government policy initiatives, and did not figure in any social policy strategy. In May 1997, with the election of a Labour government, all this changed. Although to increase its likelihood of election the Labour party had avoided emphasising the poverty theme – for example, the reversal of the adverse poverty trend did not figure among its five 'key election promises'[22] – the government once elected made a clear commitment to bring poverty down and in particular to halve child poverty by 2010.[23] This commitment, in a further break with the practice of previous governments, did not come only from ministers associated with social welfare but from the Chancellor of the Exchequer, Gordon Brown. A new office, significantly named the Social Exclusion Unit, was set up within the office of the deputy prime minister with the remit of coordinating the anti-poverty effort. However it is to be borne in mind that the core of the Labour Party's renewed attack on the 'five giants' and specifically on poverty in all its forms did not reside within the Social Exclusion Unit, but rather in the 'active labour-market' strategies, such as New Deal, Working Families' Tax Credit and Sure Start, deployed by the Treasury during the late 1990s in order to reconcile welfare with competitiveness on a scale which outran what was being attempted in other countries of Europe.[24] The thrust of its financial and social exclusion policies, at least up until the mid 2000s, can best be understood as supportive of its core strategy of making labour markets work better. It was to better achieve the objective of active labour markets, part of which involved maximising the incentive to work rather than remain on welfare benefits, that the Labour Party eventually, in 1999, committed itself to subsidise CDFIs.

One of the Social Exclusion Unit's major tasks was to produce a National Neighbourhood Strategy – a label that consciously and deliberately echoed the Labour Party's emphasis during its election campaign on community values and community cohesion by contrast with the individualistic values and social-Darwinist ethic promoted by the Conservative Party. Within the National Neighbourhood Strategy, on the recommendation of its policy action teams (PATs) dealing with jobs (PAT1), business enterprise (PAT3) and with financial services (PAT14), a government fund, the *Phoenix Fund,* was set up in 1999, explicitly to provide medium-term support for the new small business-oriented loan finance institutions that were already in being – as illustrated in Table 1.1 – and to encourage other such funds into existence. The wider purpose of this was to regenerate the environment of the decayed inner-city and sink-estate communities where most poverty was located. Indeed, the emphasis on community continued into the new generic name for this new breed of financial institutions – *community* development finance institutions (CDFIs) – and the new trade association established in the same year for them – the *Community* Development Finance Association (CDFA). The prime minister spoke up for the principle of 'looking at how small amounts of credit and capital can be made available for promoting business ideas in Britain's poorest areas'.[25] The big idea behind all of this was that business, and business thinking, was the route through which financial exclusion, and thereby poverty, should be attacked.[26]

The logic of this overall approach to financial exclusion was clear. By lending to financially excluded *small businesses*, rather than simply financially excluded people, CDFIs would be able to enable labour markets to work better and provide employment to people who would otherwise be on the dole – thereby providing a multiplier to the poverty reduction process and saving on the associated social security benefits. Evaluations of this period of CDFI development are relatively scarce, but both the government's evaluation of the Phoenix Fund (United Kingdom 2004) and a study by us (Mosley and Steel 2004), based on a very small sample of three CDFIs in Sheffield, Glasgow and Belfast, discover that this multiplier is quite substantial. Our study tracks a sample of forty-five loans granted by those institutions, and finds that those forty-five loans, of an average value of about £2,000, enabled thirty-four individuals to move out of poverty and thirty-one individuals to move out of unemployment, over the period 2000–02 – almost a one-to-one ratio – enabling a gain in individual well-being, community well-being and saved social security benefits collectively worth a great deal more than £2,000 per head (Mosley and Steel 2004: 728).

The early 2000s were good years for the British economy: not only was the economy growing but, contrary to the entire trend of the 1980s and most of the 1990s, poverty was now beginning to fall in Britain (Figure 1.1), and in the United States also, at a much sharper rate than the European average.[27] The growth of the economy was facilitated not only by the government's active labour-market policies (page 9, above) but also by a boom in financial markets, the opposite side of which coin was a very rapid growth in personal debt. And this debt was growing fastest, the Treasury noticed, among the lowest income groups who were the least capable of managing it. More than half the households with serious debt problems in 2004 were in the lowest income group, earning less than £11,500 a year at that time, and between 1995 and 2000, the ratio of debt to income for this group more than doubled, from 16 per cent to 36 per cent, a much faster increase than for any other income group (United Kingdom, Office of the Deputy Prime Minister 2004: 1). Much of this debt, it will be recalled, was owed because of financial exclusion not to banks or other fair-priced lenders, but rather to home lenders and others charging extortionate rates. And although the strategy of lending to small business-oriented CDFIs had much to commend it and much to be proud of, it could not come to grips with the problem just described. Those who had managed to exit from poverty through the operations of business CDFIs, in the Mosley and Steel study, were typically fit young men under twenty-five, with technical qualifications. Those who were continuing to sink into poverty under the weight of unmanageable debt were typically single females under thirty-five, with two or more children, without qualifications and often suffering from severe health problems. One such case interviewed in the course of our survey was:

Interviewee C2. Single mother, aged thirty-one, on second floor of three-storey council flat, Easterhouse, Glasgow, November 2009. Two children aged eight and ten. Damp running down the walls, graffiti on the outside wall and a cracked bathroom window. Total household income £125 per week, all from benefits. No savings. Had been refused a bank account in 2003 'on account of being unable to produce identification'. Owes a total of £4,500 to three finance companies (Provident, Greenwoods and Brighthouse), which she is paying off at £3 per week. During the course of the interview, the ten-year-old, who had that day been suspended from school for disrupting classes, picked up, without permission, the £10 interview fee which we had placed on the coffee table and ran off shouting in triumph. Overweight and asthmatic; on average, drinks a litre of vodka a day, sometimes neat and sometimes mixed with 'Bucky' (Buckfast tonic wine). When asked 'if you received a windfall of £1,000, how would you spend it?' her first answer was 'Christmas presents for the children' and her second 'I'd take the family away on holiday'.[28]

How could the financial services of DSL, or any of the other business-lending CDFIs listed in Table 1.1, assist a person in this position to get out of the poverty trap? The short answer is that they could not. Another approach was needed.

The new approach adopted was to change the financial product offered. At the beginning of the 2000s, various CDFIs were beginning to balance their portfolio by offering, in addition to small business loans: loans for house improvement; mortgages; loans to 'social enterprises', i.e. enterprises which had more than ten employees but nonetheless fulfilled a social purpose such as creating jobs in areas with high crime rates, poor physical environments or persistently high unemployment; and finally a new financial product called 'personal loans', which were simply small loans (generally less than £1,000) offered in low-income neighbourhoods to meet immediate consumption needs, pay off debt and in particular escape from the grasp of the doorstep lender.[29] Two of the earliest organisations to offer such loans were Portsmouth Area Regeneration Trust (PART), later to become South Coast Moneyline, in 2001, and East Lancashire Moneyline (ELM), in 2002. We shall refer to organisations offering this type of loan as *personal-lending CDFIs*; the alternative label, *consumer-lending CDFIs*, is also often used.

The government, in the shape of the Treasury, quickly came to see that these new consumer loans, administered through CDFIs, represented a promising way of tackling the debt trap head on. In its 2004 report, 'Promoting Financial Inclusion', the Treasury acknowledged the continuing persistence of financial exclusion and advocated that the problem be tackled directly, through access to affordable credit by socially and financially excluded consumers, rather than indirectly, through lending to the small number of financially excluded self-employed and hoping for spillovers into the labour market. In December 2004 it announced the establishment of a Financial Inclusion Fund, the loan part of which became known as the *Growth Fund*, to be disbursed by the Department of Work and Pensions (DWP) with an initial value of £36 million; the value of this fund was increased by successive steps between 2007 and 2009 to a value of almost £100 million. (By this time, of course, the global recession had struck; the extensions of the DWP grant represented the bottom end of the Brown administration's Keynesian initiative in mitigation of the slump.) The DWP, through this largesse, has become the key arbiter of the expansion potential of CDFIs. Some of them have used DWP money to move themselves from a local on to a regional footing: for example Derby Loans, which will be formally introduced in the next two chapters and will be used as a case study throughout the book, has now expanded into many parts of Staffordshire, Northamptonshire and Nottinghamshire, and East Lancashire Moneyline (ELM) now disburses microfinance not only across Lancashire but also holds DWP contracts for the Grimsby area, Merseyside, the Potteries and the whole of Wales. For some CDFIs, the increase in scope has involved not only geographical expansion but also the embracing of exhilarating new challenges. For instance one of the new consumer CDFIs, Scotcash, established in 2007, which will also be encountered throughout the book, announced an intention to move as quickly as possible to a scale such that the doorstep moneylender would be put in his place, building to a volume of 60,000 loans over a fifteen-year period. However, the main channel by which personal-lending CDFIs have so far been financed, namely the DWP Growth Fund has expired; it has recently (May 2011) been renewed by the coalition government as a six-month contract. This, of course, attaches a question mark to the survival possibilities of CDFIs, as we shall discuss.

To its credit, the Treasury acknowledged that combating financial exclusion was not purely a matter of money, but also a matter of knowledge. Often, highly indebted poor people, and this surely includes the anonymous interviewee from Easterhouse quoted above, dig themselves deeper into the debt–poverty trap because, instead of approaching the problem rationally and step by step, they panic, and thereby sink further into the swamp. One way of trying to incentivise a rational approach – as the Treasury acknowledged – is through the provision of debt advice. If the right advice is given at the right time and place[30] to vulnerable people, it may both save them money in the short term by deflecting them away from high-cost sources of finance, but also move them over the long term towards behaviours (savings and physical exercise being two classic examples) which protect against the shocks of life rather than leaving the sufferer more exposed to them. (This is of course simply a new line of attack against one of Beveridge's five giants – namely ignorance.) Several CDFIs, notably once again Scotcash,[31] have given money advice a key role in their strategy to build up the debt management capacity of borrowers; but others have been less forward-looking, possibly because debt advice yields no direct returns to the institution that provides or sponsors it. The question of how to create a knowledge asset through the process of personal lending, which the beneficiary can draw on over the years, will be a key concern of later chapters.

CDFIs, as illustrated by Table 1.2, grew rapidly through the early 2000s; and as they did so they shifted from a business-lending to a personal-lending empha-sis under the impetus of the new Growth Fund. Business lending by CDFIs con-tinued, but after the mid 2000s ceased to be funded by the central government Phoenix Fund and instead was supported by regional development authorities, which are themselves to be wound up in 2012. As also shown in Table 1.2, per-sonal loans, which have grown much more rapidly than other categories of loan, also have higher default rates, at least part of which extra cost has then been passed on to the borrower in the form of higher interest rates.

The data in Table 1.2 are descriptive rather than evaluative. But even the descriptives give cause for concern. The financial performance of CDFIs is not easy to infer from the table, because the concept of arrears used by the CDFA switches in 2008 from ninety-day delinquency to percentages of loans written off (cynics might say because the former figure was starting to rise alarmingly); and because, even though viability is the organisation's key preoccupation, an estimate of viability in the sense of operational self-sufficiency is provided just once, in 2005, and then vanishes. Of course, this is written in the aftermath of a deep recession, and at this short remove it is not easy to say how much of the apparent deterioration in the financial performance of 2008 and 2009 is 'struc-tural' and long term and how much of it is short term and will disappear once recovery gets under way. However, even if we set aside the probable increase in arrears and simply think in absolute terms, there is an appearance of serious inef-ficiency, which feeds into the cost and competitiveness levels which the sector can hope to achieve. The average ninety-day arrears rate for UK CDFIs is, on the average of the data for 2002–09, well into double figures, and probably still around 20 per cent; the corresponding figure for those developing countries for which the MIXmarket index holds data is of the order of 3 per cent,[32] even though in those countries incomes are far lower, operations are on a much bigger scale (for example the Grameen Bank has over eight million clients) and the physical and educational infrastructure is much worse. Exactly what is wrong is not at all clear, and it will be a major purpose of our Chapter 3 to find out what we can.

Table 1.2 Descriptives of CDFIs, 2003–09

	2003	2005	2008	2009
Number of active institutions	28	62	65	68
Size of loan book				
1 Value of loan portfolio £000				
• business loans	5,702	22,200	31,655	26,260
• personal (consumer) loans	1,048	2,097	3,025	5,812
• social enterprises	18,745	27,262	230,003	271,528
2 Number of loans in portfolio				
• business loans	1,392	3,062	3,197	4,622
• personal (consumer) loans	1,888	3,432	5,943	7,693
• social enterprises	379	627	1,709	1,522
3 = (1)/(2) average loan size (£)				
• business loans	4,096	7,249	9,899	19,136
• personal (consumer) loans	556	611	509	593
• social enterprises	49,462	43,450	134,583	184,869
Average annual interest rates (%):				
• business loans	12.9	13.5	12.8	11.8
• personal (consumer) loans	14.4	22.0	26.2	24.4
• social enterprises	9.4	12.0	11.2	9.4
Default rates (%)	(Delinquencies >90 days as % portfolio)	(Delinquencies >90 days as % portfolio)	Delinquencies >90 days (loan write-offs as % portfolio)	(loan write-offs as % portfolio)
• small business ('micro') loans	9.7	6.0	14.4	14.5
• personal (consumer) loans	7.2	18.0	28.8	13.0
• social enterprises	4.0	3.0		5.4
• all sectors	7.6	10.2		12.9
'Operational self-sustainability' (%)		36.1	19.5 (**12.2**)	39.0[1]

Source: Community Development Finance Association (2003, 2005, 2008, 2009).

Note

1 This self-sustainability figure from GHK (2010) page iv. *What can the CDFI sector deliver, and how?*

The big question, of course, is whether CDFIs can, in combination of course with the state welfare apparatus, help to overcome the five giants, and all others which stand in the way of enabling the vulnerable to get out and stay out of the poverty trap. This raises the question of duration, or sustainability, of impact, because a big worry related to the new personal-lending mode of CDFIs is that it may, unlike business CDFIs, generate only consumption benefits for the individual and not benefits which last through time or can be transmitted to others though the labour market. There is also the worry that personal-lending CDFIs, again unlike business CDFIs, may not help to wean low-income people off welfare benefits. Indeed, they may, we fear, perpetuate dependence on benefits, leading to a new version of the Field–Piachaud poverty trap. (Indeed Frank Field himself, forty years on from his original insight of 1970, was at the time of writing appointed (May 2010) as a 'poverty tsar' by the new (Liberal/Conservative) coalition administration, tasked with configuring cuts in social welfare benefits in a manner that provides the best available solution to the Field–Piachaud dilemma of balancing equity with incentives to work.) Whether CDFIs can in fact help to resolve this dilemma will be a major concern of Chapter 6.

Using these worries as a point of departure, we can now outline the intended contribution of the remaining chapters.

Chapter 2 describes our methodology, and introduces the sample of institutions with whom we have worked over the past three to four years against the background of the localities where they (and their competitors, such as loan sharks) operate; also their guiding philosophies, the innovations they have attempted to bring in and the manner in which they have adapted to shocks and opportunities. We then examine, using maps that classify the cities in which we work according to different measures of deprivation, the effectiveness of 'targeting' of CDFI interventions according to these different criteria.

Chapter 3 addresses issues of CDFI financial performance in the light of the worries addressed above. It derives a measure of viability or 'subsidy dependence' for each of the institutions in our sample and then examines how the different elements of subsidy dependence (i.e. costs and returns in relation to the break-even requirement) vary according to scale and other causes for each of our case-study institutions. This then opens up the question of whether the impact of CDFIs could potentially be influenced by measures which affect their internal efficiency – such as the wages they pay, the interest rates they charge, their publicity strategies, their training policies and their leadership.

Chapter 4 addresses the welfare (poverty) impact of community finance lending on individuals. Poverty is of course a multiple concept, and we specifically seek in this chapter to understand the effectiveness which community development finance has had, in our sample areas, in combating four of Beveridge's five giants: poverty, ignorance, disease and idleness (about the fifth, 'squalor' or poor housing, we have relatively little to say). One particular area of concern is the process by which these factors interact with others, such as debt, to produce a poverty trap. Another is to assess what has been lost in terms of long-term impact, and the development of debt management capacity, through the switch from business to consumer lending, and what has been gained in return. In this context, we are interested to see whether this form of microfinance favours women, as it does in the developing world.

Often, it turns out, the effects of CDFI interventions on individuals are related to their interrelationships with others in the community – often referred to as social capital – and this provides us with a bridge to Chapter 5, which is concerned with community impact.

Chapter 5 uses various measures of community cohesion – crime rates, intra-community trust levels, organisational membership – to assess CDFIs' contribution to community well-being. In this chapter we examine the role of specific communities, in particular ethnic minorities, and possible mechanisms which may assist social capital formation, both by CDFIs themselves and by other organisations.

Chapter 6 is concerned with the fiscal impact of CDFIs – whether they do, as was originally hoped, take pressure off the exchequer and for the first time in this country provide a self-sustaining form of social protection, or whether as now constituted they are now tending to push clients back into dependence on benefits. The composition of benefits, which has changed greatly over the years that CDFIs have been in force, is an important issue here.

A final issue, not adequately stressed in the discussion so far, is that CDFIs do not operate alone. The various levels of government, advisory and regulatory bodies, banks and other private-sector organisations, business advisers, credit unions and voluntary organisations, at a minimum, all play a part in determining the success or failure of CDFIs in addition to the role played by the management of those organisations. This issue is picked up in the concluding Chapter 7, where we seek not only to determine 'who achieved what' but also to provide ideas concerning how better support can be provided to CDFIs. This chapter also presents our conclusions and recommendations.

2 Scope and method

In Britain, by contrast with developing countries, severe poverty is urban rather than rural, and, as the Treasury's mapping of financial exclusion (reproduced in Figure 2.1) shows, it is in urban areas that most CDFIs are located. For this study, we carried out surveys of institutions in all bar one of the major conurbations represented in Figure 2.1 (south-central Scotland, Lancashire, Yorkshire, the West Midlands and South Wales),[1] excluding only greater London. Two purely business-lending organisations are examined (DSL and the 'Birmingham cluster', containing four business lenders all involved with lending to ethnic minorities), three personal-lending organisations (East Lancashire Moneyline, Yorkshire (Sheffield) Moneyline and Scotcash) and one organisation covering both modalities (Derby Loans). The individual personalities of CDFIs and their 'architectures', to adapt Kay's (1993) term for the structures of relationships in which business corporations become involved,[2] are important in determining their differential performance, and therefore impact, and in this chapter and the next we try to relate what CDFIs are able to deliver to the manner in which they are designed.

Our methodology combines, within each of our selected cities, *quantitative* methods, in the shape of analyses of impact drawn from questionnaires administered by us, and *qualitative* methods, in the shape of exploratory interviews which encourage the client to explore the motivations and the patterns of causation which determine the effectiveness of CDFI instruments and which are the cause of changes in well-being indicators. The main survey instrument consists of a questionnaire,[3] which is administered both to the treatment and to the control groups. Our fundamental research methodology is *with versus without* – that is, we seek to isolate the impact of an intervention, here the operations of a CDFI, by comparing the actual state of selected indicators of well-being with the situation which would prevail in the absence of that intervention.[4] Since the latter is hypothetical and cannot be measured directly, we simulate the situation in the absence of the intervention by constructing a *control group* (also known as a *comparison group*) – a group which has the same socio-economic characteristics as the group to which the intervention has been applied, and indeed is selected to be similar in every way to the treatment group, except for the fact that it has not benefited from the intervention. We then compare the *change* in

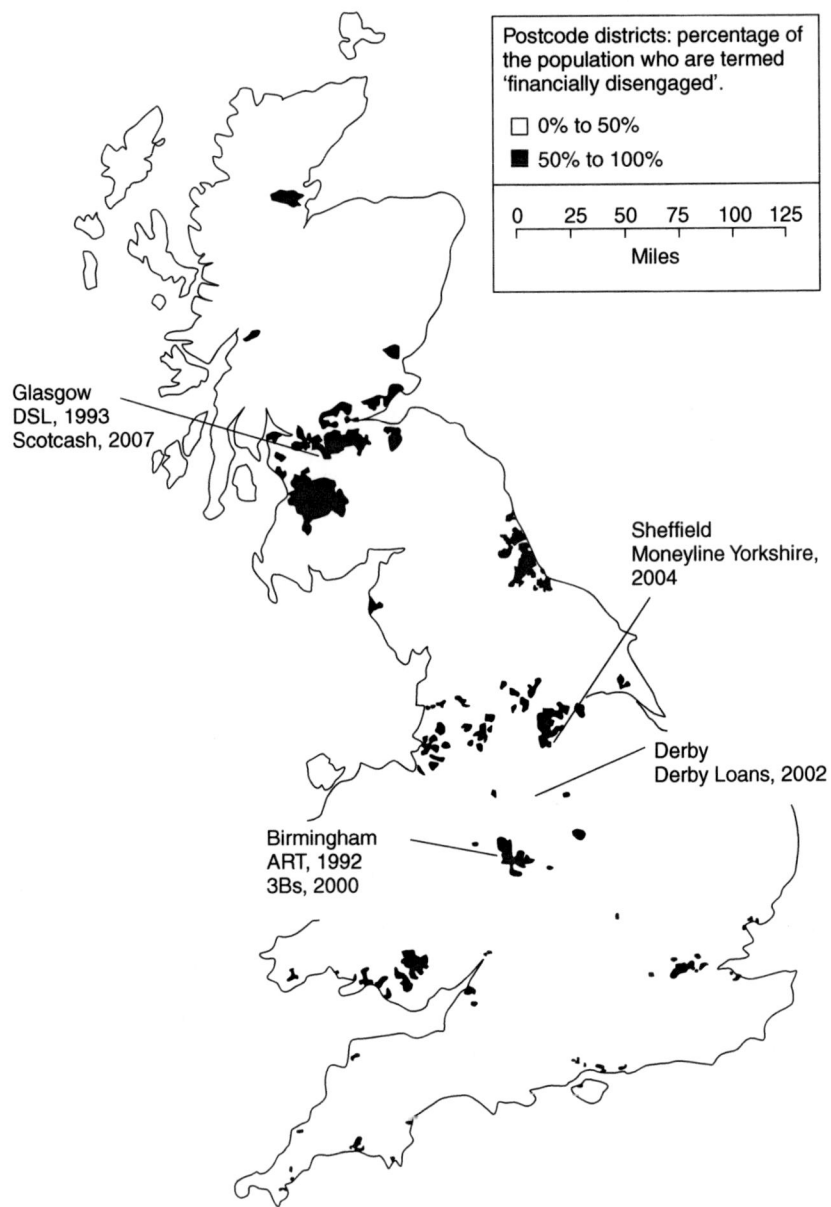

Legend on map:

Postcode districts: percentage of
the population who are termed
'financially disengaged'.

☐ 0% to 50%
■ 50% to 100%

0   25   50   75   100   125
Miles

Glasgow
DSL, 1993
Scotcash, 2007

Sheffield
Moneyline Yorkshire,
2004

Derby
Derby Loans, 2002

Birmingham
ART, 1992
3Bs, 2000

Figure 2.1 Major areas of financial exclusion (2004), with survey areas superimposed (source: adapted from United Kingdom, HM Treasury (2004), figure 1.1. Copyright of the map original rests with the Ordnance Survey and the figure is reproduced under licence number 100018617).

the well-being of the treatment group, which has received the benefit of the intervention, with the change in the well-being of the control group. If the control group is correctly identified, the difference between the change in the control group and the change in the treatment group will represent the contribution of the intervention being studied (Figure 2.2).

The approach has analogies with the experimental method used in the natural sciences in which, for example, the impact of a drug is estimated by comparing well-being and performance indicators over time as between a population who were given a drug and an identical population who did not receive it; except, of course, that in this case experiments cannot be conducted literally on the CDFI client populations, the impact on whom we are seeking to measure. In this case, the procedure we use to assess impact, not being directly executable, is simulated through the use of a control group of individuals who have not received the 'treatment' of CDFI lending, and this approach can better be described as a *quasi-experiment* (Casley and Lury 1983)

We carried out our survey twice, in 2007 and 2009, in order to assess impact over a period of time (a period, of course, which happened to coincide with a severe recession). In each 'sweep' of fieldwork (the 2007 baseline and the 2009 repeat survey), the basic questionnaires were put to clients and non-clients, and exploratory interviews were also conducted to understand patterns of causation. Our samples were selected at random for interview from lists of clients provided by the office of the CDFI; those selected were invited to choose between being interviewed face-to-face or by telephone. At all stages, obtaining informed consent has been paramount, and interviewers received training on the importance of explaining the scope of the project and allowing people to decide whether or not to participate, and also in making the questionnaire comprehensible in face of low levels of literacy and in face of distractions: the box of soft toys made available to Sheffield respondents to keep their young children happy while their parent was answering a long questionnaire was most valuable in combating the attrition problem. If a client expressed initial willingness to take part in an interview, they were asked to read an information sheet explaining the purpose of the interviews, assuring the participants of anonymity, and emphasising to them that they had the right to refuse to answer any question. Only after this information sheet had been signed did interviews proceed, which occurred in the case of about 90 per cent of personal interviews (in the case of telephone interviews, willingness to be interviewed was lower). With personal interviews, a separate room or partitioned area, was used for conducting the questionnaires, achieving a good level of privacy in a busy office environment. A payment of £10 was paid to interviewees for their time. Sample sizes for business and personal loans are given in Table 2.1.

As will be observed from the final column of Table 2.1, we experienced some attrition on the second round of the survey, especially with business-loan clients. Many respondents proved extremely difficult to contact: in many cases they had no known telephone landline, had changed their mobile telephone number since the time of the first sweep and could not be contacted in person at their home. In

Table 2.1 Sample sizes

	Treatment group numbers	Control group numbers	First sweep: timing	Second sweep: timing	Attrition rate, treatment group %
Business-lending CDFIs					
Developing Strathclyde Ltd (DSL), Glasgow	28	40	Late 2007	Late 2009	33
'Birmingham cluster': Aston Reinvestment Trust (ART), 3Bs, Halal Fund, Black Country Reinvestment Society	26	0	Late 2006	Early 2010	10
Consumer-lending CDFIs					
East Lancashire Moneyline (ELM), Blackburn	Only used for intensive interviews, not for sample survey				
Scotcash, Glasgow	125	40	Late 2007	Late 2009	35
Yorkshire Moneyline, Sheffield	136	40	Mid 2007	Mid 2009	16
Mixed business- and consumer-lending CDFIs					
Derby Loans, Derby					
Personal loans	75	40	Late 2007 to early 2008	Late 2009 to early 2010	32
Business loans	22			Late 2009 to early 2010	22

Sources: survey questionnaires (data for Scotcash, Yorkshire Moneyline, Derby Loans and 'Birmingham cluster' are online, available at: http://poverty.group.shef.ac.uk)

Table 2.2 Targeting accuracy for CDFI loans: sample data

	Numbers in sample	Postcodes of 'poorest neighbourhoods'	Percentage of client sample within 'poorest neighbourhoods' (most deprived 10% within city)	
			Borrower ('treatment') group	Control group
Sheffield (Yorkshire Moneyline) (consumer loans only)	126	S2, S3, S4, S5, S9	74	73
Derby (Derby Loans):				
Consumer loans	65	DE21, DE22, DE23, DE24	89	100
Business loans	22		60	
Glasgow:				
Consumer loans (Scotcash)	125	G15, G21, G22, G32–34, G45, G51–53	84	91
Business loans (DSL)	28		73	

Source: location of sample members from questionnaire survey, 2007–10; postcodes of 'most deprived areas' from Scottish Index of Multiple Deprivation; Office of the Deputy Prime Minister, Indices of Multiple Deprivation 2004; Derby City Council.

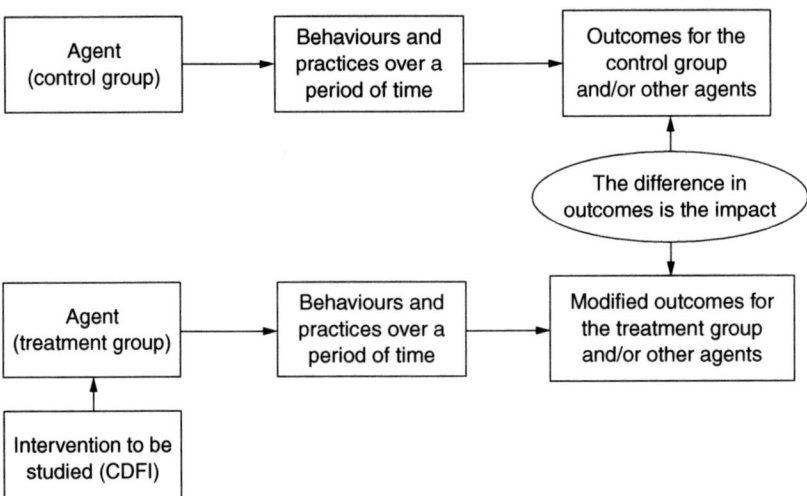

Figure 2.2 The conventional model of the impact chain (source: adapted from Hulme (2000)).

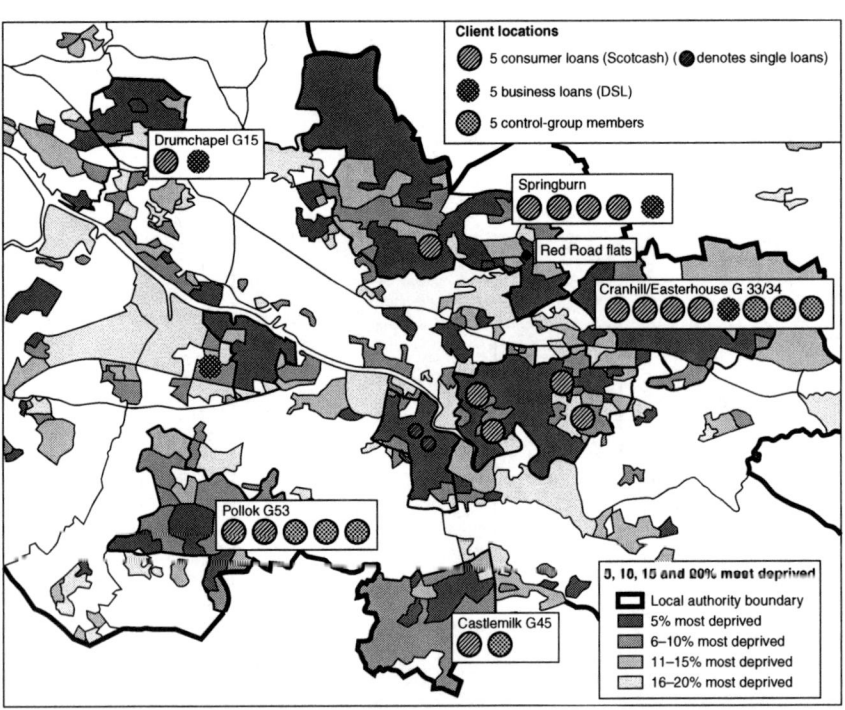

Figure 2.3a Glasgow: locations of Scotcash and DSL clients (source: adapted from deprivation maps published by Glasgow, Derby and Sheffield City Councils. Copyright of the map original rests with the Ordnance Survey and the figure is reproduced under licence number 100018617).

the case of Yorkshire Moneyline (Sheffield), Derby Loans and Scotcash, the problem of attrition (i.e. disappearance of repeat interviewees) was countered by conducting further interviews covering the period 2007–09 with a fresh sample of randomly chosen individuals selected from both the treatment-group and the control-group populations who had not been previously interviewed. These new recruits to the sample were asked to answer well-being questions related both to the time of interview and also to recall those same levels of well-being two years previously. This is not ideal, as it imposes a strain on respondents' memories, but in our judgment was the best alternative to accepting what would otherwise have been ruinously high attrition rates.

In Table 2.2, we assess the extent to which clients of our sample institutions are concentrated within the poorest neighbourhoods. This picture is fleshed out for individual neighbourhoods in the three parts of Figure 2.3, which map the pattern of supply on to the local pattern of deprivation in Glasgow, Derby and Sheffield.

On the short-run evidence presented in Table 2.2 and the deprivation maps (Figures 2.3a, b and c), our case-study institutions achieve quite a high degree of

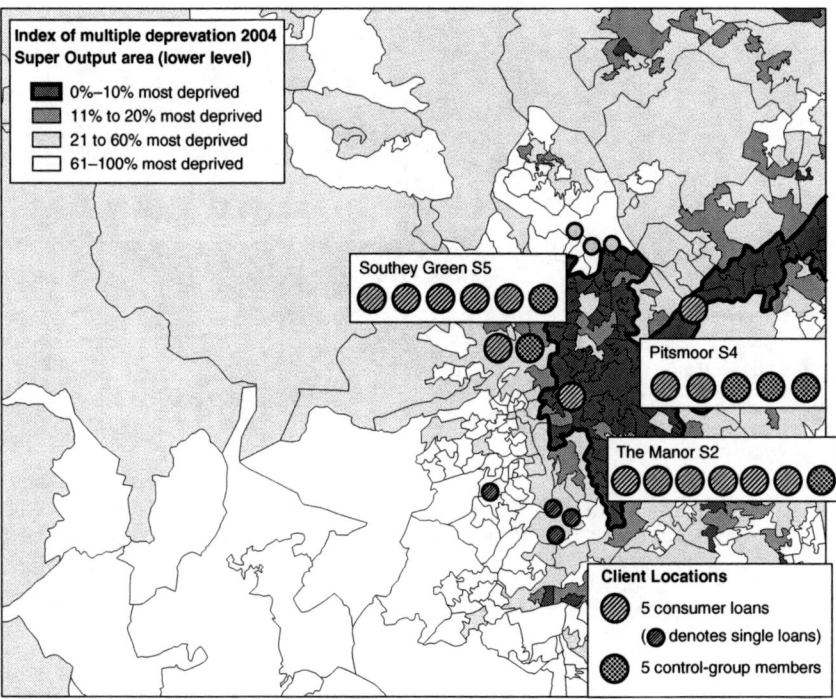

Figure 2.3b Location of Moneyline Yorkshire clients (source: adapted from deprivation maps published by Glasgow, Derby and Sheffield City Councils. Copyright of the map original rests with the Ordnance Survey and the figure is reproduced under licence number 100018617).

targeting accuracy on the poorest postcodes. On first appearance, the consumer-lending institutions are better targeted than the business-lending institutions, and it is certainly true that, within our sample, they have a stronger first-round impact. However, this begs the question of what spin-off effects they are able to achieve, through the labour market, through social networks and other routes, and these issues are discussed in Chapters 4 and 5.

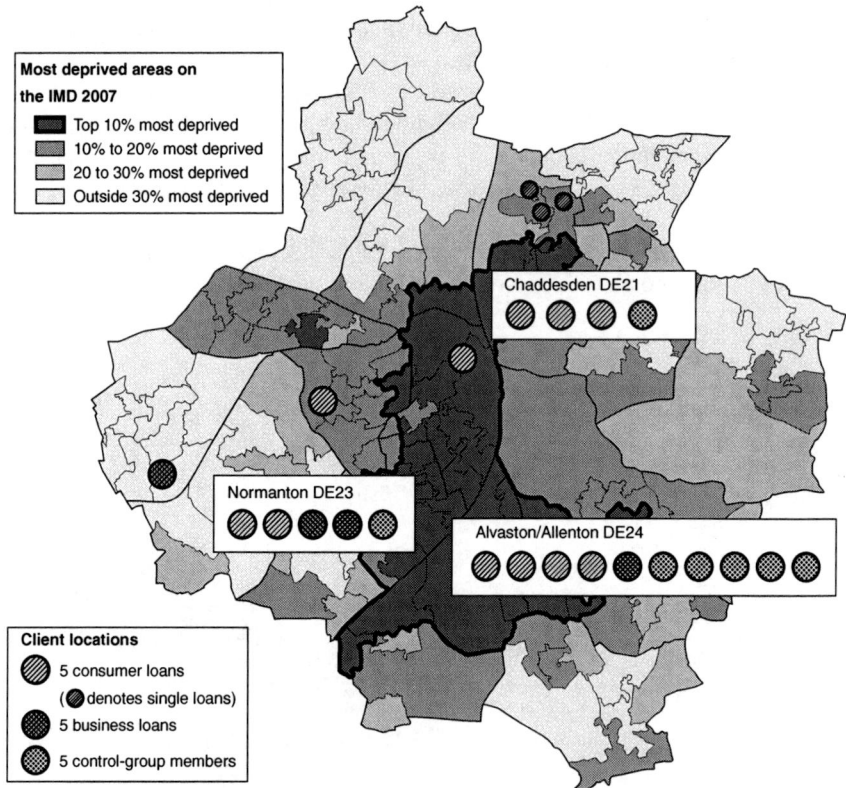

Figure 2.3c Location of Derby Loans clients (source: adapted from deprivation maps published by Derby City Council. Copyright of the map original rests with the Ordnance Survey and the figure is reproduced under licence number 100018617)

3 Financial performance of CDFIs

Outreach

In developing countries, a major reason why many microfinance institutions were able to reduce poverty on a substantial scale was that they were able to grow rapidly, without putting their finances at risk. The mere fact that BRAC and the Grameen Bank of Bangladesh, for example, were able to reach six million borrowers by the millennium, and Bank Rakyat Indonesia twenty-seven million savers,[1] was an important factor underlying the success of those institutions in reducing mass poverty.

In Britain, as we have emphasised, the market for microfinance, in the sense of the numbers of people who experience financial exclusion, is not on this scale.[2] However, in Britain as across the world as a whole the *outreach* of CDFIs – the speed at which they can grow and support their market – is an important determinant of the degree to which they can reduce poverty and deprivation. The social impact which they achieve, in fact, is simply their outreach – the number of people they manage to reach – multiplied by their impact margin – the average amount by which a CDFI increases the well-being of its clients. In this section, we examine and seek to explain the outreach of the UK CDFIs in our sample. We then go on to discuss the evolution of their financial performance.

Unlike commercial businesses such as banks, UK CDFIs are generally non-profit organisations;[3] but they also need to cover their costs if they are to survive long term. What determines their degree of success in covering costs and progressing towards viability? A point of departure is provided by John Kay's analysis of business corporations (1993), which identified four distinctive capabilities associated with corporate success. These he defined as *strategic assets* or initial advantages, *reputation*, capacity for *innovation* and, finally, what he called *architecture*, or the network of relationships and incentives which the institution is able to negotiate both within the organisation and with external partners such as sponsors, support agencies[4] and clients. Many of these relationships, both in commercial firms and in CDFIs, are based on informal trust-relationships rather than formal legal contracts.

Kay's book was concerned with modern business corporations with mainly commercial objectives – including profit maximisation but possibly also other purposes such as corporate growth, share price maximisation and deterrence of competition.[5] These are likely to differ from the objectives of CDFIs, which are not commercial corporations but charities (formally, in the terms of the Financial Services Authority's rule-book, most of them are 'Industrial and Provident Societies').[6] In particular, CDFIs need to achieve objectives associated with combating financial exclusion and poverty in local communities, as we have discussed. However, unless they raise enough finance to keep going, CDFIs like commercial firms cannot survive; and all of Kay's 'foundations of corporate success' are relevant to the performance and outreach of CDFIs, as they are to corporations. We now specify the way in which they are relevant.

Most obviously and directly, CDFIs need, if they are to achieve outreach, to be *innovative* in confronting their core problem, which is that lenders who cannot take collateral are defenceless until they design institutions to protect themselves. We described in Chapter 1 the manner in which the developing-country pioneers built their defences, through working out ingenious new incentives, such as peer pressure, to make the behaviour of debtors transparent and thereby control the cost of default. In the CDFI context also, bankable clients need to be identified, deterred in a cost-effective way from defaulting, mentored when their morale fails and motivated to save and accumulate capital. In an experimental environment in which 'what works' is not clear, this combination of requirements has not been easy to fulfil, and many CDFIs, as we shall see, have fallen by the wayside.

As we shall discover through our case studies, an important complementary asset in successful CDFIs has been the construction of an *architecture* of trust-relationships, or 'social capital networks' as they are sometimes known. In Chapter 4, we shall show that for CDFI clients, membership of social networks was often the key to whether they emerged from the poverty trap or failed to do so; and sometimes, as we shall show in Chapter 5, these social networks were able to reproduce themselves through initiatives from those clients. For CDFI managers, social networks are also of vital importance in determining success and failure. The types of networks which are relevant for determining progress down the cost curve and towards viability are of three kinds:

1   *Horizontal within-group linkages*, or what is sometimes known as 'bonding social capital' (see Woolcock and Narayan 2000) links of mutual support amongst the staff of the CDFI and sometimes also amongst CDFI clients within the community. In some CDFIs, the chemistry is such that the workforce is more than the sum of its parts, and low-paid staff nonetheless volunteer to perform vital tasks such as savings mobilisation in overtime; in others, internal inefficiencies persist and fester because of within-group rivalries and resentments, with the consequence that some CDFIs over a period of years simply do not know the state of their profit and loss account and therefore are powerless to improve it (see Case Study 3 for the contrasting cases of ELM and Yorkshire Moneyline).

2 *Horizontal between-group linkages* between CDFIs. This is the case where one CDFI learns from another and thereby improves its effectiveness. The scope for this kind of social capital-building has until recently been rather restricted. As described above, CDFIs initially grew up in a localised atmosphere in which there was one CDFI at most for each large conurbation, which did not stray outside the city limits, as shown in Chapter 1. In this atmosphere what has emerged, almost as in medieval Italian cities, has often been civic and institutional pride and rivalry rather than collaboration and information sharing. However, there do now exist institutions to overcome this, notably the Community Development Finance Association (CDFA), which maintains a research and administrative staff and runs an annual conference attended by a majority of CDFIs. As described on page 10 (also note 26, p. 186), the ethos of the association has in recent years become noticeably less social exclusion oriented and more business-oriented.[7]

3 *Vertical linkages* between CDFIs and their sponsors and clients. From the point of view of realising economies of scale, these are the crux. In seeking to broaden their market, less ambitious CDFIs (such as Yorkshire Moneyline) have relied on word of mouth to expand the market and have expanded slowly; more ambitious CDFIs such as Scotcash and Derby Loans have made widespread use of commercial advertising and have expanded much more rapidly.[8] And in the development of their financial base, some CDFIs have remained trapped within their existing civic affiliations, whereas others, notably ELM and South Coast Moneyline, had shown considerable enterprise in capturing Department of Work and Pensions (DWP) and local authority contracts on the basis of their expanding network of contacts in central and local government, and now cover much of the map. Thus, as described in Chapter 1 (pages 11–12), CDFIs now operate within different structures: some (such as Salford and Yorkshire Moneylines) still operate purely within their originating civic networks whereas others (such as ELM and Derby Loans) operate within networks which are already regional and in the former case are on the verge of becoming national.[9]

Between them, architectures and incentive structures lay the base for reputations and 'brands' to be built, a process which in CDFIs, most of them less than ten years old, is barely incipient.

Strategic assets, finally, are also highly relevant to the creation of successful CDFIs. One important strategic asset is, of course, money: Scotcash, one of the newest CDFIs, was born with a silver spoon in its mouth, in the sense of generous corporate sponsorship from the Royal Bank of Scotland and the city authorities that has enabled it to operate, by contrast with most of its CDFI competitors, a beautiful office which is a pleasure to do business in, and to be able to provide loan advice to clients deemed not to be eligible for loans, a service which is not directly remunerative and therefore needs a sponsor to provide a capital base.

However, strategic assets are not just things which CDFIs are born with, but things which they accumulate through reputation, and reputation in turn emerges from performance and from the architecture of relationships with policy makers. ELM did not begin with a large capital base, but has over the years built a reputation as an organisation which can be trusted with, in particular, local housing authority and DWP Growth Fund contracts, and its responsiveness in executing these contracts has enabled it to spread way beyond its home base. Derby Loans (now Midlands Community Finance) also began with a very modest base but has been able on the basis of its reputation to capture contracts from the DWP and regional development authorities which have given it a presence across the South and West Midlands. In other words, access to policy makers and subsidy is an important strategic asset which contributes to the determination of performance, and which as we shall see in Chapter 7, is determined at multiple geographical levels. Performance itself – ability to grow and to progress towards financial sustainability – is, of course, also a crucial strategic asset, and we analyse this in the final section of the chapter. The relationship between distinctive capabilities, size and cost is thus as in Figure 3.1.

We now present a brief portrait of each of our case-study organisations, with a view to highlighting the major features which have caused their initial conditions, their incentive structure and architecture, and thence their level of outreach, to be as they are. Our discussion is summarised in Table 3.1. The level of outreach achieved by our organisations is summarised in the left-hand column of the table, and some of the key causes of this, as we see them, are summarised in the right-hand columns.

Case-study organisations

DSL (Developing Strathclyde Ltd), based in Glasgow, is one of the pioneer CDFIs of the early 1990s, established in 1993 as a direct response to the challenge of creating self-employment opportunities for the long-term unemployed in the West of Scotland. It was initially capitalised by elements of the West of Scotland public sector (Scottish Enterprise, the Glasgow City Council Regeneration Fund and the Strathclyde Regional Council) and later attracted contributions from the European Union regional fund and from various private

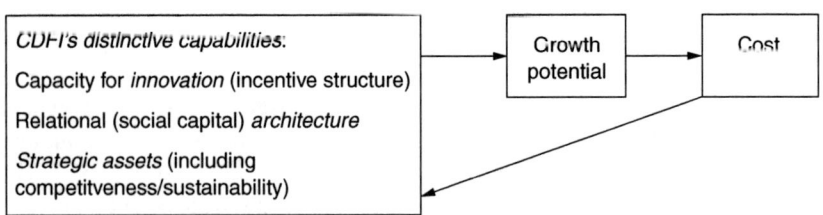

Figure 3.1 Distinctive capabilities, costs and financial performance (source: own model, derived from Kay 1993).

sector organisations. During its first ten years, it attempted to balance between the more social objective of lending to micro-scale, even start-up, businesses and the more commercial objective of lending to small, even medium-scale enterprises.[10] From the late 1990s onwards, DSL was assisted by a pathbreaking set of public–private partnership organisations in Glasgow, known as *Local Economic Development Companies* (LEDCs), which we shall encounter again in Chapters 5 and 7. One of these companies was created in each of the areas of high unemployment and deprivation within the city, both the peripheral estates such as Castlemilk, Drumchapel and Easterhouse, and inner-city areas such as Govan and Bridgeton (Figure 2.3a). They were given the job of providing technical support and advice to all enterprises assisted by DSL and other not-for-profit lenders (for a time, in the early 2000s, loans were disbursed through the LEDCs with DSL simply exercising financial supervision). The partnership between DSL and the LEDCs (Mosley and Steel 2004) was a key element in the architecture which, initially, enabled financially excluded entrepreneurs to access credit from DSL, and eventually to catalyse money out of the commercial banks, and then provided advice on which they could fall back in times of crisis, as we further document in the business-lending case studies of Chapter 4.

During a period of expansion between 2004 and 2006, there was a deterioration in arrears and other measures of financial performance. Under the management of a new chief executive, Eunice Lancaster, a number of corrective measures were taken. The number of employees was cut from six to four; several functions, in particular the IT and accounts functions, were outsourced from DSL to private companies; and the enterprise began energetically to broaden its market and to make linkages with complementary enterprises: its market now extends into Edinburgh, Fife and the Scottish borders. A notable step towards greater financial security for DSL was achieved in 2005 when the enterprise was brought within the government's Small Firms Loan Guarantee (SFLG) scheme,[11] which provided insurance for it against the cost of loan write-offs and other hazards. However, partly on account of the minimum loan-size limit of £5,000 applied by the SFLG, partly simply for reasons of cost competitiveness,[12] DSL has abandoned its previous policy of supporting very small businesses; there are those, including staff of the Regeneration Agencies (as the LEDCs are now known) who regret this, on the grounds that this makes things harder for vulnerable low-income entrepreneurs.[13]

The birth of *Derby Loans* originates with the city council, and with the failure of its attempts in the mid 1990s to get a city-wide credit union up and running. The leader of Derby City Council at that time was from a welfare rights background, and was aware of the existence of the CDFI model (as operated, for example, by Salford Moneyline). He commissioned a social survey in 2001 which illustrated the extent of financial exclusion in the city (see Derby Loans (now Midlands Community Finance) *Report to Shareholders and Funders*, January 2008 to December 2009) and recommended that an institution should be established to counter it. The new enterprise was able to raise long-term capital from the Derbyshire Building Society, as well as Derby Homes and the regional development authority, the East Midlands Development Authority. Initially it favoured the business-lending strategy for combating social exclusion: it was to Rolls-Royce, the city's chief employer, that the city council turned in looking for a chief executive to run the prospective anti-financial exclusion venture, and it was from Rolls-Royce that a manager, Andrew Baker, was recruited to run the company. The new company, Derby Loans, 'managed to catch a bit of Phoenix Fund money [in 2003–04] before the door shut'.[14] Derby Loans has always wished to pursue a portfolio balanced between personal and business loans. However, in 2008 it lost a contract to supply business loans from the East Midlands Development Authority, leaving it with only one source of financing for business loans, Advantage West Midlands. This has forced the enterprise, since 2008 renamed Midlands Community Enterprise to reflect its broader ambitions, to become more proactive within the personal loans market.

But there was always a willingness to diversify and to embrace any strategy which worked,[15] and both Andrew Baker and Melanie Andrew, who joined him as chief executive in 2007 and eventually replaced him on retirement, were keen to emulate National Provident's ability to achieve market share and indeed to compete with doorstep-lending agencies by any possible means. Initial expansionism was directed northwards, towards the coalfields of north Derbyshire and north Nottinghamshire, and a new branch of Derby Loans was opened in the high-unemployment neighbourhood of South Normanton, fifteen miles north of the city, in 2006. However the approach of opening the South Normanton branch one day a week did not work well commercially, and Derby Loans' expansion strategy soon switched towards south of the city – to Swadlincote, also a former coal-mining area, and to the larger town of Burton-on-Trent. Derby Loans has been highly successful in pursuing Growth Fund contracts from the DWP, and its major recent coup, in 2009, has been to win a DWP contract to cover the whole of Northamptonshire outside the county town, with new lending centres being established in Kettering, Corby and Peterborough, and two new loan officer posts being recruited.

The composition of demand for CDFIs has shifted over the eight years that Derby Loans has been in existence, and in particular ethnic minorities have penetrated many areas of low-income housing in Derby. The main street of Normanton, where Derby Loans' base is located, has evolved in seven years from a dour working-class alley to an ebullient multi-ethnic neighbourhood, with seven Polish/Kurdish/Pakistani mini-supermarkets, a minaret newly adorning the largest South Asian restaurant, and melons, mangoes and oranges spilling onto the pavements in midwinter. In the process, there has been a demographic shift: Derby Loans' core market for personal loans, like Scotcash's (see below) is 'poor white', not Asian, and its centre of gravity has shifted over time from Normanton (DE23) to the neighbouring postcode, DE24 (see Figure 3.1b), which is ethnically less diverse. For small business, the ethnic shift has been in the opposite direction, and a case study of CDFI lending to ethnic-minority business in Derby is presented as Case Study 6 (p. 104).

The distinguishing features of Derby Loans' architecture are pragmatism (in relation both to financial products and to the locus of geographical expansion), the strength of links with local business and the weakness of links with banks and, in particular, credit unions: one attempt to achieve a partnership with the Derby Credit Union was formed and dissolved in 2003, and in 2009 the credit union went bankrupt. Thus savings development strategies have had, in the main, to be pursued through other channels; the option of developing basic bank accounts through Trusted Partnership status with the Royal Bank of Scotland is being pursued. The character of policy has changed over time to reflect the balance of controlling interests: on the board, there are now fewer city councillors, and more accountants and business people. However, the continuing influence of city councillors is reflected in decision making on interest rates, which remain at a maximum of 24 per cent in spite of the organisation's desire to price according to risk and to charge more than 30 per cent for some loans, as the management would wish and as several CDFIs are already doing. Interest-rate strategy is further discussed below.

Unlike other CDFIs in this book, *Moneyline Yorkshire* (to give it its proper name; we shall generally and inaccurately refer to it as 'Sheffield Moneyline') is not a free-standing organisation but rather a CDFI organisationally linked to a credit union. It originated, in September 2004, from a merger between three credit unions around the city of Sheffield to form a new Sheffield Credit Union (SCU). This merger was accompanied by pressure from several mainly church-based non-governmental organisations (NGOs) in Sheffield to provide for a lower social stratum by establishing a new lending vehicle for severely indebted people without assets, to be known as Moneyline Yorkshire (MY). It was intended that clients of MY would be provided with loan advice and positive encouragement to save, to be provided by a new NGO known as Financial Inclusion South Yorkshire (FISY), and that these services would enable them to 'graduate' over time, as they built up savings, to become members of the credit union: by this means a unique one-stop shop for financial inclusion would, it was hoped, be provided for the city, and eventually across the whole of the South Yorkshire conurbation. Initial grant financing for this structure was provided by Barclays Bank and, after 2004, from the DWP's Growth Fund, with loan finance from the social enterprise funder, the South Yorkshire Key Fund. Sheffield City Council has also provided grant financing from the start, but more in a supportive role than in the propulsive, entrepreneurial role that we observe in ELM and Derby Loans. Within the architecture of Moneyline Yorkshire, business influence is therefore weaker, and the influence of credit unions stronger, than in any of the other institutions in our sample. In the role of Chief Executive of the three linked organisations, the appointments committee[16] recruited a banker, who, however, became increasingly constrained by loyalty to the credit union and to the city council. Originally, business lending, along with housing lending, was in the prospectus, but it was rejected by the chief executive as risky and a likely road to financial ruin; housing lending continued in principle as a 'runner', but a runner that never materialised; and there has been no attempt at geographical expansion of Moneyline outside Sheffield.[17] Thus the possibility of funding from the regional development authority, lucrative for Derby Loans and DSL, vanished, in an environment in which local authority funding remained weak. As a source of seedcorn funding, this left the organisation heavily dependent on the DWP Growth Fund contracts; Moneyline became an entirely consumer-lending operation. However, even in this role, it remained vulnerable, partly because of its inability to control its arrears but even more because its architecture, with Moneyline in the grip of a dominant credit union, rendered it vulnerable to a financial squeeze. In 2006, it was announced that the DWP Growth Fund contract for Sheffield had been transferred from Moneyline to the Sheffield Credit Union, in order to provide financial support for the credit union. Moneyline Yorkshire was thus bereft of its main source of funding; and since that time, Moneyline's viability has dwindled.[18] As a result of the weak performance and expiry of grants that were intended to support the loan advice function, the services of FISY had fallen away to almost nothing, and Moneyline clients were left with sparse mentoring services. Arrears rates at this time were about average for CDFIs at around 15 per cent, but the organisation's IT facilities were so poor that it took four years to demonstrate that this was so, which did nothing for its reputation with sponsors. Moneyline's structure was further weakened when the chief executive of the three now merged organisations was seconded to Sheffield City Council as a Financial Inclusion Champion in 2009 and not replaced, leaving a leadership void for the organisation's board and professional officers to fill as best they could. In the midst of a global recession, and with the balance of power within the organisations having veered towards the credit union, the stage seemed set for Moneyline to be wound up. This course of action was in fact recommended by the organisation's auditors in February 2010.

The story, however, contains a further twist. Growth Fund funding from the DWP, originally planned to end in March 2011, has now been extended for eight months until November 2011. Lending through credit unions is capped by law at an interest rate of 24 per cent, a constraint which does not afflict (Yorkshire) Moneyline.[19] At the time of writing, the board of the merged organisations is now seeking to refloat Moneyline by escaping from the credit union's interest-rate cap and on-lending interest payments repaid to it in the form of top-up loans through Moneyline at an interest rate which reflects the risk costs of lending, likely to be just around 100 per cent per annum. This is still, of course, highly competitive with the 300 per cent plus annual percentage rates charged by home credit providers, as described in Chapter 1. The CDFI–credit union alliance, in other words, has already experienced both an unexpected downside and an unexpected upside, both of them completely unforeseen by this author and director of Moneyline.

Scotcash, established in April 2007, is the newest of the institutions considered in this study. As of the time of writing it had provided a cumulative total of nearly 3,000 loans (about 1,000 of these in 2009), which makes it, already and in spite of being only three-and-a-half years old, one of the larger CDFIs in Britain.[20] It already supplies about one-eighth of the loans made by UK CDFIs (excluding credit unions), and under its ambitious expansion plan, aims to provide financial services to over 60,000 people over twenty years, thereby breaking the hold of the doorstep moneylender (Scotcash 2008). Scotcash is sponsored not (as in most cases in both the industrialised and developing worlds) by an NGO but by a public–private triumvirate – Glasgow City Council, the Glasgow Housing Association (GHA) and the Royal Bank of Scotland – providing it, as discussed above, with a clear strategic asset. (As in the case of DSL, one notices a stronger role for the state in the establishment of CDFIs than that found south of the border.) One rationale for this particular form of sponsorship, which applies to all local authorities, is that Scotcash, if able to help clients manage their debts better, may be able to reduce the GHA's overdues also. The financial strength deriving from this pattern of sponsorship has enabled Scotcash to afford effective publicity, inviting and attractive premises, a salary package some 25 per cent above the going rate, and the innovation of a comprehensive loan advice service as described in Case Study 1. All of these, as we shall see, have impacted favourably on Scotcash's ability to grow and to keep its arrears under control.

Case Study 1 Loan advice in Scotcash

Scotcash is selective in its allocation of loans to the financially excluded. After interview and financial appraisal, many applicants for financial support from Scotcash are deemed not to be eligible for loans, but for money advice only. As of September 2010, 1,730 clients – about two-thirds of the number who had received loans – had received money advice, but only seventy-five of these advice clients had gone on to take loans.[21] The advice function is executed by two senior advisers (one of them formerly an insolvency administrator and the other formerly an accountant, both with more than twenty years' experience), seconded to Scotcash from the Glasgow office of the Citizens' Advice Bureau (CAB), and working full-time within the Scotcash office. Their assistance, which takes the form not only of advice with financial planning but also of practical help with rescheduling overdue loans by home credit providers and claiming welfare benefits owed to clients, is available to all who apply for Scotcash services. Often, for example, if a loan advice session reveals a client to have an unmanageable level of debt as a consequence of having contracted multiple loans from different home lenders, a loan adviser will contact the home lender to arrange a temporary reduction or stoppage of repayments. 'They will usually grant this relief, as they soon realise that they can't get money out of a stone.'[22] Loan advisers can also check the range of welfare benefits which a client is currently claiming against those to which she is entitled, and advise her of any additional benefits to which she is entitled. In addition, advice is given on financial planning and saving, with a view to achieving a long-term improvement in debt management capacity. Both loan and advice clients are encouraged to take out savings accounts with the Glasgow Credit Union. The fact that the two advisers, although working on Scotcash premises, are still formally attached to the CAB and thus providing *independent* financial advice is clearly publicised by Scotcash and for vulnerable borrowers is an important asset which gradually enables them to build up trust-relationships ('linking social capital') with the advisers.[23]

Between 2008 and 2010, it was estimated that by these means a sum of £1.8 million was saved for Scotcash clients. There are longer-term behavioural effects as well. Some clients, in the experience of the advisers, have got out of chronic debt and have been so traumatised by the experience of being in it that they have determined never to borrow again. Others have experienced an increase in their self-confidence to manage money, and have got themselves on to a sustainable borrowing path. One of these, previously a domestic violence victim with multiple debts to loan sharks, was assisted by the loan advisers to get a mortgage, after getting her debts down to a reasonable size. Another was able, with the help of the loan advisers, to achieve an increase in her tax credits and, after an industrial tribunal which the advisers encouraged her to attend, to get her job back. The experience of other Scotcash clients is discussed in Chapters 4 and 5 below.

This approach points the way towards an entirely new approach to advice, in which that advice is treated not as a complement to lending, but as a separate service responding to a different kind of need, providing a consolation prize (and a ladder into loan services) for those not accepted for loans, and a screen, increasing the quality of loans, for the lender.

Emulating widespread practice in the developing world, Scotcash, consciously influenced by ELM[24] (discussed below) offers incentives, in the shape of larger loans and lower interest rates, to those who have a track record of repaying on time: as lenders become better acquainted with their market, they acquire knowledge which enables them to better screen out good from bad borrowers and thereby to reduce the cost of lending. The organisation is seeking to diversify its product from loans into house contents insurance, and geographically to expand beyond Glasgow into Lanarkshire and Dundee.

Two further elements of the relational atmosphere of Scotcash are worth elaborating. The office layout is at the opposite pole from the glum benefits-office atmosphere of many CDFIs, and its open-plan, stripped-pine, brightly lit environment evokes more the feeling of an up-market architect's office than that of a jobcentre or even a bank: and a vigorously participatory and can-do culture, with team meetings every morning, is encouraged by the general manager. These aspects of the organisation's architecture – its literal architecture in this case, not just its relational architecture – are supportive of long-term trust-relationships within the organisation and thereby help to bring down the organisation's long-term cost structure, as we discuss below.

East Lancashire Moneyline (ELM) arose out of awareness in the high-unemployment East Lancashire area of a market for fair-priced financial services amongst financially excluded people depending on doorstep lenders for personal finance. Support for this idea was provided by local authorities, especially housing offices beset by arrears problems. Initially, ELM's expansion was laterally from its base in Blackburn along the Colne valley (the M65 corridor) to Accrington and Burnley, and also Bury. Building on this base, however, ELM quickly gained a reputation for the provision of 'back-office' services, including IT and training (including the training, in 2004, of the loan officers of the incipient Yorkshire Moneyline),[25] which helped to supplement the fee income part of its business. ELM was also highly proactive in winning DWP contracts, after these were opened to outside tenders.[26] Between 2005 and 2009, ELM won contracts to supply personal loans far outside its East Lancashire base – in Merseyside, Grimsby, Staffordshire and across the whole of South Wales – and currently has a loan book of about £2 million and an 'outreach' (Table 3.1) of about 3,000 loan clients in 2009. It is thus, in terms of turnover, the most successful of all CDFIs to date, and the first to achieve something like a nationwide presence. In its low-key style, avoiding rhetorical mission statements, glossy publicity and other PR devices, its maintenance of close informal ties with clients and sponsors, and its rigorous pursuit of arrears coupled with great flexibility in face of clients' personal circumstances, it emulates the idiom of both the inspirational microfinance institutions of the developing world and the most successful of the UK home-credit lenders such as National Provident. In two other areas of under-performance for most CDFIs – arrears control and savings mobilisation – ELM has also excelled, principally by designing an effective incentive structure. These are issues of great importance for understanding outreach and productivity, and we return to them below.

CDFI architecture and the determinants of outreach

Thus the personal lenders, Scotcash and ELM, achieved an initial strategic asset through their initial links with local government and housing offices (and, in the case of Scotcash, also their generous capitalisation derived from their additional links with the Royal Bank of Scotland), which were then built into a relational architecture which provided a platform for future expansion. In Derby Loans, the city council was also present as an inspirer, but private businesses (including the 'local' Derbyshire Building Society) were much more to the fore, and the city housing office (Derby Homes), although present, was present in a more recessive role. In Sheffield Moneyline, the architecture was different again, in the shape of a partnership between the CDFI, a group of local credit unions and various mostly church-related charities. ELM and Scotcash, and to a lesser extent Derby Loans, then built on their initial asset base through the development of innovative services and incentives (such as Scotcash's advice service, ELM's savings incentives, and publicity initiatives and geographical expansion in all three organisations). Through their entrepreneurial approach, ELM and Derby Loans were able to expand outside their home community. By contrast, Moneyline Yorkshire found itself marginalised by its own architecture, stifled rather than supported by its parent credit union, until it suddenly in 2010 perceived the scope for reprieve by taking advantage of its room for manoeuvre on interest rates. Other organisations not represented in Table 3.1 have used other approaches to achieve outreach; for example, the founding consumer-lending organisation, Portsmouth PART (now South Coast Moneyline), has now largely diversified out of consumer lending into small-scale housing lending, and now holds local authority contracts for this function covering much of southern England.

Table 3.1 Outreach of CDFIs and possible determinants

Institution	'Outreach'		Strategic assets: initial capitalisation (£000)	'Architecture': internal relationships within enterprise, and external relationships with sponsors and clients	Incentives to innovation			Geographical coverage
	Number of loans made in 2009	Size of loan book (May 2010) (£000)			Product coverage	Commercial strategy	Financial discipline and savings	
Business-lending and hybrid-lending organisations								
DSL (1993)	105	2,445	300 Initial capitalisation from Glasgow CC regeneration fund (later European Union social fund also).	1998–2005: all loans given in partnership with LEDCs (local economic development companies) which provided technical support to clients. 2005 to date: only small businesses (i.e. sole traders) supported by LEDCs (now Regeneration Agencies); larger businesses supported through Business Gateway.	Business loans only.	Leaflets, local newspapers and others (e.g. regeneration agencies) (Note: since 2007, Scotcash also publicises DSL).		Glasgow and West of Scotland, with links to Edinburgh, Fife and Scottish borders.
Derby Loans (2002)	20 (business loans only)	150 (business loans only) 500 (consumer loans only) 650 (total loan book)	150	Initial impulse from Derby City Council and Derbyshire Building Society. Board was chaired by a local businesswoman until 2008, and business representation on the board has increased since that time. Notably weak links with credit unions (see text). More recently, partnerships being sought with commercial banks.	Initially business loans; consumer loans added after 2003.	Leaflets, local newspaper adverts and other (e.g. Arriva buses).		2004: expansion into former coalfield areas of north Derbyshire and north Nottinghamshire. 2007: expansion into south Derbyshire and north Staffordshire. 2009: expansion into Northamptonshire (DWP Growth Fund contract).

Consumer-lending organisations

East Lancs Moneyline (ELM) (2002)	3,250	£2 million		Linkages to local (East Lancs) district councils provide strong funding base.	Initially (until c. 2005) provided business, housing and consumer loans; now business loans only.	Leaflets, local newspaper adverts.	(1) Encouragement to all borrowers to save £1 in every £10 (see Chapter 4, Case Study 3). Appointment of full-time Debt Recovery Officer.	2002–05: from initial base in Blackburn, new branches opened in Accrington, Burnley and Bury. 2006: new branches opened in Grimsby and Merseyside. 2008: new branches opened across South Wales.
Scotcash	1,500	1,200	415	Jointly sponsored by Glasgow City Council, Glasgow Housing Association and Royal Bank of Scotland. Provides specialist loan advice, typically to clients who have not been granted loans (see Case Study 1) Strong linkages to Glasgow Credit Union.	Consumer loans only.	Leaflets, local newspaper adverts and other (e.g. local housing offices). Note: also advertises the services of DSL and other microfinance providers within the Glasgow area.	(1) Free loan advice available to all clients. (2) Interest-rate discounts to on-time payers.	Glasgow metropolitan area only.
Derby Loans	See above							
Moneyline Yorkshire (2004)	200	250	110	Partnership between Moneyline Yorkshire (MY) and Sheffield Credit Union (SCU), with the former providing unsecured loans to the lowest income groups.	Initial capitalisation through Barclays Bank and Church Urban Fund; subsequent finance from DWP Growth Fund (80%) and Sheffield City Council.	Leaflets only.		Sheffield metropolitan area only.

Source: Developing Strathclyde Ltd, Derby Loans, East Lancs Moneyline, Scotcash, Derby Loans (trading as Midlands Community Finance) and Sheffield Credit Union (incorporating Moneyline Yorkshire), *Annual Report and Accounts*, 2009 or latest available year.

Note

Birmingham business-lending organisations are not represented here but are listed in the discussion of ethnic-minority lending in Chapter 5.

Business lenders have found it more difficult than personal lenders to build market share in the UK,[27] and have dealt with the problem in a variety of ways. Derby Loans, as discussed above, has switched into consumer lending and thereby built up its loan pot, reduced its average loan size and increased its ability to target the poor (see Figure 3.1b). Some institutions not represented in this list, such as Aston Reinvestment Trust (ART) in Birmingham and Black Country Reinvestment Society (BCRS) in the West Midlands, have gone up-market, refusing to make loans of less than £10,000. DSL's combination of cost-cutting, geographical expansion and achievement of shelter under the Small Firms Loan Guarantee Fund umbrella has enabled it also to balance financial self-protection with a policy of continuing to nurture small and vulnerable entrepreneurs, although not on such a generous scale as previously.

CDFI costs and viability

To protect their long-term solvency, CDFIs need to find a means of covering their costs on a long-term basis. The preceding paragraphs discussed the factors on the demand side which determine a CDFI's scope for expansion. We now examine the other half of the viability story, the factors underlying the structure of costs.

There are three main categories of cost that a CDFI has to cover: the interest it pays on the loan capital it borrows, the costs of operating the organisation (or administrative costs) and the costs it incurs as the result of having to write off loans that go bad and are not repaid. Between them, these costs define the 'break-even' charge which a CDFI must make for credit if it is to cover its costs, which is:

$$r^* = \frac{(a+i+p)}{1-p} + K \qquad (3.1)$$

where a=operating costs (sometimes known as 'administrative costs'), i=the cost of acquiring funds to on-lend,[28] p=the cost of loan write-offs – all of these defined as a percentage of the CDFI's portfolio – and K=the cost of capitalising the CDFI. (The variable p representing costs of default appears in this relationship both in the numerator and in the denominator since if default occurs, the 'good' debtors who are continuing to service their loans have to pay both the lost interest and the lost principal on the 'bad' accounts in order to enable the CDFI to break even.) This relationship, first developed by Henderson and Khambata (1985) illustrates three propositions of great importance concerning CDFIs' interest-rate policy, the first very obvious and the other two less so.

The first proposition is that ability to control default is the crux. If a CDFI wishes to keep interest rates to the borrower at a moderate level (say below 50 per cent APR on a twelve-month loan) and at the same time wishes to break even, then it *must* keep write-offs due to default low (say below 12 per cent) – which most UK CDFIs, recall Table 1.2 above, have not succeeded in doing.[29]

Otherwise, it must admit defeat and, to be sustainable, it must charge interest rates well above those which have normally prevailed – and well above those which CDFIs' boards of directors, especially those dominated by charitable interests, are typically willing to tolerate.

Although most CDFIs, to date, have failed in the task of keeping arrears low, the task is not impossible, and has in fact been accomplished by the majority of microfinance institutions in the developing world (see Chapter 1, p. 13). The way to do it is, as we recall from Chapter 1, first to exert continuous pressure to repay on borrowers, either directly from the lender to the borrower by telephone and/or indirectly through Grameen-style peer groups, and second to keep the loan size very low until the borrower has proved her ability to sustain repayments. The exerting of this pressure on clients, of course, causes a temporary upward bump in the lender's administrative costs (a in equation (3.1)) – the payments made to those who supervise the loan repayments. But, because the relationship between a and p in equation (3.1) is non-linear, the 'bump' more than pays for itself in lower default costs (p). There is evidence that ELM and Scotcash in particular have begun to appreciate this logic and to reap dividends from applying it. ELM has appointed a director of credit control who has implemented a policy of telephone reminders for all those who go even a day overdue, followed by home visits for those who still do not pay, and Scotcash have taken the radical step of parting company with the debt collection agency whom they previously employed, making loan officers directly responsible for their own arrears. In both organisations there has been an improvement performance, and Scotcash's arrears now stand at 4.8 per cent, far better than the UK average (see Table 1.2) and perfectly respectable in relation to a global performance measure.

The third proposition is a little more complex. CDFIs generate benefits (revenues) not only to the CDFI itself which enable it to break even, but also benefits to others and in particular clients – benefits which include improved health, improved employment prospects, improved community cohesion, improved links with the financial system and other dimensions of well-being which accrue to people outside the CDFI. Indeed, a major purpose of Chapters 4 through 6 of this book is to calculate these 'external' benefits. However, to reap many of these external benefits, further costs over and above those contained in the administrative cost (measure a in equation (3.1)) have to be incurred – they require a prior investment in support activities such as loan advice and mentoring, on the Scotcash model, which most CDFIs because of their low initial capitalisation cannot afford. How is this obstacle to be got round?

For now, rather than attempt to answer this question directly, we shall leave it hanging (we finally get round to it in Chapters 4 and 7), and focus on relationship in equation (3.1) in its simplest form. Figure 3.2 illustrates the relationship between costs and scale of production for our sample of CDFIs over the course of the 2000s.[30] It illustrates the presence of powerful economies of scale. Average costs (measured as a percentage of portfolio) in Moneyline, with a loan book of under £100,000, are some thirty times those in DSL, with a loan book of £2 million.[31] These cost levels, high by global standards for all CDFIs and astronomical for the smallest, constitute one of the biggest barriers to the expansion of CDFIs. Even the institutions which are big by UK standards, ELM and Scotcash, are pygmies in global microfinance terms, and most CDFIs, not having been able to go to scale to the extent that ELM and Scotcash have, are currently, in face of the global recession and the impending withdrawal of DWP Growth Fund money, having difficulty retaining a long-term footing even in their local markets.

However, for none of the organisations studied has experience consisted of a simple linear progression down the cost curve, and there are other factors at work which influence costs and possibilities for expansion.

One factor which has emerged with the evolution of 'nationwide' CDFIs is *sequences of expansion and consolidation.* As discussed above, successful microfinance institutions gradually overcome the asymmetric information problem by getting to know their market, expanding their relationships with those whom they can trust and limiting or eliminating their relationships with those whom they cannot. Within a city or neighbourhood, this process can enable CDFIs to travel down the cost curve quite quickly. But, especially in UK conditions, the market quickly becomes saturated, and this has obligated CDFIs that wish to grow quickly, such as Derby Loans, South Coast Moneyline and ELM, to seek out other markets – which, by hypothesis, they do not know as well as their 'parent' market. Doing this inflicts on them two kinds of costs: on the one hand, the set-up cost of finding new premises, advertising for staff and paying

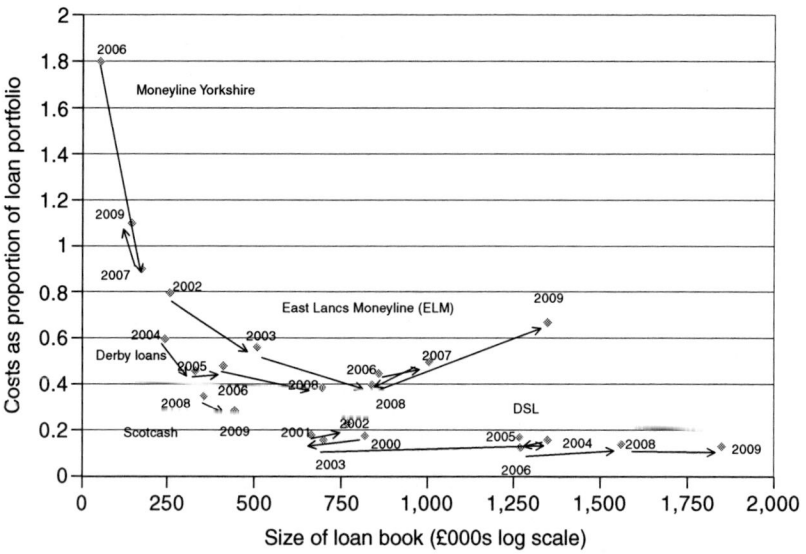

Figure 3.2 Cost functions for four CDFIs, 1995–2009 (sources: Developing Strathclyde Ltd, Derby Loans, East Lancs Moneyline, Scotcash, Derby Loans (trading as Midlands Community Finance) and Sheffield Credit Union (incorporating Moneyline Yorkshire), Annual Report and Accounts, 2009 or latest available year).

the running costs of new lending centres from which no revenue is coming in, and, on the other, the likelihood that default costs in new areas will in the short term also be higher than in established areas, precisely because trust-relationships between lenders and borrowers have had no time to gel. For these reasons, we observe on Figure 3.1 an upward bulge in the cost ratio of ELM in 2009 as its lending programmes in Grimsby, St Helens and Wales come on stream and a smaller upward movement in Derby Loans' costs in 2008 with the expansion into south Derbyshire and Staffordshire.

Second, there is scope for influencing cost levels through policy actions. Within DSL, as described above, there was a disturbing increase in arrears to over 30 per cent in 2006, which forced a temporary stoppage of lending and which if not contained could have brought the company down. A solution to the problem was found by bringing the company within the ambit of the Small Firms Loan Guarantee Scheme (now Enterprise Guarantee Scheme), which provides protection against the consequences of loan write-offs affecting small firms, subject to specific conditions (e.g. DSL no longer supports start-ups or loans under £5,000). This protection, as shown in Figure 3.2, has straightened out what was threatening to become a dangerous kink in the cost curve.

Third, the key element in the cost structures of microfinance organisations is, as discussed above, *arrears and default on loans*, and this may vary between firms for reasons quite independent of economies of scale. Indeed, as will be recalled (p. 7, above) it was with the devising of a technology that would 'sub-stitute for collateral' and thereby restrain loan arrears even among very poor, assetless people that microfinance began. This involved harnessing a whole range of social pressures into playing the role of discouraging debtors from defaulting – including bringing bank staff face-to-face with them every week to pay their weekly instalments, organising them in solidarity groups, exposing debtors to social pressure, offering discounts in exchange for a track record of on-time repayment and providing them with buffers which might protect them against having to default, such as savings and insurance.[32] Many of these devices involved setting up administrative structures, notably networks of mobile banking services and repayment centres within clients' villages and urban loca-tions, and these of course added to the administrative cost associated with lending. But, since the gap between costs and revenues rises linearly with the level of administrative cost but exponentially with the default rate (equation (3.1)), the bargain was always likely to be a good one if conscientiously applied – and so it has proved. Scotcash invested administrative resources in bringing its default rate down; its outreach is growing. Yorkshire Moneyline, Sheffield, did not; its outreach is shrinking.

In Britain and other industrialised countries, it might be expected that the whole problem of controlling default would be easier to solve: by contrast with the case in developing countries, CDFI clients in industrialised countries are never more than a day's drive from the creditor institution, can be quickly traced by telephone and can be required to set up a direct debit out of their bank account, from which loan repayments are automatically debited on pay day. In practice, as we have observed (Table 1.2 and surrounding discussion) the reverse is the case: the default rates of UK CDFIs are on average some seven times what they are in developing countries, and as a consequence most CDFIs are chronically weak. One reason for this may be that in Britain, the range of substitutes for collateral falls far short of what is attempted in LDCs. Early experiments with group lending have mainly been abandoned[33] and exposing debtors to social pressure has scarcely been tried, but there has been imaginative use of 'progressive lending' – i.e. scaling up loan size in exchange for a track record of on-time repayment. However, as we have already observed, British CDFIs do vary greatly in their architectures, and it is therefore important to try and understand which available features of loan recovery technology feed effectively into lower default rates. In Table 3.2, we seek to relate the default rates of our case-study institutions to the investments they have made in efforts to control arrears.

CDFIs' practice in recovering delinquent loans does vary widely, as Table 3.2 illustrates. Best practice is represented by ELM and Scotcash, both of which aim to initiate telephone contact with all clients who are behind on their repayments within forty-eight hours of the repayment falling overdue. (Artistry is required in doing this effectively, since many CDFI clients have only a mobile telephone rather than a landline, and defaulters are likely to instantly disconnect as soon as the CDFI's landline number appears on the read-out display of their mobile.) ELM, in addition, have recently appointed a full-time debt-recovery officer, and follow up telephone contact with home visits if repayments are not resumed. ELM calculate that in 85 per cent of cases, home visits occur within fourteen days.[34] There is a huge performance gap here between the leaders and the laggards, Derby Loans and Moneyline Yorkshire, who neither make use of home visits nor (until September 2010, in the case of Yorkshire Moneyline) have a dedicated loan recovery officer. But at least Derby Loans and Moneyline, even if not using best practice, are aware of the arrears problem and (on the evidence of 2009–10 data) their loan recovery performance is improving. By contrast, 3Bs (Birmingham) has gone out of business and South Coast Moneyline has an arrears rate of 77 per cent, so that de facto it is more of a grant-giving than a financial organisation, and its survival must be in doubt when DWP finance terminates in 2011.

Other methods of controlling default are practised by members of our sample. Scotcash, as we have observed (Case Study 1, pp. 33–34) follow the strategy that prevention is better than cure, and screen out all those applicants for loans who appear on appraisal not to be likely to keep up repayments, compensating them with the offer of loan advice: thus their client base is more preselected than the others in our sample, and Scotcash's relatively low default rate, a third of that for consumer CDFIs in the UK as a whole, may be associated with this. DSL demand personal guarantees from those clients whom they believe to be high risk, which as a business-lending organisation they are relatively well positioned to do; and their achievement in coming under the government's Small Firms Loan Guarantee umbrella has provided additional protection. Some CDFIs have recourse to debt-collection agencies. In addition, the initiatives taken to encourage savings by a number of organisations, and outstandingly by ELM (see Case Study 3) provide

Table 3.2 Case-study organisations: loan delinquency and possible causes

Institution	Default rate as % of portfolio, 2009	Measures to keep down default	Administrative costs as % of portfolio, 2009
Business-lending and hybrid-lending CDFIs			
DSL	6.4	Personal guarantees; insurance through Small Firms Guarantee Scheme	12.9
Derby Loans	17.0	Progressive lending; telephone calls to defaulters	24.7
Business loans: CDFA average	14.4		N.A.
Personal-lending CDFIs			
East Lancs Moneyline (ELM)	23.0	Progressive lending; incentivised interest rates; home visits to defaulters; appointment of a specialist loan arrears officer	41.2
Scotcash	8.6	Progressive lending, incentive interest rates	57.6
Derby Loans	17.0	Progressive lending; telephone calls to defaulters	24.7
Moneyline Yorkshire:			
Moneyline only	20.2	Attachment of bankers' orders to benefits	39.6
All unsecured credit	13%		
Personal loans: CDFA average	28.8		N.A.

Source: Developing Strathclyde Ltd, Derby Loans, East Lancs Moneyline, Scotcash, Derby Loans (trading as Midlands Community Finance) and Sheffield Credit Union (incorporating Moneyline Yorkshire), *Annual Report and Accounts*, 2009 or latest available year. CDFA average rates are derived from *Inside Out* (various issues), and are reproduced from those reported in Table 1.2.

clients with an asset which protects them from the debt-default trap. Savings mobil-isation is a real key to better long-term financial performance by CDFIs, and is discussed in detail in Chapter 4.

There is no free lunch. All of these approaches to the control of arrears – like the rather different ones practised by microfinance institutions in developing countries – involve an increase in administrative cost for the CDFI, which may be seen as an investment in lower default rates in the future, which will take time to mature. The figures in Table 3.2 should be read with this lagged effect in mind. In particular, the sudden increase in ELM's costs in 2008/09 is due to expansion into new regions, one consequence of which has been an increase in arrears, to which some of the arrears-control measures discussed above are a response. Thus, in 2009, ELM experienced *both* an increase in arrears rates *and* an increase in administrative costs per unit of portfolio. It hopes and expects that, as has occurred in other CDFIs and as it has already experienced in its Blackburn office, additional expenditure on arrears control now will yield better ability to discriminate between good and bad borrowers, and thus lower arrears rates, in the future. It may be that other approaches to loan recovery may also be effective – in particular the payment of incentives to loan officers linked to loan recovery rates so that a part of their salary becomes performance dependent.[35]

We now consider more broadly the factors underlying financial sustainability, expressing these, in Table 3.3, in the form of a subsidy dependence index.[36] Of the institutions studied, none is financially viable, and only ELM (in some of its branches, notably the Blackburn branch) is operationally viable. Apart from small scale and failure to contain default, which have already been considered, the main reasons for this are inflexibility in the setting of interest charges, includ-ing the costs of default, and failure to provide performance incentives to staff and, in some cases, clients also.

These results parallel those achieved in other industrialised countries. In the United States also, 'no microfinance programme has achieved outreach [which we can interpret as market share comparable to that of the doorstep lenders], and none has turned a profit' (Carr and Tong 2002: 6).[37] In general, it would appear that not only in Britain, but across the whole range of industrialised countries, CDFIs are finding it more difficult to achieve financial viability, and much harder to keep arrears down, than microfinance organisations in developing countries exposed to far more severe resource constraints. In their review of opportunities and chal-lenges for microfinance (for small businesses) in the United States, Schreiner and Morduch ask, 'Why does microfinance in the United States appear to be so much more difficult than microfinance in Bangladesh, Bolivia and Indonesia, three very different countries that boast large, dynamic microfinance sectors?' (Carr and Tong 2002: 22). They provide an answer in terms of the small size of the microen-terprise sector, the continuing, albeit eroded, existence of a social welfare safety net, competition from established lenders, tight regulation of those lenders and limits to the formulation of joint-liability groups.

In the presence of sponsors willing to subsidise microfinance institutions over a generous period of time until viability is achieved, this would present no

Table 3.3 Estimates of financial viability/subsidy dependence ratios, 2009

Institution	1 Break-even interest rate[1]	2 Current interest rate (% APR)	3 = 2/1 Estimate of financial viability[2]	4 Subsidy dependence index[3]
Business-lending and hybrid-lending CDFIs				
DSL	28	12	0.42	2.38
Derby Loans	67	25	0.37	2.70
Personal-lending CDFIs				
East Lancs Moneyline (ELM)	64.9	39.9	0.62	1.61
Scotcash	87.0	48.5	0.55	1.81
Derby Loans	67	25	0.37	2.70
Moneyline Yorkshire	81	24	0.29	3.44

Sources: Developing Strathclyde Ltd, Derby Loans, East Lancs Moneyline, Scotcash, Derby Loans (trading as Midlands Community Finance) and Sheffield Credit Union (incorporating Moneyline Yorkshire), *Annual Report and Accounts*, 2009 or latest available year. CDFA average rates are derived from *Inside Out* (various issues), and are reproduced from those reported in Table 1.2.

Notes
1 Annual percentage rates. For all organisations, the APR quoted is that related to a six-month loan of £500 (for consumer lending CDFIs) or a two-year loan of £5,000 (for business-lending CDFIs).
2 Financial viability is the ability of a microfinance institution to cover all its costs (including the payment of interest) on all the capital it has to raise.
3 Subsidy dependence indices. The SDI is calculated as:

$$\frac{A(i^* - r) + (Ei^* - p) + K}{rX}$$

where i = borrowing interest rate, r = lending interest rate, X = loan portfolio, E = value of bank's equity capital, A = value of institution's borrowed funds outstanding, p = profit before tax, K = non-interest subsidies and i* = interest rate which the institution would pay for access to concessional funds were eliminated.

problem. However, support both from banks and from governments has been radically cut in the wake of the global financial crisis, leaving CDFIs very exposed and in many cases unable to undertake new lending. In Britain, the coalition government has indicated that the regional development authorities (RDAs), which provide the bulk of support for business-lending CDFIs, are to be terminated in 2011, and in that year the DWP Growth Fund will probably also close. As a consequence, it is likely that those CDFIs with small revenues to plough back into the business and few alternative funding sources to draw on will find it difficult to survive. We return to this predicament in Chapter 7.

Summary of argument

We may tentatively summarise the argument of this chapter as follows. There is a wide performance gap between the best and the worst CDFIs, which has been able to persist over time because CDFI survival is only to a limited degree determined by market processes, and much more by success in acquiring grants from government and other sources. This is important for understanding the impact of CDFIs, since that impact is determined by the number of clients that CDFIs are able to reach ('outreach'), as well as the margin they can achieve on each loan, and the outreach of specific CDFIs is performance sensitive. If the performance gap can be closed, more financially excluded people can be reached in the future. We draw a profile of our CDFI sample, and then, borrowing from the literature on the modern business corporation, we analyse the performance of CDFIs in terms of their 'strategic assets' (including their cost effectiveness), their ability to build their reputations and design incentives to good performance, and their architecture of relationships with clients and with sponsors (the last of these especially important in the CDFI context). The outreach achieved by CDFIs correlates with each of these: faster-growing CDFIs have better incentives for staff and clients and better relationships with sponsors, and these have fed into their reputation and their ability to build their market through both publicity and relationship building with potential sponsors.

Over time, the ability to hold down costs and move towards viability itself becomes a strategic asset which contributes to the CDFI's reputation. In 2010, following a change of government and a financial crisis, CDFIs have been put under pressure to move towards viability a great deal more quickly than they foresaw in the growth period of the mid 2000s; they have been forced to draw on their architecture of support networks with sponsors and others to try and achieve this. Costs are significantly and negatively associated with outreach, and hence the relationship between CDFI performance and outreach is circular: growth of outreach, over the long term, generates lower costs, which if sustained becomes a strategic asset making the CDFI more competitive. In the short term, however, the process of expansion may cause upward blips in costs, as it has done for ELM and for Derby Loans, and in such an event measures to control costs are vital. The most important of these are measures to control arrears, which are the largest element in costs.

4 CDFI clients

Impacts on individuals

Approach

We now assess the ability of CDFIs to influence well-being – a process which works at several levels, including their impact on the individual client, on the community in which they live and work, and on the national economy. In this chapter, we consider only the impact on individuals; impact at the level of networks and communities is considered in Chapter 5, and impact at the level of public-sector revenue and publicly provided benefits in Chapter 6.

For the individual CDFI client, moreover, we are seeking to assess only one dimension of impact – the *impact margin* – which is the measured influence of a loan or other financial intervention on individual well-being per beneficiary. This is not the same as the overall impact of a CDFI. Overall impact is the product of the impact margin and the number of beneficiaries (or outreach), which was analysed in Chapter 3.

Our purpose is to assess the impact of CDFIs on various dimensions of well-being – income, human capacities and intra-community relationships in particular. Our income measures have both a current (or short-term flow) and an asset (or long-term stock) dimension. The asset dimension is wide, encompassing stocks of physical capital (such as buildings and equipment), financial liquidity (savings), human capital (education, applied knowledge and health) and social capital (the benefits to be derived from personal relationships and membership of networks), one aspect of which is *empowerment* (e.g. ability to manage debt, or escape from dependence on moneylenders).[1] *Vulnerability* is another measure often used to capture the capacity of an individual to withstand current and future shocks, which typically relates some measure of assets to a measure of the shocks which the individual is likely to experience (see Moser 1998; Dercon 2006). In this study, we experiment with a range of asset and vulnerability measures, of which we argue below that the most robust are savings, education, health-seeking behaviour and dependence on doorstep lenders. Between them, the promotion of these indicators may be seen as a concerted attack on the 'five giants' – poverty, unemployment, squalor, ignorance and disease – which Lord Beveridge announced his intention to slay through the establishment of the welfare state nearly seventy years ago.

In Table 4.1, we present descriptive measures of the initial conditions (in 2007) of both our treatment and our control groups. As previously discussed, the consumer-lending clients 'start', from the point of view of our surveys, within a much lower income and educational stratum than the business-lending clients. Business-lending clients have higher levels of asset ownership, in the sense of being more likely to own a car and their own house, derive most of their income from self-employment and have on average higher levels of income and health. Consumer-lending clients have lower levels of income, car ownership and health, are most likely to live in rented accommodation rather than owning their own house and derive a much higher share of their income from welfare benefits than from work. However there is much more dispersion of income for business- than for consumer-lending clients, and at the bottom end of the scale some business-lending clients experience severe levels of deprivation. Most of these are sole traders with no employees.

In what follows, our approach is to examine the degree of success of our sample institutions in achieving specific welfare objectives – raising low-income individuals above the poverty line, improving their financial and other management capacities, and inducing health-seeking behaviour; and, in the next chapter, constructing intra-community linkages and developing community well-being. We do this principally through a comparison of clients' case histories – we compare clients who have done well, and made perceptible contributions to community well-being, with clients who did badly, and ask what difference CDFIs, in the context of all the other factors which determine performance, have made. (The database used for comparisons between 'risers out of poverty' and 'fallers into poverty' is set out in the Appendix.) In particular, we focus on those CDFI clients who have been able to escape from poverty, in spite of the recession, during the survey period 2007–09, and ask what initial conditions and support measures distinguished them from those who fell into poverty during that survey period.

Because the clients of business-lending CDFIs begin from different starting points from consumer-lending clients, require different skills to get where they need to get and wrestle with different decision problems, we examine the two types of organisation separately. We begin by comparing success and failure, in the sense discussed above, among business-lending CDFIs, and then move on to the case of consumer-lending institutions, using both qualitative and formal analytical methods. However, it turns out that some factors, such as financial management capacity and membership of social networks, are generic and apply across both forms of CDFI. We conclude with a comparative treatment of the two kinds of organisation.

Business-lending clients

All of the sixty-four business clients whom we examine started small, inexperienced and financially vulnerable; indeed, so vulnerable that, as shown in Table 4.2, more than nine-tenths of them experienced financial exclusion and had to

Table 4.1 Sample descriptives (as of loan start date, 2007)

Institutions	Personal characteristics				Household income (£/annum)[2]				Assets		Savings:	
	% female	% with no education	% financially excluded[1]	% borrowing from National Provident or other doorstep lender	From self-employment	From employment	From benefit	Total income £	House ownership %	Car ownership %	% saving	Average value £
Clients of business and mixed lenders												
DSL (n=28)	47	4	91	13	20,230	4,540	2,820	27,590	67	88	73	1,820
Derby Loans (n=22)	38	0	82	10	23,050	4,702	2,409	30,161	50	94	75	1,520
'Birmingham cluster'[3] (n=21)	53	11	75	26	8,999	2,500	4,850	16,349	75	84	32	2,992
Business clients, average	46	5	83	16	17,426	3,914	3,359	24,700	64	89	59	2,110
Clients of consumer lenders												
Derby Loans	60	55	54	57	1,002	2,948	6,727	11,066	0	15	40	114.6
Scotcash	77	34	67	37	609	3,404	7,134	10,518	17	36	17	26.4
Sheffield Moneyline	91	26	54	60	234	1,496	9,083	10,857	0	14	15	44.6
Personal lenders, average	76	38	58	51	615	2,616	7,648	10,813	6	22	24	61.8

Sources: survey questionnaires (online, available at: http://poverty.group.shef.ac.uk). For the questionnaire proforma see www.poverty.group.shef.ac.uk.

Notes:

1 'Financially excluded' means ever refused a loan by a high-street or other bank.

2 Income data are for *equivalised* household income. Equivalised household income is calculated by adjusting the total incomes of each member of the household, before housing costs, by the following coefficients:

First adult	0.67
Spouse	0.33
Other second adult	0.33
Third and subsequent adults	0.33
Child aged under 14	0.20
Child aged 14 and over	0.33

The method, known as the *OECD equivalence scale*, aims to adjust incomes according to need on the basis of household size and composition to express all incomes as the amount that a childless couple would require to enjoy the same standard of living (see, for example, Brewer *et al.* 2009: Appendix Table A.1).

3 'Birmingham cluster' comprises clients of Aston Reinvestment Trust (ART), Black Business in Birmingham (3Bs) and Halal Fund.

turn to CDFIs for help. In a majority of cases they have stayed small: only eleven of them, at the time of writing, employed any full-time staff, and of these only six (DSL1, 2, 7 and 8, B19 (ART) and Derby Loans 95) have experienced continuous growth and are now free of the need to borrow on subsidised terms. Of the remaining fifty-eight, eleven are known to have ceased to trade: most of these are small subsistence businesses, sometimes known as 'lifestyle' businesses, but one (DSL17) was a medium-sized business with ten employees, described in more detail in Case Study 2c.

Our principal concern is with CDFIs as an instrument of poverty reduction. In Table 4.2 we assess their effectiveness at achieving this, comparing those borrowers who emerged from poverty during the survey period (or whose employees did) with those who fell into poverty.

Overall, Table 4.2 suggests that among the business-loan clients in our sample, poverty has been reduced at an impressive rate in spite of the recession, with about 0.8 *net* exits from poverty per loan made. However most of the exits from poverty are concentrated among just six firms (DSL1, 2, 7 and 8, ART19 and Derby Loans 85) which are both fast-growing and intensive in the labour of low-income people; the last three cases are discussed in detail as Case Studies 2a and 5. There is a strong correlation between initial size, initial income and ability to reduce poverty, as portrayed in Figure 4.1: most of the very small loan-supported businesses, with no employees, have achieved low impact,[2] and most of the big impacts are achieved by firms which are already small- to medium-sized and have cash reserves to back them. Firms which manage to grow fast from a subsistence base are very much the exception rather than the rule.

This pattern is not difficult to explain. Those who are poor and vulnerable do not like to take risks, because of the grave consequences if the risk does not come off. If an important debtor defaults, or the market suddenly collapses, the operator of a micro-business will be forced to sacrifice or mortgage the few assets she has and possibly put her family's livelihood at risk, whereas a better-off business can simply dip into its savings account. Typically, therefore, start-up businesses begin with a technology which is tried and tested and avoids risk, including the risk of hiring labour or expensive equipment, leaving more established businesses with better reserves to make experiments. But it is in the process of making the experiments that the high yields accrue, and, as shown in Figure 4.1, all of the six firms which were able to achieve high impact and take some of their employees across the poverty line had incomes and assets above the average. Most of the subsistence or 'lifestyle' businesses remained trapped at the left-hand end of the curve. What is crucial is to understand how those few who do escape from the trap manage to escape.

In seeking to understand this, we focus on five causal factors: the management of the loan-supported business; two elements of what in Chapter 3 we called 'architecture', namely the structure of relationships within the company and the social networks in which the company is enmeshed (both those which connect it to its mentors and markets and those which provide social support and technical skills and advice); the financial support which the business is able to

Table 4.2 Business CDFIs: upward and downward income transitions, 2007–10

Institutions	Employer identities	Number who crossed poverty line	Average household income, 2007	Average household income, 2009	% upward transitions across poverty line (as % of loans 2007–09)
Upward transitions					
DSL:					
Entrepreneurs	G6, G22	2	29,550	34,500	0.12
Employees	G1*, G2*, G4*, G7* , G8*	22	9,861	13,978	1.37
Derby Loans:					
Entrepreneurs	D72	1	24,456	27,850	0.06
Employees	D74, D83*, D85*	7	10,077	12,641	0.43
'Birmingham cluster' (ART, 3Bs and Halal Fund):					
Entrepreneurs	B2, B9, B12	3	16,865	19,850	0.15
Employees		8	11,045	13,650	0.40
Downward transitions					
DSL:					
Entrepreneurs	DSL17*, 18, 19, 25	3	28,520	26,560	0.13
Employees	DSL17*	4	15,100	9,806	0.05
Derby Loans:					
Entrepreneurs	Derby12, 14	2	11,500	4,500	0.12
Employees	None	0	N.A.	N.A.	N.A.
'Birmingham cluster' (ART, 3Bs and Halal Fund):					
Entrepreneurs	B1, 5	2	17,850	13,500	0.10
Employees	ART21*	2	13,550	11,500	N.A.

Source: surveys, 2007–10. Data are summarised in the Appendix and available online at: www.poverty.group.shef.ac.uk.

Note:

* Denotes medium-sized firm with more than five employees.

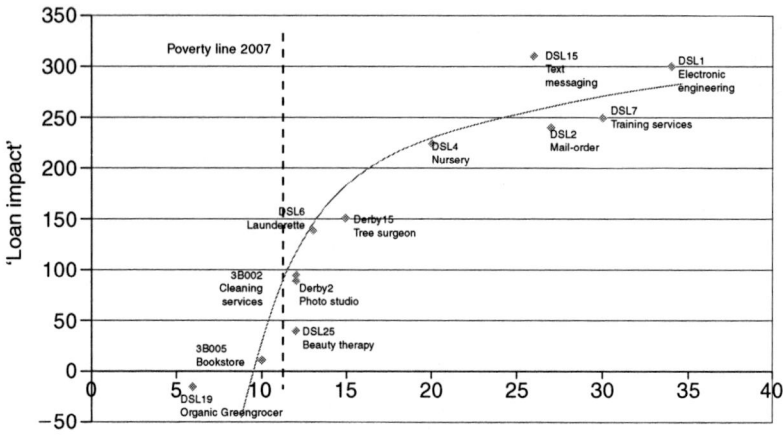

Figure 4.1 Business-lending CDFIs: impact (2007–09) in relation to initial income (2007) (source: surveys, 2007 and 2009).

Notes
Poverty line 2007=£11,500 per capita (60 per cent median income, measured as a family with two adults and two children). 'Impact' is measured as change in the business's net income (2007–09) as a percentage of the change in the control group's net income over the same period.

extract from the CDFI and other sources; and, finally, the sheer resilience, pride and bloody-mindedness which are often the only thing which stop the entrepreneur from throwing in the towel in bad times. Indeed, we focus particularly on what happens to clients in times of crisis, and why under that stress they sometimes expire, sometimes thrive and sometimes just keep their nostrils above the water. Although our analysis will sometimes be quantitative, it is impossible to infer from our bare data the amount of skill, ingenuity, blood, sweat and tears which have gone into mere survival – in other words into protecting and preserving livelihoods rather than promoting them. Substantial use is therefore made of case-study material.

As a metaphor depicting the struggle for small-business survival, we use the diagram presented in Figure 4.2, which relates the return from investment in a small business, measured on the vertical axis, to the risks associated with that investment. The starting point is within zone A on the diagram, at a point such as A*. The client is financially excluded, and existing on a low income. She has few assets that she can use as collateral. She has obtained a loan from a CDFI, which enables her to acquire assets which aim to increase the productivity of her or his business. Thus she moves to point B*. By comparison with the starting point, this yields higher returns, but it also inflicts risks – associated with acquiring and holding a market, making the technology work and, not least, servicing the debt incurred with the CDFI and other lenders.

Figure 4.2 illustrates three stylised cases of what can happen next. The first (case I) is 'rags to riches'. Everything works, or anything which does not is either anticipated or quickly fixed. As a consequence, the entrepreneur soon gets to a point where s/he has paid back all her debts and no longer needs to borrow, at any rate from a CDFI. This kind of magical outcome does happen, as we shall illustrate (see Table 4.3). But, as Tolstoy reminds us on the first page of *Anna Karenina*, 'all happy families are alike, but each unhappy family is different in its own way',[3] and we are likely to learn even more from the unhappy families – especially those which manage to escape from their predicament.

The second case on Figure 4.2 (case II) is the more typical case where the entrepreneur, initially, survives but struggles to keep risk and return in balance. We are particularly interested in the case, illustrated on the diagram, where s/he encounters an unexpected shock, which puts her survival at risk. In our case studies, these shocks took many forms: global recession (which indeed hit many CDFI clients during the period of this study in 2008–09), localised market collapse, fire, vandalism, illness or accident, failure of a large debtor or insurer to pay on time, divorce and consequent decapitalisation. However, some firms, listed in Table 4.3, coped with these shocks, to the extent that they or their employees moved out of poverty, whereas others (case III) did not, failed to keep up loan repayments, as a consequence lost their CDFI line of credit and, having lost this resource, then moved downward across the poverty line. Case Study 2c provides a narrative account of one of these cases.

It is clearly critical to understand why the different responses to crisis adopted by CDFI-assisted firms, and their consequences, result in such diverse outcomes. In Table 4.3, we illustrate how the enterprises which we have characterised as 'risers out of poverty' and 'fallers into poverty' responded to the varying crises which they encountered – recession and seasonal fluctuations (DSL6), market collapse followed by ill-health (Derby Loans) default by a major debtor (Derby Loans 85), destruction of the factory by fire (DSL8), fire followed by website problems followed by cancer (DSL20). These shocks would have defeated most people – the authors certainly. That they did not in these cases was important for the ability of the CDFIs studied to reduce poverty. We classify the manner in which they did this according to the five categories listed above – organisational capacity, technical support, financial support, social capital and personal resilience.

Organisational capacity was important in achieving the survival of enterprises Derby Loans 85 (Collstream), DSL20 (Able2Wear), DSL6 (Soapy Bubbles), DSL8 (MacVicar), and in the last three cases critical. In each of these instances, the organisation of the business as a *partnership* gave the entrepreneur first in the firing line the opportunity, when the initial shock hit, to transfer some of the strain to the other partner, to brainstorm with them about the way forward and maybe most importantly gave them the resilience to keep going rather than quit. In the case of Collstream, the crisis – the refusal by a key debtor to pay on time – was fairly short term. The partnership (Case Study 2a) practises fairly rigorous division of labour, and when the crisis hit, the partner 'out of the firing

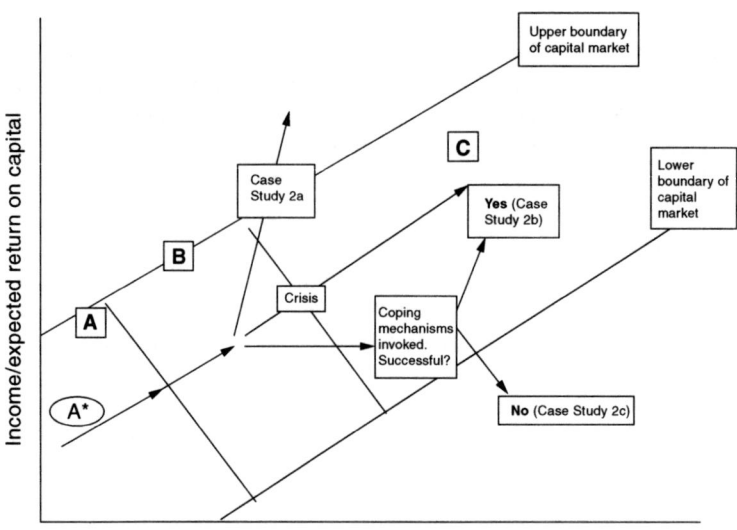

Riskiness/vulnerability of borrower's portfolio

Figure 4.2 Response to shocks as a determinant of client trajectories.

Notes
Zones of the capital market and patterns of borrower behaviour:
A Low risk, low income, client probably unemployed and possibly living in a hazardous (crime and vandalism-threatened) environment, very low income and asset levels, extreme perceived need for risk-protection devices, including equity and insurance; social and human capital increments particularly critical within household portfolio.
B Moderate risk, moderate yield, financial services demanded mainly for working capital with very small fixed capital investment.
C High risk (unless insurance available), high average yield, financial services demanded for fixed capital equipment (especially housing and vehicles) and labour hiring as well as fixed capital.

Possible outcomes for individual borrowers:
1 (Case Study 2a) – the 'super-ladder': yields so high (or augmented by a windfall) as to enable the borrower to dispense with microfinance services
2 (Case Study 2b) – the normal ladder: borrower balances yield and risk through a sequence of loans, with stable or increasing levels of labour and capital input. Coping mechanisms are capable of achieving exit from crisis with
3 (Case Study 2c) – 'the snake': coping mechanisms unable to cope with increased levels of risk; borrower quits the capital market.

line' (Chris, the IT and technical specialist) did not immediately try and take over from the partner in the firing line (Ian, the sales and finance specialist). But he was there when needed, and gave support on the phone, which 'along with a few pints of beer', as Ian relates, gave him the moral support he needed to chart the way through to a strategy which would buy the company time until the debtor paid up. In case DSL20, Able2Wear (Case Study 2b), there are three con-secutive crises between 2007 and 2009 – failure of the website, factory fire and the senior partner, Patricia, being hit by cancer – and the story is much more long-drawn out; but in each of these cases the junior partner and technical director, Harry, is able to take some of the day-to-day pressure off her, and to give her the reassurance that the company unique selling point, specialist clothes for disabled people, will win through. In case DSL6, Soapy Bubbles, what the two partners have to confront is not so much a crisis, in the sense of a sudden catastrophic event, as a slow erosion of demand, in the shadow of the projected closure and relocation of many of the tenants of the Red Road tower-block complex (see further Chapter 5); but it is their decision to confront the situation proactively, by becoming leaders in the local community (Case Study 4) which provides them with the contacts which eventually enable them to stabilise and expand the market for their launderette business. Finally, the partnership between John Gibson (DSL7) and James MacVicar (DSL8) (Case Study 5) is a partnership between organisations, rather than within an organisation; but here too, when MacVicar was hit by the catastrophic fire of April 2004, the fact that he was in a partnership was an asset which gave him support and motivated him to revive the company rather than let it go under.

In all of these cases, therefore, two heads proved to be better than one, even if it was a desire for independence which had made the entrepreneur move from employment to self-employment in the first place. *Emergency financial assistance* was also crucial, notably in setting MacVicar and Able2Wear back on their feet after their respective fire emergencies. Even more crucial, we would argue, was *social capital*, in the sense of the use of social networks to compensate for deficiencies in other resources and to buffer against shocks. We are using the term social capital here in a slightly specialised sense. It is quite an elastic phrase, meaning simply social relationships which may yield material benefits to those involved in them, but, of course, social relationships have multiple layers, and some relationships are destructive rather than constructive. Here we are concerned, in particular, with three layers of relationships formed by CDFI business clients: with their *market* (which provides them with feedback on what lines to persist with and which ones to pull out of), with their *fellow-entrepreneurs* and with *support agencies* such as regeneration agencies, Business Links and Gateways and financial institutions, including but not confined to CDFIs. Overall, the literature takes the view that social capital is a particularly crucial asset where market linkages are weak or missing (Putnam 1993; Knack and Keefer 1997; Whiteley 2000). In the context of small business development and survival, the idea of social capital has been developed notably by Brook (2005) and Shaw *et al.* (2005); and our concern, drawing on their work, is to understand how the way it was used varied as between the successful and unsuccessful clients in Table 4.3. We find there that the 'risers' used social capital in three particularly imaginative ways to recover from crisis:

1   *As an incentive to lateral thinking.* The fact that the 'riser' companies spread their net of contacts wide and did not remain encased within their existing social web was valuable when the crisis consisted of a technical problem which that web could not resolve. After Able2Wear (Case Study 2b) had made three unsuccessful attempts to make their website work interactively,

Table 4.3 Business CDFIs: analysis of income transitions

Organisation	Nature of business	Nature and date of crisis	Nature of response				Debt to assets ratio (and date of 'peak')	Remarks
			Business management and 'architecture'	Technical support, training and mentoring	Financial support	Social networks		
Risers out of poverty								
DSL1	Electrical engineering	No crisis						
DSL2	Mail order	Minor crises only during survey period (but see Mosley and Steel 2004 for cases in early 2000s)						
DSL5	Nursery	Minor crises only during survey period (but see Mosley and Steel 2004 for cases in early 2000s)						
DSL6 Soapy Bubbles	Shop and launderette	(1) Seasonal: decline in demand in April (at end of football season) (2) Structural: out-migration from Barmulloch area, and threat to close	Search for long-term contracts for launderette (eventually successful, 2009)	New DSL loan, June 2004	Informal cover arranged to keep business open.	Joint leadership of Barmulloch Community Association: campaigning against closure of library and bus routes	22% (July 2006)	See Case Study 4
(Employees of) DSL8 MacVicar (April 2004)	Printer	April 2004: factory fire, destruction of nearly £700,000 of equipment	Improvisations by loyal workforce (including all-night work) during immediate aftermath of crisis	Decision to buy and install new equipment, to demonstrate loyalty (financial gamble, dependent on financial support in next cell)	DSL emergency loan, May 2004, plus additional financing from banks	Partnership with client G7, q.v.; broader support from local Catholic community organisations to which MacVicar had supported.	15% (April 2004)	See Case Study 5
DSL20 Able2 Wear (2009)		(1) Factory fire (2) Proprietor's illness	Downsizing of space – move to restricted premises after fire, 2007		Reallocation of work to senior partner		28% (April 2008)	See Case Study 2b

Derby72	Photographic studio	(1) Slump in demand for weddings after 2007 (2) Proprietor's illness	Photographic training course, Mackworth College, 2005	Took on part-time job, 2009	35% (September 2008)	See Case Study 2b
Derby74	Chain of ethnic foodstores	No crisis				See Case Study 7
Derby85	Text messaging service for mobile phones	Minor crises only during survey period				See Case Study 2a

Fallers into poverty

(Employees of) DSL17 Mactag	Highlandwear manufacturer	(1) Collapse of demand, due to 2008/09 recession (2) Competition from Far Eastern and Irish highlandwear manufacturers	Overexpansion of labour force, 2007, even when demand was falling.	Supplementary DSL loan, 2007 (plus attempts to expand Bank of Scotland overdraft)	150% (March 2008)	See Case Study 2c
DSL19	Wholefood retailer	Demand shrinkage, 2008		Failure to control debts	85% (June 2008)	
DSL25 Soul Therapies	Beauty therapist	(1) Collapse of demand, due to 2008/09 recession (2) Increasingly tense working relationship with landlord, culminating in split		Found part-time work .... through contact of her sister's.	145% (September 2009)	

Source: see Appendix 2.

they did not give up; they learned, through a friend, of a Norwegian contact who both had the skills to solve the technical problem and some experience of the problems of specialised clothing for the disabled which is Able2Wear's market niche. This Norwegian 'white knight', as Patricia Watson refers to him, cracked the problem through a programme of which the existing range of suppliers were unaware. Similarly Soapy Bubbles constantly added new retail products to its product range, installed a phone booth and a mini-lending library, and by these means built up the comparative advantage of their shop as a haven to which their customers could always turn for advice or simply for exchange of information, which in turn gave them ideas about what new products to introduce. Often, in these cases, the lateral thinking that was needed came from a support or mentoring agency such as the Glasgow Regeneration Agencies, and the role of these support agencies is considered in Chapter 7.

2   *As a reciprocal investment.* What is significant about the social capital drawn on by Soapy Bubbles, Able2Wear and MacVicar is that it did not come out of the sky – it represented the return on an investment which these enterprises had been making for years. Soapy Bubbles, as we saw, made a specialism of developing their shop as an information exchange, and then took the information exchange out into the community, becoming leaders of the Barmulloch Community Association and fighting within that association for the preservation of local libraries and bus services, and assisting with the multiple consequences of the expected closure of the thirty-storey Red Road flats. MacVicar (Case Study 5), apart from providing employment to a depressed local community, provided leadership to Catholic charities in the east end of Glasgow. Having in this way set a lead in creating community linkage and cohesion, those linkages were then there for them to use as an asset when bad times arrived. They provided, in return, social solidarity, commercial contacts and ideas on which they able to draw in order to rebuild after their crises.

3   *As a warning of future problems, which enables crisis to be anticipated rather than responded to.* With a wide and candid enough range of contacts, client firms gain an extra pair of eyes which enable them to see trouble coming and prompt them towards measures which will head it off. The fact that these forms of social capital were not utilised by the 'fallers' has, we believe, a part to play in explaining differential poverty outcomes in the two groups of business clients. In particular DSL17 (Case Study 2c) did not, in the crucial winter of 2007/08, have the breadth of social networks to warn them that they needed to trim costs, diversify their product range against the threat that their existing products were succumbing to Far Eastern competition and diversify their sources of financing. A similar failure to foresee that debts were getting out of control also beset Fressh (DSL19), which also went out of business during the 2008 recession. A useful leading indicator of danger is provided by the *debt-to-assets ratio*, or ratio of outstanding debt (principal) to income.[4] This is listed for all companies in the sample

in the penultimate column of Table 4.3. None of the companies which survived allowed the debt service ratio to go over 50 per cent. In DSL17 and Fressh, the two that failed and had dependent employees, it went over 100 per cent.

Social capital, therefore, is not just an objective in itself, in the sense of friendship and social contact, but a means by which other objectives can be achieved and missing resources, especially information, foresight and capital, substituted for. Where it is lacking, as it was for Sallie Powell of The Studio (Case Study 2b), whose hearing is bad and who therefore had to operate much more on her own than the other case studies considered here, that puts more stress on individual capabilities and resilience.

Of the case studies summarised above, cases 2a, 2b and 2c, representing growth, crisis confronted and failure, respectively, are presented here. Case Studies 4 and 5, describing the formation of social capital, are presented in Chapter 5.

Case Study 2a Take-off

Collstream Ltd, Derby, is a texting agency, which sends messages via mobile phones – interestingly for this study, these messages are often sent by financial institutions to debtors. Ian learnt his skills working for the credit-card institution Egg (a subsidiary of Prudential), and went freelance in 2005.

The business is highly competitive but uses very little physical capital (a mere £50,000 worth of fixed assets in 2009) to achieve a turnover in that year of nearly £1 million. Most of its capital is embodied in the skills of the workforce. It is for this reason that Collstream was financially excluded, or at any rate financially obstructed, at the beginning of its life: the collateral which it could offer consisted purely of the skills of its employees and not of marketable assets. Banks 'do not like to lend against staff'.[5] Hence the firm needed to turn to Derby Loans for their initial capital injection of £10,000 in 2007.

The company is a partnership between Ian (who takes primary responsibility for marketing, finance and staff) and Chris (who takes primary responsibility for product design and IT). The two are different and complementary personalities, the one more outgoing, entrepreneurial and a 'people person', the other more thoughtful and office-bound. The division of labour between the two is clear, but during the company's one big crisis, when a big debtor threatened to default, Chris while leaving it for Ian to take the lead in handling the crisis made it clear that he was there if needed.

Collstream achieved continuous growth during the 2008–09 recession – during which, of course, debt became unmanageable for many – and has now 'broken through': turnover doubled in 2010. It ascribes its success to 'working sixteen hours a day, six and a half days a week', and to being able to provide a workable technology which enables its business clients to achieve repayment of their debts. Collstream is now a member of 'Derby 500', an elite group of companies within the city, and a sponsor of Derby County Football Club.

Case Study 2b Discovering a niche and hanging on

In both of these cases, the skill which was made marketable was artistic. The women who manage the enterprises have very different social backgrounds and financial strengths. Both were hit by an exceptional sequence of shocks; both made an exceptional success of coping, by very different means.

1 Able2Wear, Glasgow (interviewee G20). The entrepreneur, throughout her career, has been a seamstress and textile manufacturer. With her business partner, she formerly made uniforms for the police: now she is retired, she sold that company in 1991, and looked for a new niche. She now owns the only company that designs and makes clothes for wheelchair users and disabled people. She described the origin of her idea as follows:

> One policeman friend came to me about fifteen years ago and said – my wife's got multiple sclerosis – what can we do for her? I thought, there aren't any companies around which meet this need. I went to the Mitchell Library in Glasgow and there was nothing. Once I started to research the idea seriously, I found that the demand was overwhelming – from basketball teams needing tracksuit trousers without pockets to swimming accidents, you have no idea of the amount of business I've had from swimming accidents! I think the demand was always there, it is simply that disabled people have notoriously found it difficult, not to express themselves, but to express themselves in a way which makes contact with the people who hold the power. (The press are particularly bad for ignoring stories involving disabled people.) Then we tried some designs out on the friends who has suggested the idea, and the idea took root. Through the 1990s we just about managed to break even.[6]

Needing a large injection of capital, she joined a pharmaceutical group, who got 5 per cent of the equity in return for putting money into the business. But that arrangement came to an end, and she started again as an independent manufacturer in April 2004, with the help of a £20,000 loan from DSL and £5,000 from Glasgow City Council. She drives herself extremely hard and at her first interview in 2007 described herself as 'exhausted, working eighty hours a week with no time to take holidays', putting all her savings into her business. There have been two particularly critical moments in the life of the new company: in 2006, when critical delays occurred in establishing a website, and, in April 2008, when a fire in the adjoining factory spread into her premises – luckily, it was insured, but the company incurred substantial costs arising from a financial dispute with her insurers and the need to move into new premises. Counterpointed with these business crises, or maybe partly the consequence of them, there have been two health crises – in 2005 she suffered a burst appendix; then at end 2008 she fell ill with cancer and in consequence had to put huge reliance on her chief designer and partner. (He is highly protective of her and it was not easy to get an interview.)

The lessons Patricia draws are patience in working out designs ('you can visualise and design a problem-solving garment, but until it has been worn and tested by a wheelchair user you can't promote it to the disabled market'); adaptability in response to evolving awareness of needs and specific orders; and the right help, often very specialist, at the right time – notably the 'white knight' a disabled British ex-serviceman now living in Norway who sorted out her website; June her designer; and Harry, her business partner most of all. Her three children have also been conscripted in less specialist roles. But the biggest lesson is simply courage and resilience when everything was going wrong. At one stage she wrote to one hundred of her best customers and said 'if you are thinking of ordering again in the next few weeks, please could you do it as soon as possible, as we have a slightly tricky cashflow situation.' The strategy worked.

2 The Studio (interviewee Derby2). Sallie Powell is a gifted sculptor, graphic artist and photographer. She supports a fourteen-year-old son alone.

At the point when she approached Derby Loans, she had been discouraged from applying to the commercial banks by her lack of capital. Her business enterprise is photography, principally wedding photography. This market is bunched (with the bulk of takings around Christmas), highly specialised, volatile and under severe competition from 'mass-production' high-street photographic agencies such as Comet and Currys. She took out her loan (for £4,000) in 2006, and used it to rent a studio in Mackworth, a lower middle-income area of south-west Derby (Figure 2.3b), some way away from her main market. Nonetheless, takings in that year were exceptionally good, in the neighbourhood of £25,000. But business dropped off dramatically in subsequent years, and by the late 2000s was down to £2,500. Until recently, as we discuss below, her main source of income has been from Working (formerly Working Families') Tax Credit.

In 2009 there was a revival in business, during which she took on a trainee. It proved to be neither the right time nor the right person, and he had to be laid off within the year. The problem throughout was to deal with a very rigid set of commitments in face of a highly unstable income which was on a declining trend. This she did first by abandoning her lease on her studio and going freelance (various plans including establishment of a photo booth had to be shelved at the same time), and eventually, when revenue continued to decline, by taking a job in Comet, which of course offers photographic services itself. Ironically, therefore, her key coping mechanism has been to take employment from one of the major organisations which is undermining her self-employment.

She has not often had to reschedule her debt, but when she has, Derby Loans, about whom she has been very complimentary ('if it wasn't for Derby Loans, I wouldn't be here [in this studio]') have themselves been adaptable.

She continues to do freelance work when she can, but this is not often, and she has been further hampered by the need to have an operation in March 2010. Paradoxically, even though her job satisfaction has decreased over the period of her Derby Loan, her annual income has increased (from about £10,000 to about £18,000) and at the same time become more stable. It is not the compromise she would have wished to make, but by making it, she has hung on.

Both of these cases of survival in face of multiple shocks were artistically gifted women operating in highly specialised markets. Sallie got much less social and technical support, and expressed less outward self-confidence. Both believed fiercely in what they were doing. Both were willing to adapt to less-than-optimal lifestyles and work patterns to reduce their financial vulnerability.

Case Study 2c Overcommitment and failure

DSL17, *Glasgow*. DSL17 is one of the few export industries to have been supported with the help of a CDFI, and possibly also one of the few CDFI clients
whose chief executive holds an MA in drama (from Goldsmiths', University of
London). Established in 1991 with the intention of making clothing accessories
for the textile trade, DSL17 diversified into highlandwear (belts and tartan
jackets, shirts and kilts) in 1996, initially buying supplies from subcontractors
and then, when these proved unreliable, manufacturing them itself. In 2005 the
company was forced to move its premises when its landlord sold the business
premises to housing developers. This was unforeseen and, due to the urgency of
the move, proved to be very costly. Suitable premises, within the catchment area
of the specialised staff, proved hard to come by and expensive. However, in spite
of its debt exposure, DSL17 increased its staff, with the assistance of a £25,000
loan from DSL, from fourteen to twenty-three between 2005 and 2007. When we
interviewed the managing director of DSL17 he explicitly criticised Marks and
Spencer and other retailers of tartan scarves for sourcing their products outside
the UK.[7] At that time, 60 per cent of production was exported, mostly to the
United States. With characteristic bravado, he described himself that day in April
2007 as 'the Jaguar of the Highlandwear industry', paying himself a salary of
£35,000 per annum.

   In common with many people, DSL17 failed to foresee the 2008–09 global
recession. However, the company's previous actions had put it in an exposed
position because of its failure to control both its overheads and its labour costs.
It was now caught between the upper millstone of imports from the far east, and
also from Ireland, at half its own price (now made worse by the gathering global
recession) and the nether millstone of demands from the Bank of Scotland, itself
under pressure to call in its outstanding loans, to reduce its overdraft from
£50,000 to £5,000 between December 2007 and March 2008.[8] DSL17 had no
equity to fall back on (all the shares being in the hands of the owner's family)
and gradually began to default on its debt. When it called in the liquidator in
May 2008, it had £67,000 of unpaid trade debts, and accumulated losses over the
year of £267,000.

The general lessons from this set of case studies are that business survival
depends on the business's architecture (its design and the web of relationships
surrounding it), flexibility in anticipating and dealing with face of shocks and the
courage of its leadership. Without adaptability and resilience there is nothing –
and where those come from is not at all clear, although on the evidence provided
here social capital is useful in supporting both.

   Useful ideas related to the impact of business lending on dimensions of well-
being other than poverty, including financial capacity, education and health-
seeking behaviour, are also found in Table 4.3. However, many of these ideas
also relate to personal lending, and are discussed below.

Personal-lending clients

We now turn to the case of personal-lending CDFIs; our concern, once again, is to measure and explain impact, and to do this through a comparison of those whose welfare improved, relative to the control group, with those whose welfare diminished. However, because the modus operandi of personal-lending CDFIs is different from that of business-lending CDFIs, namely to improve well-being by building the client's financial capacity rather than their business skills and assets, we scan a different set of causal factors when trying to understand variations in fortunes, and focus on how such financial capacity should be defined and built up.

In Table 4.4, we examine the over-time change in income of our sampled CDFIs. A significant positive impact of CDFI loans is visible only in the case of Scotcash; in Derby Loans and Sheffield Moneyline, impact is positive but not statistically significant. However, in all three institutions loan impacts are very diverse as between across different types of borrowers; and we wish to understand the causes of this, and our approach will be to compare the borrowers who emerged from poverty during the loan period with those who failed to do so, and to try and discover what is different between the two groups.

In Table 4.5, we extend the scope of our enquiry from income and assets to health, and examine the effect of CDFIs on various health indicators.

We may first note some disturbing characteristics of the absolute values of these health indicators. One respondent in twenty, in 2007, had gone short of food in the previous week, or their children had. Moreover, only a minority of respondents (48 per cent) across the sample, reported general health in 2007 which was 'good', 'very good' or 'excellent'. By 2009, after two years of recession, this percentage had declined further, but only fractionally, to 46 per cent.

When we start to draw comparisons between the treatment group and the control group, we find few differences in health trends between the treatment and the control groups: during the recession period of 2007–09, self-reported standards of general health as we saw declined slightly across all three consumer CDFI groups in both treatment and control groups, although there was also a decline (from insignificant levels to near zero) in the proportion of respondents reporting going short of food across the board. In none of these cases is the difference in trends between treatment and control groups significant. However, when we examine differences in *health-seeking behaviour* (as distinct from general health trends) there is one significant finding: in Scotcash (which as can be recalled from Table 4.4 had a larger increase in average income than any of the other client groups), there is a significant decline in the proportion smoking and a significant increase in the proportion engaging in vigorous activity in relation to the control group. This significant contrast between treatment and control group experiences is not to be found in the case of Derby Loans or Sheffield Moneyline, and indeed the client group in Sheffield Moneyline increase their smoking sharply between 2007 and 2009, a behaviour not observed in the control group. This difference in health-seeking behaviours becomes much more

Table 4.4 Consumer-lending CDFIs: income dynamics and possible causes, 2007–10

Institutions	Income, 2007		Income, 2009 (change as % of 2007 in brackets)[1]		Change in components of income[1]			Change in financial capacity, 2009/10 as % of 2007/08 borrower sample (control group in brackets)	
	Borrower group	Control group	Borrower group	Control group	From employment and self-employment	From benefits	Savings	Doorstep lender dependence	'Rationality' of coping response in face of shock (from Deakin scale)[2,3]
Scotcash: (n=125)	10,518	11,830	12,906 (+22.7%)	12,024 (+1.6%)	+4.6%	+19.2%	+224%	−41%	1.02
Derby Loans: (n=75)	11,066	12,020	11,940 (+7.8%)	12,536 (+4.3%)	−22.4%	+17.4%	+61%	No change	1.32
Moneyline Yorkshire: (n=126)	10,857	11,044	12,815 (+18.4%)	11,430 (+3.5%)	−8.1%	+3.6%	+45%	−29%	1.12

Source: surveys, 2007–10. Data are summarised in the Appendix and the full data array is online, available at: www.poverty.group.shef.ac.uk.

Notes

1 Here and throughout the report, a state of 'poverty' and 'transition out of poverty' are defined in relation to the standard Office of National Statistics poverty line of 60% median income. The value of this poverty line varies by region and household composition. In 2007 the national average level of the poverty line was £11,506 per annum, rising to £12,088 in 2009, for a household with two adults and two children.

2 The shock simulated in our questionnaire was: 'Suppose that you suddenly had a financial emergency and needed £1,000 in a hurry, what would you do?' The question was first asked as an unprompted question, and then the nineteen possible responses listed in Moore (2003) were reviewed, and the respondent's answer was coded on a scale from 1 (for the answer 'never') to 5 (for the answer 'always'). High values for this component of the Deakin scale thus connote low levels of rational response in a crisis.

3 Our concept of a 'rational' coping strategy is adapted from the Deakin coping scale devised by Moore (2003). In our survey questionnaire, we ask 'If you had a financial emergency and needed £1,000 in a hurry, what do you think you would do?', and,after leaving time for an unprompted response, code the respondent's subsequent replies according to the nineteen suggested responses on the Deakin scale, which appear as question 29 of that questionnaire. We define the 'rationality' of the respondent's response pattern as the ratio of the 'rational' responses: 2 ('analyse my reaction to the problem'), 5 ('get more information about the situation'), 6 ('identify the source of the problem') and 7 ('take control of the situation') to the 'emotional' responses: 12 ('feel miserable about the situation'), 13 ('keep my fingers crossed that it will go away'), 14 ('pray for it to go away') and 15 ('hope for a solution to appear'). Values of this ratio above 1 suggest a predominance of rational over emotional coping mechanisms in the respondent, and values below 1 imply the reverse.

Table 4.5 Consumer and business CDFIs: health, health-seeking behaviour and other non-income dimensions of well-being, 2007–10

| Institutions | Indices of health-seeking behaviour 2007: | | | | | | | | Index of health-seeking behaviour 2009: | | | | | | | | Change in health indicators over two year period (absolute difference between client group change and control group change)[5] | | | |
| | Borrower sample | | | | Control group | | | | Borrower sample | | | | Control group | | | | | | | |
	Self-reported general health[1]	% went without food in previous week[2]	Exercise[3]	Smoking[4]	Self-reported general health[1]	% went without food in previous week[2]	Exercise[3]	Smoking[4]	Self-reported general health[1]	% went without food in previous week[2]	Exercise[3]	Smoking[4]	Self-reported general health[1]	% went without food in previous week[2]	Exercise[3]	Smoking[4]	Self-reported general health[1]	% went without food in previous week[2]	Exercise[3]	Smoking[4]
Scotcash	48	7	41	48	38	8	32	60	46	5	48	45	36	2	30	65	0	–5	**+9***	**+8***
Derby Loans	45	2	22	62	37	3	26	64	45	0	27	61	34	0	27	67	–3	–1	+4	+4
Moneyline Yorkshire (Sheffield)	47	5	25	47	44	4	31	68	46	3	27	60	43	2	32	67	0	0	+1	**–12****
Average, 3 institutions	47	5	29	52	36	5	30	64	46	3	32	49	32	2	30	66	–3	–1	+3	0

Notes

1 'Self-reported health': proportion who described their health during week previous to interview as 'excellent', 'very good' or 'good'.

2 Respondents were asked separately whether they or their children had gone short of food in the previous week. If the answer to either of these questions is yes, a yes answer is recorded.

3 'Exercise': proportion who engaged in some form of *vigorous* exercise in the previous week. In our questionnaire, examples of vigorous exercise were given as going to the gym, cycling, swimming, running or weightlifting.

4 'Smoking': includes all those who smoked at all in the week previous to interview.

5 *Illustration.* In Scotcash, smoking in the treatment group fell from 48% to 45%, or –3% (compare column 12 with column 4) whilst smoking in the control group increased from 60% to 65%, or +5% (compare column 16 with column 8). Hence the absolute difference in smoking rates between the treatment group change (–3%) and the control group change (+5%) is (+5)–(–3), i.e. 8%.

Bold numbers indicate the existence of a significant difference between the treatment group trend and the control group trend. Asterisks denote levels of significance: * denotes significance at the 10% level and ** indicates significance at the 10% level.

salient when, in the next section, we contrast between those who rose out of, and those who fell into, poverty.

The Scotcash case in Table 4.5 suggests, and the comparison between 'risers' and 'fallers' in Table 4.8 will confirm, that both health-seeking behaviour and behaviours which increase financial management capacity are quite strongly correlated with the likelihood of income progression. The link between the three often operates through worry, which in its extreme form, panic, destroys the ability to think through financial problems rationally, or in the language used above, causes emotion-based responses to predominate over rationality-based responses; and worry, as we have illustrated using the nationwide sample of the Families' and Children's Survey, damages not only psychological but also physical health (Lenton and Mosley 2008). The important implication for Scotcash is that it has been seen, in a number of testimonies, as an institution whose main professed influence is precisely to reduce worry. One quotation illustrative of this principle was given above. Here are some more: 'I have less money worries because Scotcash is an option now and it is an affordable option. It also means that I can get used to paying a loan back to get the discipline of it' (loan client 106). 'Better sleep: have been worrying less about meeting repayments. Less worry about creditors knocking on the door – I can now relax at home' (loan client 110).

Impacts on business and personal-lending clients compared

In Table 4.6, we bring together our results on the impact of CDFIs, over the recession period 2007–09, on business-lending institutions (Tables 4.1 and 4.2) and on personal-lending institutions (Tables 4.4 and 4.5). The results suggest a paradox. On the evidence of Table 4.6, CDFIs tentatively have not been able to provide a 'win–win' route out of poverty, in the sense of both reaching a large proportion of the poor and taking a high proportion of them out from poverty. Business-lending CDFIs are relatively good at providing a ladder out of poverty for those whom they manage to reach – the ratio of people taken out of poverty between 2007 and 2009 to total clients, if employees of those clients are taken into account, is over 80 per cent; but, as Table 4.6 shows, business CDFIs only reach at most a couple of hundred clients per lending institution and that ladder has only been provided for a select few. Moreover, the business-lending route is a much bigger gamble for the client, in the sense that there is a much bigger risk of taking a CDFI loan resulting in a sharp drop in income: from the data in Table 4.6, the coefficient of variation of income (ratio of standard deviation to mean value) was 84.8 per cent for the two business lenders, DSL and Derby Loans, whereas for the three personal (consumer) lenders, Sheffield Moneyline, Derby Loans and Scotcash, it was 46.9 per cent. By contrast, some consumer-lending CDFIs have grown much more rapidly, and in some cases now reach well over 1,000 clients, most of them in a far lower income stratum than those reached by business-loan clients (see Figure 2.3a for the geographic relationship between CDFI clients and zones of deprivation in the case of Glasgow). But they take

Table 4.6 Estimated CDFI impact on income (2007–09): summary table[1]

| Institutions | Average income 2007 (£/annum) | | Average income 2009 (£/annum) | | 'Impact margins' | | | (7) Number of new loans, 2009 | (8) Forecast of impact[4] |
	(1) Client group (st. dev.)	(2) Control group	(3) Client group (st. dev.)	(4) Control group	(5) 'Impact margin 1'[2]	(6) 'Impact margin 2'[2,3]			
DSL (entrepreneurs and employees combined)	27,522 (19,867)	11,830	30,282 (25,162)	12,024	2,566	109.1 (24 exits from 22 loans)[5]		78	200
Derby Loans (bus) (entrepreneurs and employees combined)	21,251 (13,134)	12,020	25,531 (22,115)	12,536	3,764	60.0 (9 from 15)		25	94
Scotcash	10,518	11,830	12,906	12,024	2,194	17.5 (14 from 80)		900	1,974
Derby Loans (consumer)	11,066 (5,470)	12,020	11,940 (5,847)	12,536	358	19 (9 from 46)		250	89
Sheffield Moneyline	10,857 (6,336)	11,044	12,815 (5,056)	11,430	1,572	8 (5 from 65)		86	135

Sources: surveys, 2007–09.

Notes

Data arrays for poverty exits are provided in the Appendix, and full dataset is online, available at: www.poverty.group.shef.ac.uk.
Income data are for *equivalised* household income, for the calculation of which see Table 4.1.
1 Impact margin 1 calculated as columns ((3)−(1))−((4)−(2)).
2 Impact margin 2 calculated as the number of exits from poverty (2007–09) as % of sample.
3 Overall impact 1 calculated as columns (5) × (7) £000/p.a.
4 The twenty-four exits include direct and indirect effects in the case of business loans; in several cases one loan achieves exit from poverty for several employees.

Table 4.7 The samples: poverty dynamics 2007–09

	Business-lender clients			Personal lenders			All cases	
	DSL	Derby Loans	'Birmingham cluster'[1]	Scotcash*	Derby Loans*	Moneyline Sheffield*	Numbers	Percentage of total
Exited from poverty 2007–09	6	3	3	14	9	5	40	16
Entered into poverty 2007–09	4	2	4	7	5	7	29	12
Remained poor	6	6	4	49	25	40	130	53
Remained nonpoor	7	3	5	9	7	13	44	18
Total cases	23	14	16	79	46	65	243	100

Source: questionnaire survey, 2007–10, questions 52, 55 and 57 (labour income, self-employment income, other income and benefits)

Notes
1 'Birmingham cluster' is a small sample (n=21, five non-respondents) of business-lending clients drawn from the following CDFIs: Aston Reinvestment Trust (ART), Black Business Birmingham (3Bs), Halal Fund.

only a small proportion of them, about one-fifth on our estimate, above the poverty line. Of course, these results are based only on a small sample of borrowers from six of the seventy CDFIs in Britain, and on a relatively short period only; there is also significant variation around the mean impacts recorded in Table 4.6, as we shall illustrate.

Nonetheless, the results presented in Table 4.6 correspond to the basic economic intuition that growth in income depends on capital formation. Business CDFIs, as we have discussed, place a physical capital asset – often a machine, a vehicle or office premises, frequently accompanied by technical advice and expertise – in the hands of their clients, and if productive these assets raise the client's income. In addition, some CDFI-supported businesses create jobs for low-income people, and this provides an additional channel by which incomes can be raised above the poverty line. None of these pathways for increasing income is available to consumer-lending CDFIs, which operate in a quite different way. Typically, they do not finance the acquisition of physical capital assets, but rather they finance the purchase of consumption goods – Christmas presents, holidays, baby clothes and toys, and household improvements such as decorating being, in that order, the most important functions to which consumer CDFI loans were committed.[9] Their technology, in A.K. Sen's terminology (Sen and Dreze 1989), is *protectional* rather than *promotional* of clients' livelihoods. However, they do at least have the potential for creating assets in a less tangible sense. First of all, they seek to terminate clients' financial exclusion, by providing them with access at least to basic bank accounts; which, it is hoped, will reduce their dependence on doorstep lenders and other exploitative and high-cost sources of credit; which in turn will give them the ability to save and protect themselves against future shocks, or indeed to accumulate capital. These assets, if they materialise, are, of course, much more ethereal assets than the vans, electric motors and computers financed by business-lending CDFIs – they are *relational assets*, or capacities, rather than physical assets. Whether or not they do materialise, we suggest, is crucial to the question of whether consumer CDFIs provide a sustainable or a purely ephemeral benefit, and may, we argue, be related to their failure, on average, to produce a significant increase in income.

Table 4.7 illustrates the poverty dynamics of our samples, listing the numbers of clients who entered into or exited from poverty over the period 2007–09. We have already mentioned the tendency of business CDFIs to generate a higher proportion of exits from poverty than consumer CDFIs, but it is notable that there is also variation in the rate of exit between different kinds of consumer CDFI: Derby Loans, for example, achieves a rate of exit from poverty more than twice that of Yorkshire Moneyline.

As Table 4.7 shows, most of the sample, during the recession period analysed, did not cross the poverty line; but forty individuals, or about one-sixth, climbed above the poverty line during this period, whereas twenty-nine, or one-eighth, fell below it. To gain an initial foothold on the poverty dynamics of CDFI clients as a whole, we shall initially focus on these sixty-nine individuals, and ask why the risers rose and the fallers fell.

In what follows, we examine this question through a comparison of clients' case histories – we compare clients who have done well, and made perceptible contributions to community well-being, with clients who did badly, and ask what difference CDFIs, in the context of all the other factors which determine performance, have made. This approach has a great deal in common with that adopted by the Joseph Rowntree Foundation research project on *Routes out of poverty* (Kemp *et al.* 2004), which also breaks down individuals' poverty dynamics into their component parts, examining the entire range of snakes and ladders which determine ups and downs in individual well-being and not confining itself to any single policy intervention. These snakes and ladders it divides into *income events* (such as getting or losing a job), *demographic events* (such as getting or losing a partner, or having a child) and *health events.* In the Rowntree study, for people as a whole and especially for those in work, income events and specifically labour-market events are the most important cause of exit from poverty; but for pensioners, non-income factors (including ill health, loss of a partner, etc.) dominate income factors as a causal influence.[10]

As discussed above, business and consumer CDFIs seek to influence these events in very different ways. Loans to business CDFIs are used to create physical assets which aim to generate immediate growth in income; loans to consumer CDFIs create relational assets which, if they raise income at all, do so only over the long period. The key capacity which consumer CDFIs seek to influence, as described above, is the ability of clients to manage money and thus to accumulate assets – typically in the form of savings – within another institution (CDFIs, it will be recalled, are not authorised to accept deposits, and the farther their clients are from a post office, credit union or other institution to which they are happy to entrust their savings, the higher their transactions costs and the less their motivation to start to save).To achieve this, or even to think it feasible, requires motivation, which is easily paralysed by exhaustion and failure: it is not easy to get to first base.[11] In explaining how these obstacles are overcome by some clients, we find it useful to think in terms of three groups of factors:

1   *initial conditions* – including prior levels of education and in-built coping mechanisms;
2   *social influences* – including as an important special case, relations with advisers who are in a position to help clients manage debt;
3   *power-relationships* – and in particular, for many, the relationship between the client and the provider of home or doorstep finance, which if sufficiently powerful may crowd out any possibility for a low-income client to save.

We wish therefore to explore the hypothesis that a client's progression out of poverty – in particular, the difference between those who exited from poverty and those who fell into it in Table 4.7 – is determined by ability to accumulate capital, with demographic, health and labour-market shocks acting as confounders, or disturbances, to that relationship. In the case of a business-lending client, capital is accumulated in both physical and financial form, but in the case of a personal-lending client, only in the financial form of savings. In either case, the interaction between initial conditions, the social influences on the client and the power-relationships to which she is subject is crucial to the outcome. Figure 4.3 summarises these different ways in which CDFIs can potentially provide a financial ladder out of poverty:

It will be the task of subsequent sections to determine whether those potential pathways out of poverty have actually been followed. We seek to understand, in the light of our examination of the poverty dynamics of our personal lending CDFIs, Scotcash, Derby Loans and Sheffield Moneyline, the levers which may enable a larger number of clients of consumer CDFIs to graduate out of poverty.

Determinants of the process of exit from poverty

The approach we shall now take is to compare the individuals in Table 4.7 who escaped from poverty – a minority within the sample – with those who did not, in terms of the factors listed above – labour-market events, health and demographic shocks and the factors which determine the ability to accumulate capital. In Table 4.8, we observe that individuals who escaped from poverty, by contrast with individuals who fell into poverty:

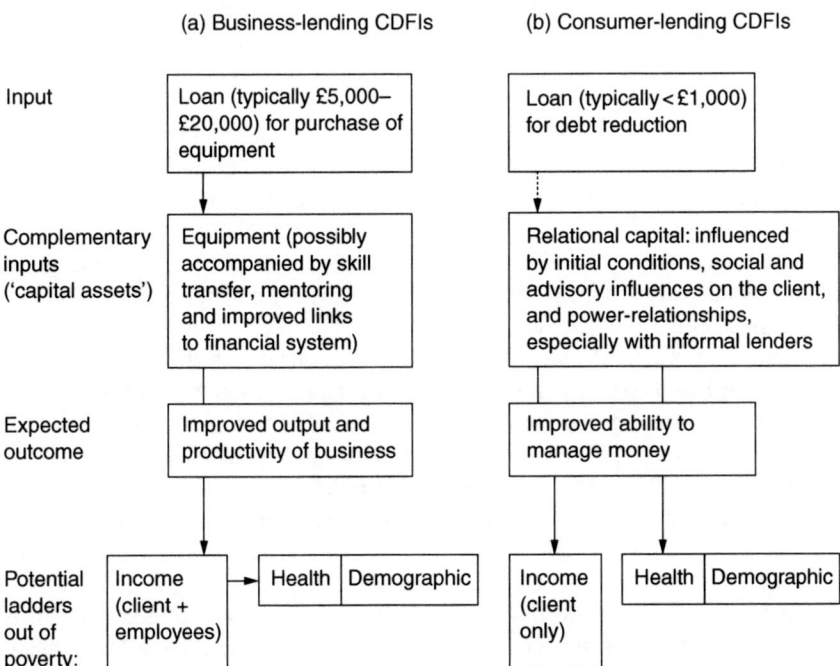

Figure 4.3 Business-lending and consumer-lending CDFIs as contributors to ladders out of poverty.

1   Were more likely to save. Savings rates among those individuals who exited from poverty, as Table 4.8 shows, are many times higher than among individuals who stayed poor or fell into poverty. In some cases, as we illustrate graphically in Figure 4.5 (see p. 79), individuals within the severe poverty category nonetheless managed to save, in contradiction of the common proposition (e.g. Dearden *et al.* 2010: 31) that saving is seldom undertaken by, and by implication impossible for, those who are out of work.[12]

2   Had higher initial qualifications and more 'rational' coping strategies[13] in face of a shock. Whether clients take an emotional or a rational attitude may be critical in determining whether they are able to sustain their links with financial institutions when their ability to cope with a shock (for example, to keep up repayments to a CDFI when their finances come under pressure, as at Christmas) is put to the test. These attitudes, in some cases, can be favourably changed by advice (e.g. Scotcash clients 23 and 64 in the Appendix, whose attitude to saving in 2007 was that it was impossible but who changed that view under the influence of Scotcash advisers). In addition, we argue, the balance between rational and emotional coping mechanisms is influenced by more informal social influences, including the social groups of which the client is a member; those influences are multiple, but our informal impression from case-study interviews is that the denser the social networks in which clients are involved, the more likely it is that they will not only maintain discipline on loans and keep up repayments[14] but also use them promotionally as a means of deliberately promoting themselves up the income ladder, rather than merely protectionally as a way of protecting their own household's and especially their children's consumption.[15] The key relationship here is that between attitude structure, loan advice and financial management capacity. *Attitude structure* is measured by calculating the ratio of 'emotion-based' responses to an imagined shock[16] (such as 'feel miserable about the situation' and 'keep my fingers crossed that the problem will go away') to 'rational-based' responses, which may either involve working out a rational response inside oneself (e.g. 'analyse my reaction to the problem') or sharing the problem with others (e.g. 'seek advice from others'). In the 'improver' group of borrowers (and to a lesser degree in the control group), rational-based responses predominate over emotion-based responses, whereas in the 'decliner' group the reverse is the case.[17] The implication is first that loans will have higher impact in more fertile soil – that is, in individuals in which rationality-based responses predominate over emotion-based ones – but second that in the cases where they can influence those responses, in particular through their loan advice function, that in turn may have a positive impact on their income trajectory. As loan advisers in Scotcash emphasised to us, sometimes a meeting with a loan adviser can be the catalyst which turns the trauma of financial incapacity into a purposive approach, and make an effective vow never to get into debt again; and in other cases not. 'There are a few compulsive non-copers for whom bankruptcy is the best option', they commented, 'but these are a small minority'.[18] Often the fact of advisers

being able to achieve some initial coup, however small, which eases financial pressure – whether getting the Provident to ease its demands, or demonstrate a client's entitlement to welfare benefits of which s/he was not aware, or in one case simply enabling a client to find a suitable house – can initiate a process of building trust-relationships which eventually brings about a fundamental change in attitudes.

3   Had more labour income, and had increased their earnings from work between 2007 and 2009, whereas those who fell into poverty had reduced them.

4   Had higher levels of social capital, in the sense of membership both of business-related organisations (a very untypical behaviour for clients of consumer CDFIs) and purely social organisations;[19] Table 4.4 also suggests the existence of a link from community involvement to loan discipline and income progression. As shown in Table 4.8, several loan recipients, for example Scotcash 23, 64 and 114, ascribed their progression to involvement in their local communities, which added a multiplier to their desire to exhibit themselves as successes (in particular financial successes) rather than failures. The fact of being an organisation member, rather than the type of organisation, seemed to be the defining influence: membership of neighbourhood watch committees (respondent 76), of parent–teacher associations (respondent 64), and of tenants' associations (respondent 114) alike spoke, in intensive interviews, of membership in the association as being a defining factor influencing their shift to planning their money proactively. Those with high community involvement, as Table 4.8 also shows, are much more likely to experience high impact from financial contact with the lender, either through loan or advice, than those with minimal membership of social networks. The implication that we derive is that community involvement acts as a powerful reinforcer to capacities which cause lending to have high impact. It does this, we argue, by making behaviour more public and open to exposure, and thereby increasing the perceived penalty attaching to behaviours which might lead to a slip back into the debt trap, such as default on payments to CDFIs, increased dependence on loan sharks or alcohol addiction. In other words, it reinforces fear of failure and increases the incentive to 'progression' – and thus adds a public social and reputational penalty to a private financial one. In this way, much more indirectly than the peer-pressure mechanisms of third world microfinance institutions, it acts as a collateral substitute, and protects the capital of its sponsors. An implication might be that consumer lenders could buttress their effectiveness by making contacts through networks rather than just through individuals – for example by directing publicity through social clubs and organisations, as well as by broadening its existing and very valuable links with the Glasgow Credit Union into other credit unions with collection points nearer to members' homes. We take up this theme again in our final section.

5   Had made greater use of money advice, provided either by voluntary organisations or by CDFIs themselves.

6 Finally, had been more proactive in reducing their dependence on doorstep lenders. As illustrated by Figure 4.4 for Glasgow, doorstep lenders are not evenly spread across all areas of deprivation and financial exclusion within a city, but tend to cluster in particular areas (in the case of Glasgow, Govan, Bridgeton and Easterhouse).

These initial indications are a beginning. Before we move to a formal econometric test, however, it is useful to examine the extent to which the variables in Table 4.8 can be varied by adjustments of policy and institutional design.

One key variable determining progression out of poverty in Table 4.8 is the ability to save. As the table shows, Scotcash was more successful in mobilising savings than either of the other two institutions in our sample, but it is possible that all CDFIs can learn from the experience of the still more successful ELM, described in Case Study 3.

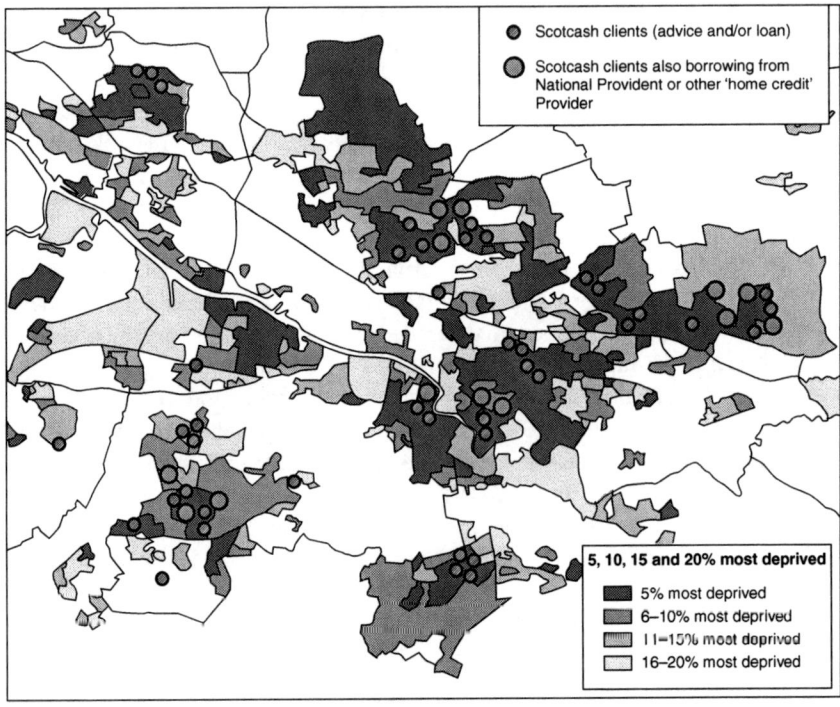

Figure 4.4 Glasgow: mapping of CDFI clients and doorstep lenders in relation to zones of multiple deprivation (source: adapted from deprivation map published by Glasgow City Council using the Scottish Index of Multiple Deprivation (SIMD). Copyright of the map original rests with the Ordnance Survey and the figure is reproduced under licence number 100018617).

Case Study 3 Savings mobilisation in ELM

East Lancashire Moneyline (ELM) has been more successful than any other CDFI in the mobilisation of savings, which is a crucial element in the development of financial capacity. Over the last five years, ELM has opened new savings accounts at a rate of more than one for each loan account opened – something like ten times the rate achieved in the average CDFI.[20] How has it done this?

The approach chosen is very different from that adopted in Scotcash and in Moneyline Yorkshire, where the recommendation is for CDFI clients to save with the local credit union.[21] Rather, loan clients are invited, at the point that they are setting up the direct debit for the repayment of their loan instalments, to commit a part of the repayment – typically 20p in every pound – to savings with ELM's savings partner, Halifax Bank of Scotland (HBOS). On being asked why they should do this, the loan officers reply: it will enable you to cope better with emergencies, and achieve a measure of financial independence. The loans officer to whom I spoke, Sharon Willis – a more successful recruiter of savings accounts than any other CDFI employee – explained that her first approach would be to emphasise that savings accounts can shelter clients against having to return, in case of a sudden shock, to the doorstep lender – as a single parent herself, she can certify that saving got her out of the debt trap. Once persuaded, her next step the second is to work out a savings plan that is affordable for the client.[22] The fact that there is no minimum limit on savings accounts is important in this context – 'the other day, I opened a savings account for 2p'.[23]

The crux in Scotcash, as in ELM, often lay in involving the client not simply in a short-term transaction but in a plan to scale down debt. This in turn often reduced worry:

> We have no debt now so more peace of mind. Also we had just moved so did the house up. Also we decided after paying off Scotcash loan we would not borrow again, now we save up if we want anything.
>
> (respondent 100, married with two children, forty-five, G32).

But sometimes the relationship went the other way: one Scotcash borrower (with an exemplary repayment record) claimed that the availability of loan finance reduced, rather than increased, her incentive to save.[24]

One key variable is loan advice and mentoring (which, we observe, was accessed by 41 per cent of 'risers out of poverty' and only 21 per cent of 'fallers into poverty'). Across our samples, there is very great variation in the manner in which loan advice is provided, whether by voluntary agencies such as Citizens' Advice Bureaux (CAB), Surestart, Local Authority agencies, National Debtline and various church organisations including Christians against Poverty, in the case of small business borrowers by Business Links, or by the CDFI itself. In Derby Loans and DSL, loan advice and mentoring are not provided in-house but are subcontracted to external agencies. In Moneyline Yorkshire (Sheffield) loan advice is available in-house but only on a

Table 4.8 Poverty transitions analysed by possible cause

Indicators of debt management capacity....	Exit from poverty 2007–09 N = 40	Became poor 2007–09 N = 29
Initial conditions		
% no educational qualifications[1]	0.24	0.29
Ratio of 'rational' to 'emotional' coping mechanisms on Deakin scale[2]	1.38	0.88
Financial management capacity		
Savings: % with positive savings accounts[3]	73	7
Average value £(2009)	998	107
Average change in savings 2007–09 (£/annum)	952	–333
Labour market		
Monthly income from work (2009)[4]	720	161
Average change in labour income 2007–09 (£/annum)	641	–334
Access to knowledge		
Access to loan advice[5]	0.41	0.21
Social relations		
% using doorstep lender[6]	32	22
Change %	–35	+8
Member of social organisation or network in 2009[7]	0.59	0.12

Sources: survey questionnaire, 2007 and 2009.

Notes and definitions

1 *Educational qualifications*: responses are coded according to the five-point scale: 0, no qualifications; 2, GCSE, O levels or equivalent; 3, A levels, Scottish Highers or equivalent; 3.5, other further education or vocational qualification; 4, university degree.

2 *Ratio of 'rational' to 'emotional' coping mechanisms*: taken from the Deakin coping scale, see Table 4.4.

3 *Savings*: self-reported savings in cash and kind in the seven categories 'bank or building society deposits', 'credit union deposits', 'Christmas club or similar run by a local shop', 'informal deposits with work colleagues, friends or the committee system', 'putting money by in a jar or envelope', 'asking a relative or friends to save or look after money for you', 'lending money to friends or family as a way or saving' and 'savings deposited with a lender, e.g. credit card lender or catalogue lender such as BrightHouse', see question 15 of questionnaire surveys 2007 and 2009.

4 *Labour market earnings*: monthly take home pay after deductions.

5 *Received loan advice*: takes the value 1 if the respondent received advice on managing money during the period 2007–09, whether from the lending institution itself or from an external agency such as the Citizens' Advice Bureau; 0 otherwise.

6 *% using doorstep lender*: includes the categories of pawnbroker, 'home lender' such as National Provident or Greenwoods, 'catalogue lender' such as BrightHouse or loan shark; see question 19 of survey questionnaire.

7 *Membership of social networks*: takes the value 1 if the respondent was a member or organiser of any of the nine types of social networks specified in question 21 of the survey questionnaire (social club, Women's Institute, community group (choir or orchestra, tenants' organisation, community centre, neighbourhood watch), church, mosque or religious organisation, political party, school parent–teacher organisation, support group or welfare organisation, hobby or interest group, pensioners' club or lunch club, other groups) specified in question 22 of the survey questionnaire; 0 otherwise.

small scale, in the shape of two junior part-time staff financed by a commercial bank, and then only to groups and not to individuals. In Scotcash, the loan advice function is a great deal more intensive, and two senior advisers, seconded from the Citizens' Advice Bureau, are on hand full-time. The assistance takes various forms: assistance with budgeting; advice on opening and managing savings accounts; advice on benefit entitlement and employment possibilities; in the case of Scotcash, direct negotiations with National Provident and other doorstep lenders with the aim of mitigating demands for loan instalments; and general moral support. It will be clear from our previous argument that the function of encouraging clients to open savings accounts with other agencies, in an environment where saving is a minority activity and CDFIs are not empowered to accept deposits, is a crucial one. In Scotcash and Moneyline Yorkshire, the invitation to save is a completely voluntary one, but there exist interesting models outside our sample where heavier persuasion is applied. Over the last five years, ELM has been more successful than any other CDFI in the mobilisation of savings. Over the last five years, ELM has opened new savings accounts at a rate of more than one for each loan account opened – a far greater rate than that achieved in Yorkshire Moneyline or Scotcash. The approach is that loan clients are invited by *loan officers* (not money advisers), at the point that they are setting up the direct debit for the repayment of their loan instalments, to commit a part of the repayment – typically 20p in every pound – to savings with ELM's savings partner, HBOS. On being asked why they should do this, the loan officers reply: It will enable you to cope better with emergencies, and achieve a measure of financial independence.[25]

The second key variable which *potentially*, and we stress potentially, is capable of stimulating savings and money management capacity is membership of social groups. The data of Table 4.8 suggest that 59 per cent of risers out of poverty (by contrast with 16 per cent of fallers into poverty) were members of some kind of social network, and in Figure 4.5 we build on this idea by displaying scatterplots of the relationship between savings and income, both for the whole sample and for Scotcash.

It is apparent that especially among the lowest income groups, ability to save, which was a minority phenomenon,[26] was often related *both* to membership of social groups and, especially within the Scotcash sample, to access to loan advice. These characteristics, of course, were provided completely independently of one another. However, in cases where these two characteristics came together, they often produced dramatic results, in particular by eliminating the need to borrow from the doorstep lender and thereby giving the borrowing room for financial manoeuvre. The testimony of Scotcash client 14, pictured on Figure 4.5b, is graphic. This client, with the support of Scotcash money advisers, made not a single but a double transition – from incapacity benefit to part-time work for a paints company and from a £2,000 debt with National Provident (and zero savings) to positive savings with the credit union:

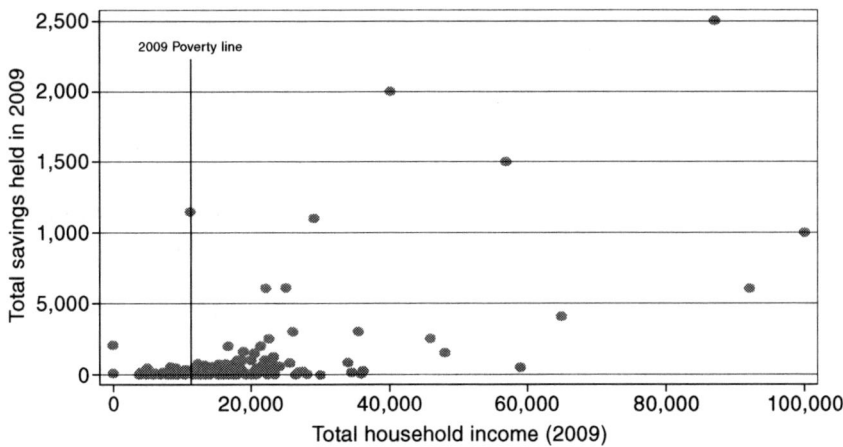

Figure 4.5 Scatterplots of saving in relation to income, whole sample (source: surveys, 2007 and 2009).

INTERVIEWER: You already mentioned you had to go to the Provident to get the money to send your son to his football. So do you still have any debts with other lenders like that?

RESPONDENT: No, that's me I'm clear. That's me clear now.

INTERVIEWER: So that is since you've got your job and you can afford to pay it off.

RESPONDENT: Aye.

INTERVIEWER: And are you a member of a credit union at all?

RESPONDENT: Yes I am. ... I find it brilliant, I've got my wee boy joined in it and everything, do you know what I mean.

(transcript of interview with client 14, 5 May 2008, thirty-five, G45, female, one child age twelve)

However, just because membership of social networks appears to be an important element in many poor people's escape from poverty, it does not follow that such networks can necessarily be created in this or other industrialised countries for the purpose of making CDFIs more effective. In developing countries, 'solidarity groups', typically clusters of a dozen or fewer individuals (five in the case of the celebrated Grameen Bank of Bangladesh) are routinely used to enforce peer pressure, provide an incentive to clients not to default and, more positively, to provide solidarity and mutual moral support within the group (Hulme and Mosley 1996). However, in industrial countries individual lending is the norm, and solidarity-group lending is uncommon, and where tried, for example in the cases of the NGOs ASPIRE, Belfast and the Scottish Microfinance Programme, has failed (Mosley and Steel 2004; Hermes and Lensink 2007). Interestingly, it has been announced that the Grameen Bank is to open an experimental branch in

Glasgow in 2011; and it is the case that in some urban environments, for example in New York, Grameen has been successful in lending with the use of a peer-group model.[27] At the time of writing, however, we know of no UK cases where social networks have been successfully *engineered* (by contrast with existing networks being gratefully drawn on) in support of CDFI operations.

In the light of this discussion, we build and test a model of the determinants of escape from the poverty trap. The sequence of causation that we shall seek to investigate is that indicated in Figure 4.3: social capital relationships and the design of the CDFI, in particular the nature of the advice provided alongside the loan, determine motivation to save, which then, in conjunction with other factors, in particular demographic and labour-market experiences, determines the likelihood of exit from poverty. Dependence on doorstep lenders also enters this savings function, as a factor which may influence both the amount of spare cash which the client has left over from spending on immediate necessities and in a longer-time perspective the client's perceived control over her allocation of resources, or financial management capacity.

Thus, in Table 4.9, we estimate a savings function, in which the right-hand side variables are simply the factors informally associated, in Table 4.8, with the likelihood of exit from poverty:

savings = f (loan advice, membership of social networks, degree of dependence on doorstep lenders, controls including initial formal education and coping strategy)   (4.1)

Savings, thus estimated, then becomes an independent variable in an 'escape from poverty' equation in which the other major factors identified by the Rowntree team (Kemp *et al.* 2004) as key ladders out of poverty, labour-market events, health shocks and demographic events, figure alongside savings capacity and the CDFI's own input as determinants of the likelihood of transition out of poverty:

change in client income = f (CDFI loan size, savings, change in labour income, health and demographic shocks, controls)   (4.2)

This equation is valid, we believe, for clients of consumer CDFIs but needs to be modified for the case of business CDFIs, whose productivity depends not only on their savings but on other kinds of assets, notably physical capital and equipment. In addition, as noted above, clients of business CDFIs are more likely to go bankrupt than clients of consumer CDFIs – indeed, as we have seen, eleven of the fifty-three business clients in Table 4.6 did so within our observation period, admittedly a period of acute recession. Hence, we include a measure of riskiness (the debt to capital ratio or 'risk ratio') in our poverty equation for business-lending CDFIs only:

change in client income = f (CDFI loan size, savings, physical capital, risk ratio, change in labour income, health and demographic shocks, controls)   (4.2a)

Finally, we need to control for 'selection bias': the possibility that the process by which recipients of microfinance services are selected may be endogenous and thus distort our measure of the impact of financial services (Khandker 1998; Hamid *et al.* 2010). We do this by using, as instruments for the size of the loan received, the index of multiple deprivation (IMD) of the postcode zone in which they are situated and their level of equivalised household income as measured by our survey.

CDFI loan size = f (index of multiple deprivation, client's income level, controls) (4.3)

The model consisting of relationships (4.1)–(4.3) is estimated by instrumental variables methods in Table 4.9. The Sargan-Hansen test statistic suggests that the instruments are adequate and that the system of equations (4.1), (4.2) and (4.3) is well identified.

As we observe from the third and fourth columns of Table 4.9, income transitions within our sample are influenced positively by savings rates and by increased inclusion in the labour market;[28] demographic and health shocks, although having the right sign, are not significant. Part of the reason for this may be that the operation of the benefits system tended to buffer the income of people suffering health and demographic shocks, and there were even cases, such as client Derby 61, where an upward transition across the poverty line came about as a result of a client experiencing a negative shock (in this case a household member becoming severely disabled and as a consequence receiving big increases in disability living allowance and in incapacity benefit). Benefit-led increases in income, although neither as numerous nor as durable within our sample as capital – and labour-market led transitions, nonetheless represent significant ladders out of poverty in the short term.[29]

A major objective of our study has been to understand the causal factors underlying changes in poor people's assets, represented within our business-CDFI sample partly by physical capital such as buildings, vehicles and equipment but in our larger consumer-CDFI sample purely by individuals' often sparse and painfully accumulated savings. Two factors emphatically, and two others less robustly, emerge in the final two columns of Table 4.9 as significant influences on savings. In the first place, *attitudes* are important: a one-point increase in our 'relative rationality measure', the extent to which people in response to shocks react calmly and rationally rather than by panicking or avoiding the problem, translates (column 5 of Table 4.9) into a significant increase in savings of about £111, which then, substituted into our income regressions, converts into an increase in income of around £500 per annum, or about 5 per cent. But, of course, coping ability is not an unvarying parameter, and one of the things which clearly influences it, on the evidence of our case-study material, is the availability and quality of *loan advice*, which is the other variable in column 5 of Table 4.9 robustly associated with changes in savings. Where, as often in our sample, it worked to achieve a turnaround in the

Table 4.9 The determinants of exit from poverty (estimation method: 3SLS)

Dependent variable Regression coefficients on independent variables:	Loan size[1]		Change in income 2007–09[2]		Change in saving 2007–09[3]	
Constant	358.8 (1.31)	394.2 (0.82)	−273 (0.31)	155.0 (0.32)	−143.8 (1.40)	−29.4 (0.23)
Instruments for loan size (participation in CDFI):						
Index of multiple deprivation[4]	−12.1 (0.21)	−177.7 (1.45)				
Equivalised household income, 2009[2]	0.025* (1.76)	0.122*** (8.45)				
Causal influences on exit from poverty:						
Change in saving 2007–09[2]			7.84*** (4.01)	2.92*** (3.06)		
Change in labour income 2007–09[3]			0.58* (1.93)	0.95 (1.59)		
Loan size[1]			2.77 (1.40)	0.96 (1.59)		
Educational qualifications[5]			−742** (−2.15)	−467.59 (−1.13)		
Health shock dummy[6]			509.8 (0.73)	828.7 (0.34)		
Demographic shock dummy[7]			593.9 (0.79)	1405.1 (1.56)		
Causal influences on saving:						
'Termination of borrowing from doorstep lender' dummy[8]					168.8** (2.43)	248.2 (1.40)
Membership of social networks[9]					89.0 (0.90)	451.6** (2.14)
Received loan advice[10]					244.8** (2.21)	492.0** (2.19)

'Rational' coping strategy[11]							111.1** (1.95)	
Number of observations	115	217	115	217	115	217	115	217
'R²'	0.15	0.31	0.15	0.31	0.15	0.31	0.15	0.31
Hansen–Sargan overidentification statistic		0.13		0.13		0.13		0.13

Sources: questionnaire survey, 2007–09, online, available at: www. poverty.group.shef.ac.uk.

Notes

Figures in parentheses below coefficients are Student's t-statistics: *** represents significance of a coefficient at the 1% level, ** at the 5% level and *at the 10% level. Second equation in each column excludes choice of coping strategy as explanatory variable.

Variable definitions:

1 *Loan size*: the value in pounds of all CDFI credits received by the client between 2007 and 2009. If loan size is 0, the implication is that the respondent was turned down for a loan and received only loan advice during these periods.

2 *Change in income 2007–09*: equivalised to compensate for variations in demands on the respondent's income. For details of the formula used, see Table 4.1, note 1, and for further notes on this approach see Institute for Fiscal Studies (Brewer *et al.* 2009).

3 *Change in saving 2007–09*: self-reported savings in cash and kind in the seven categories 'bank or building society deposits', 'credit union deposits', 'Christmas club or similar run by a local shop', 'informal deposits with work colleagues, friends or the committee system', 'putting money by in a jar or envelope', 'asking a relative or friends to save or look after money for you', 'lending money to friends or family as a way or saving' and 'savings deposited with a lender, e.g. credit card lender or catalogue lender such as BrightHouse', see question 15 of questionnaire surveys 2007 and 2009.

4 *Index of multiple deprivation*: a measure of deprivation according to indices such as income, asset ownership, house condition, crime, unemployment and educational standards, originally standardised by the Office of the Deputy Prime Minister and now collected by city councils and by the Scottish and Welsh governments and displayed on those authorities' websites (for the Glasgow data used here, see online, available at: www.scotland.gov.uk/simd2006). In the four cities for which we present data, we rank the respondent's postcode in one of five descending categories of deprivation according to the values the index of multiple deprivation (IMD) for that area, as follows:

	Glasgow	Sheffield	Derby	Birmingham
5 *(most deprived category)*	G32–34	S5	DE23	B20
4	G5, G21, G40	S2, S4	DE24	B9
3	G22, G31, G45	S3	DE21–22	B18
2	G15, G51–G53	S8, S13	DE1 (part)	B11
1 *(least deprived category)*	All other postcodes	All other postcodes	All other postcodes	All other postcodes

continued

Table 4.9 continued

5 *Educational qualifications*: responses are coded according to the five-point scale: 0, no qualifications; 2, GCSE, O levels or equivalent; 3, A levels, Scottish Highers or equivalent; 3.5, other further education or vocational qualification; 4, university degree.

6 *Health shock dummy*: takes the value −1 in the event of a serious negative shock, e.g. severe illness such as cancer or injury causing withdrawal from the labour market; +1 in the event of a positive health shock, e.g. recovery enabling respondent to re-enter the labour force; and 0 in all other cases.

7 *Demographic dummy*: takes the value −1 in the case of a demographic event with negative implications for the respondent's income or assets, e.g. divorce from or death of a partner, or birth of a third or subsequent child; +1 in the case of an event with positive implications for the respondent's income or assets, e.g. marriage, getting employment after a period of unemployment or movement from part-time to full-time; and 0 in all other cases.

8 *Termination of borrowing from doorstep lender*: takes the value 1 if respondent moved, between 2007 and 2009, from borrowing from a high-cost lender (pawnbroker, doorstep lender such as National Provident or Greenwoods, or loan shark; see question 19 of survey questionnaire) to no borrowing from such sources; takes the value −1 if respondent increased her borrowing from these sources between 2007 and 2009; and takes the value 0 in all other cases.

9 *Membership of social network*: takes the value 1 if the respondent was a member or organiser of any of the nine types of social networks specified in question 21 of the survey questionnaire (social club, Women's Institute, community group (choir or orchestra, tenants' organisation, community centre, neighbourhood watch), church, mosque or religious organisation, political party, school parent–teacher organisation, support group or welfare organisation, hobby or interest group, pensioners' club or lunch club, other groups) specified in question 22 of the survey questionnaire; 0 otherwise.

10 *Received loan advice*: takes the value 1 if the respondent received advice on managing money during the period 2007–09, whether from the lending institution itself or from an external agency such as the Citizens' Advice Bureau; 0 otherwise.

11 Our concept of a '*rational*' *coping strategy* is adapted from the Deakin coping scale devised by Moore (2003). In our survey questionnaire, we ask 'If you had a financial emergency and needed £1,000 in a hurry, what do you think you would do?', and after leaving time for an unprompted response, code the respondent's subsequent replies according to the nineteen suggested responses on the Deakin scale, which appear as question 29 of that questionnaire. We define the 'rationality' of the respondent's response pattern as the ratio of the 'rational' responses: 2 ('analyse my reaction to the problem'), 5 ('get more information about the situation'), 6 ('identify the source of the problem') and 7 ('take control of the situation'), to the 'emotional' responses: 12 ('feel miserable about the situation'), 13 ('keep my fingers crossed that it will go away'), 14 ('pray for it to go away') and 15 ('hope for a solution to appear'). Values of this ratio above 1 suggest a predominance of rational over emotional coping mechanisms in the respondent, and values below 1 imply the reverse.

self-belief of particular clients, it served in effect as a very practical and applied fusion of human and social capital.[30] The ability of clients, in these cases, to adopt the savings ladder out of the poverty trap derived almost entirely from the relationships of empathy and trust which loan advisers were able to build with them to experiment with a change in the way they allocated their resources.

Membership of social networks has been found both in industrialised and in developing countries to be strongly associated with savings and growth (Putnam 1993; Knack and Keefer 1997; Whiteley 2000) and, using the rather wide definition of social networks adopted by Putnam, we too find that ability to accumulate assets in the form of savings is significantly associated with membership of social groups (column 5 of Table 4.9; N.B. savings insignificant in column 6). The significance of these linkages is, in our view, both negative and positive. Membership of social groupings places members in a goldfish bowl in which all aspects of their behaviour can be observed and commented on including their ability to repay debt; and this transparency, or potential for exposure, acts as a sanction which motivates group members both to repay their debts and to accumulate defences against the risk of not being able to repay, such as savings – as of course happens much more explicitly in the peer-group lending schemes of the Grameen Bank and other developing countries. In a more positive sense, membership of social groupings provides a potential reinforcement to fellow members whose morale and fortunes are down not to despair and to sustain their long-term ambitions including the savings on which those ambitions depend – a reinforcement not available to the socially isolated. Finally, on the evidence of our case studies, many clients only perceived themselves as able to save once they had loosened the hold on them of agents who deprived them of room for financial manoeuvre, and in particular doorstep moneylenders, pawnbrokers and other forms of loan shark. We find that the dummy variable for clients who detached themselves from doorstep lenders between 2007 and 2009 ('Termination of borrowing from doorstep lender', column 5 of Table 4.9) is significantly associated with increases in savings; note however that this variable ceases to be significant when a 'rational coping strategy' is not included in the model.

In Table 4.10, these propositions are further tested through the use of a probit specification, which directly measures the likelihood of escape from poverty. As in Table 4.9, we instrument for loan size by means of the index of multiple deprivation and income level, but in this specification, in the light of our previous discussion of the impact of welfare benefits, we factor these, and also log of outstanding debt, into the story. Once again the significance of loan advice is confirmed as a predictive variable.

All of our instruments are shown in column 1 to be significant in explaining the probability of being a borrower in our sample. The marginal effects reveal the significance of loan advice as a predictive variable: the acceptance of loan advice is associated with a statistically significant 14 percentage point increase in the likelihood of escape from poverty.

Table 4.10 Likelihood of escape from poverty: Heckman probit estimates and marginal effects.

Dependent variable	Borrower		Probability of escape from poverty		Probability of escape from poverty	
	Coefficient	Std error	Coefficient	Std error	Marginal effect	Std error
Regression coefficients on independent variables:						
Constant	-6.59***	(1.88)	-2.26***	(0.30)		
Index of multiple deprivation	-0.14*	(0.08)				
Log outstanding debt	0.23***	(0.37)				
Total benefits	0.003**	(0.00)				
Log household income in 2007	0.74***	(0.21)				
House ownership dummy			-0.00***	(0.00)	-0.00***	(0.00)
Loan advice dummy			1.10***	(0.28)	0.14***	(0.05)
Membership of social networks			0.34	(0.28)	0.03	(0.02)
Change in income			0.0001***	(0.00)	0.00***	(0.00)
'Off loan shark' dummy			0.37	(0.28)	0.03	(0.02)
Highest qualification			0.20	(0.28)	0.02	(0.02)
Observations	252		252		252	
Rho	0.997					
Wald chi²	52.57					
Prob> chi²	0.0000					

Note
*** Represents significance of a coefficient at the 1% level, ** at the 5% level and *at the 10% level.

Conclusion: is a 'win–win' technology available for CDFIs?

Potentially at least, CDFIs represent a striking new idea: a social welfare institution which not only contributes to well-being in the sense of increased consumption but also in the sense of asset building and, additionally, to a degree, pays for itself. It therefore extends the idea of 'asset-based welfare policy' outside the state sector, and potentially suggests, under the impetus of inspiring precedents in developing countries, that it can be implemented in a financially sustainable way.

We have examined two of the mechanisms by which the CDFI sector has functioned over the last fifteen years: the *business-CDFI* model, which aims as in developing countries to lend to small businesses which are bankable but suffer from financial exclusion, and the more recent *consumer-CDFI* model, which breaks new ground by lending not to businesses of any sort but to low-income consumers, most of them dependent on welfare benefits. Our evidence on six CDFIs during the global recession period 2007–09 suggests that they are caught on the horns of a dilemma: business CDFIs secure a fairly substantial average benefit for a small number of people, whereas consumer CDFIs secure an insignificant average benefit for a large number of people. From this point in the argument we focus on the problem of insignificant average benefit among consumer CDFIs. Our hypothesis is that this problem arises because the asset element in the process of transferring consumer CDFI loans, consisting of improved financial management capacity, has been insufficiently developed. We test this hypothesis by examining the connection between leading indicators of financial management capacity – including social capital, rationalistic attitudes and strategies to escape from moneylenders – and saving, and then the relationship between saving (in conjunction with other 'ladders out of poverty') and the process of escape from poverty.

Both our qualitative and our quantitative evidence suggest that the main mechanism which determines the ability of CDFIs to function as a ladder out of poverty, or alternatively as a snake pushing them further into poverty, is the ability to build assets in the form of savings – savings only in the case of consumer CDFIs and savings plus a range of physical assets in the case of business CDFIs – subject of course to a range of labour-market, demographic and health shocks against which savings themselves constitute a defence. This logic suggests that the independent variables which our analysis suggests to be the most effective instruments for increasing savings are the instruments which would be most effective for increasing the ability of CDFIs to climb the income ladder. These variables are, first, loan advice and, second, membership of social networks, and they are connected, because the provision of loan advice is both social capital in the sense of a social relationship which increases individual productivity and human capital in the sense of capital embodied in the transfer of relevant knowledge.

Here a public goods problem arises, and because of this an interesting divide arises between CDFIs. The provision of loan advice is in the interest of borrowers, because as we have shown it raises their productivity; but it is not in the short-term interest of lenders because no part of the outlay which they make on advice comes back to them. The result of this is that the CDFIs which attract public subsidy, in particular Scotcash, provide their own loan advice, but those whose advice function is unsubsidised, namely Derby Loans and for the most part Sheffield Moneyline,[31] simply do not promote advice proactively, and simply refer those who ask for money advice to the CAB, where they often have to wait many weeks for an appointment and sometimes receive advice which is dysfunctional from the point of view of the CDFIs (e.g. 'seek a means of wiping out your debts rather than paying them back such as an IVA' (individual voluntary agreement). As a result the uptake of money advice is much greater in Scotcash, which provides advice as an integral part of its financial product, than in other agencies, and arguably the fact that Scotcash of all the consumer-lending agencies has the highest 'impact margin' (Table 4.6) may be in part due to this. In our judgment our results justify the extension of subsidised loan advice beyond the few agencies which currently provide it, and if this occurs local authorities may find that their arrears on rents and other publicly provided services diminish – as the Glasgow City Council, which part funds Scotcash, has done. In other words, there may be a private as well as a public dividend to be derived from loan advice.

Similar considerations may also apply to the other variable impacting on the level of savings, namely institutional membership. However, whereas it is not difficult, given the availability of the requisite skills and funding, to operationalise money advice, it is not at all easy, as several experimental CDFI initiatives in Britain have already discovered, to operationalise social groups in support of loan effectiveness. Our tentative suggestion is that it might be possible at minor cost to organise meetings of borrowers specifically where National Provident is known to be strong (i.e. the blue dots on Figure 4.4) for purposes of publicity, market research and eliciting feedback. This would kill several birds with one stone: it would extend the CDFI's reach, it would provide it with feedback enabling it to improve its own operations, the groups if they keep going could act as peer group monitoring mechanisms according to the classical third-world model and, finally, further inroads could be made into the territory of the loan sharks, which in itself, as per the analysis of Tables 4.8 and 4.9, would raise saving and increase probabilities of exit from the poverty trap. This approach is experimental and may fail; but it is consistent with our basic argument that to achieve lasting gains in the fight against financial exclusion, money alone will not do the job.

This chapter has considered only one dimension of the impact of CDFIs, namely the influence they have on the well-being of individuals. Also important, of course, is whether they can influence the ability of neighbourhoods and communities to work together and create public assets such as a pleasanter and less intimidating social environment. These issues are considered in the next chapter.

5 CDFI clients

Community-level impacts

Approach

The logic of establishing community development finance institutions is to support not only individuals, with whom the analysis of the previous chapter has been preoccupied, but also, as their title implies, communities. The incoming Labour government of 1997, in its quest for a view of society which might replace the divisive tendencies of conservatism, put *community* in pride of place as an organising principle, as a 'third way' alternative to both socialism and the principle of social Darwinism, or survival of the fittest, associated with some versions of conservatism and in particular the conservatism of Margaret Thatcher (Affleck and Mellor 2006; Hudson *et al.* 2008). Although, in its election campaign, the Labour Party had put little emphasis on redistribution as a policy objective, once in power it made clear that it was a key policy objective by whose success it should expect to be judged, both at home and abroad. In the fight against domestic poverty, child poverty was prioritised, and, as will be recalled from Chapter 1, a new Social Exclusion Unit was set up within the Office of the Deputy Prime Minister, with a remit to rebuild deprived and fractured communities, in particular within the inner-city areas which are the focus of this book. Financial exclusion was quickly identified as a prime mover among the various forms of discrimination and institutional failure which constitute social exclusion, and, as described in Chapter 1, government money was provided through the Department of Trade and Industry (now the Department of Business, Innovation and Skills, BIS) in the form of a 'Phoenix Fund' to enable CDFIs to support financially excluded businesses. The intention was that through these loans jobs could be created in deprived communities, and the initiative was given Treasury support in the shape of Community Investment Tax Relief for CDFIs, with the intention of levering additional investment into the sector.

The proposition that communities and social networks were good for development and poverty reduction was, as we have already seen, not based purely on intuition or ideology. Around the millennium, the idea that membership of social groups might be key to both economic and political development gained leverage around the world, initially through the thesis of Robert Putnam's book *Making Democracy Work* that it was a higher level of participation in 'networks of civic engagement' (1993: 175), or social capital,[1] rather than a higher level of physical investment and human capital, which was responsible for the faster growth and higher living standards of northern by comparison with southern Italy. Inspired by Putnam's finding, quantitative cross-country studies, typically using intra-community trust as an indicator of social capital rather than seeking to measure the density of social networks directly, were published soon after Putnam showing that social capital across the world had a significant influence on growth even when physical and social capital were controlled for (Knack and Keefer 1997; Whiteley 2000). The idea that social capital might be a crux for poverty reduction then spread to the developing world through the efforts of the World Bank, notably through the pages of the *World Development Report 2000* (World Bank 2000). In our own case-study cities, we have observed that affinity-group membership is positive for savings and thence for poverty reduction being a member of a vibrant and supportive community normally adds, as we have already demonstrated (Tables 4.8 through 4.10), to what CDFIs are able to achieve with clients on their own.

Is this additional community impact something which simply has to be accepted as it is, or can it be enlarged and developed by the right kind of policy initiatives, including by CDFIs themselves? There is a variety of views on this. One approach is to suggest that social integration cannot be created by any kind of extraneous policy effort but arises rather from spontaneous group action at neighbourhood level. 'In this model of society', as Forrest and Kearns note, 'social cohesion is viewed as a bottom-up process founded upon local social capital, rather than as a top-down process' (2001: 213). However, there is an alternative view, which suggests that some forms of social capital, at least, can be created. The Joseph Rowntree Foundation research programme on *Changing Neighbourhoods*, for example, argues that the quality of social interaction and neighbourhood-level cohesion can indeed be changed for the better by judicious intervention. Indeed, they argue, one way of doing this is through microcredit itself: 'small amounts of unrestricted money' they claim, 'can make a big difference, particularly to smaller community groups and those just starting out' (Taylor *et al.* 2007b: 2, 13). However, they stress that the way in which this is done is important, preferring indirect 'light touch' approaches over comprehensive area redevelopment programmes, and stressing that some elements of social capital are more in need of building up than others:

> Policy-makers often speak of the need to develop 'social capital' in communities, on the assumption that community ties are weak. But many communities do have these strong bonding ties already. What they lack is the 'bridging' social capital ties across social groups/communities, both within a neighbourhood and between neighbourhoods.
>
> (Taylor *et al.* 2007b: 7)

A distinction between bonding and bridging social capital was originally made in Putnam's study of Italy (1993: Ch. 6). The contrast between the two ways of making networks was greatly developed in the context of developing countries by the World Bank's *World Development Report 2000* and in particular by one of its contributing authors, Michael Woolcock (World Bank 2000; Woolcock 1998, 1999; Woolcock and Narayan 2001) who represented bonding social capital within communities as being defensive or, in the language of the previous chapter, protectional, whereas bridging social capital was promotional, transformative and associated with processes of social advancement, such as the out-of-poverty transitions of the previous chapter. And, indeed, bridging social capital unlike bonding social capital typically requires inputs from outside the community as well as from inside; institutions against financial exclusion are an excellent example of these. In some cases, such as money advice (as provided in particular by Scotcash within our sample), bridging social capital is combined with elements of human capital, and in this case we have what is known as 'credit plus' (McKernan 2002; Karlan and Valdivia 2010; Biosca *et al.* 2010), where the 'plus' consists of the complementary inputs which seek to make credit more effective. Thus one approach towards the encouragement of community cohesion is to provide enabling inputs, typically via an indirect bridging mechanism such as advice or technical support rather than through explicit group formation,[2] which removes some barrier causing discrimination, exclusion or low productivity. This has been the approach, for example, of the New Deal for Communities, an adjunct to the government's New Deal programme of achieving greater labour-market flexibility through investment in training,[3] whose multi-faceted programme prioritised the removal of discrimination in housing. In this chapter, whilst well aware that community-building is a process much of which happens over very long time spans far beyond this book's brief two-year time snippet, we examine thirteen cases in which actions by clients, CDFIs and external actors have been successful in creating social capital of different kinds during this period, and ask how they have done it. Thus, what we investigate in the next section, with the help of both anecdotal and formal statistical evidence from our case-study cities, is the second leg of a possible two-way relationship: we would like to know whether causation runs from CDFI clients' development to the formation of social capital (the dotted arrow in Figure 5.1) as well as, as already observed in Chapter 4, in the reverse direction (the solid arrow in Figure 5.1).

Of course, social capital, both in its bonding and its bridging forms, is not a homogeneous putty-like lump, the enlargement of any part of which makes everyone better off; nor will those who see benefits from network membership and want to take it further necessarily wish to invest in 'the community' as a whole, but rather in specific interest groups. Social networks and even neighbourhoods may overlap and conflict with one another. Additionally, the strengthening of one community may threaten or undermine another (Forrest and Kearns 2001; Robinson 2005). In Robinson's view, this has caused a clash of policy agendas:

While the social exclusion and community cohesion agendas promote mobility and reject strong local communities for fear of promoting further isolation, housing and neighbourhood management promotes social

cohesion at the neighbourhood level as an essential ingredient of sustainability. In effect, the sustainable communities that housing managers are
trying to nurture – characterised as internally cohesive and possessing a
sense of solidarity and mutual support and co-operation – are the very communities problematised by the community cohesion agenda. Hence the comments of a chief executive of a black and minority ethnic (BME)-led
housing association reported by Robinson *et al.* (2004, p15), who reflects
that his most sustainable and easy-to-manage estates are mono-cultural.

(2005: 1423)

As Robinson notes, a context in which this issue is particularly relevant is the
formation of social capital amongst ethnic minorities, where community organisations established to defend one ethnic group may be perceived as threatening
and undermining other ethnic groups. We then examine the role of CDFIs in the
process of group formation and community-building in ethnic-minority communities with particular reference to our Birmingham sample. We conclude with
some ideas on policy and institution building.

Investment in social networks: case studies

We now examine the process of social network formation among our sample of
CDFIs, illustrating what it has been able to achieve across the sample. We
emphasise that this kind of social entrepreneurship is a minority activity. Not all
managers of CDFIs see it as their function to build communities, and among
clients, community-building, on our measure, is engaged in by barely 5 per cent

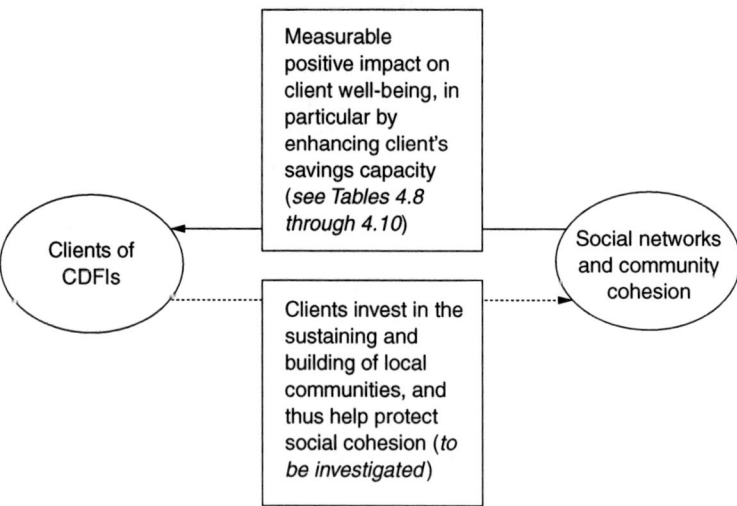

Figure 5.1 The possible two-way relationship between microfinance clients and social
networks.

of the client sample; more than this in the case of business-lending CDFIs, less in the case of consumer-lending CDFIs. However, those who do it add an important multiplier to what CDFIs are able to contribute through their impacts on individuals, and it is this which we seek to assess in this chapter.

Business-lending CDFIs

Our first example comes from outside the sample, as it provides inspiration for what remains to be done within the sample and elsewhere. One of the pioneer British CDFIs, ASPIRE of Belfast (now absorbed into Enterprise Northern Ireland) aimed to tackle financial exclusion explicitly by lending to enterprises in businesses emerging from conflict and economic decline. Established in 1999, a year after the Good Friday agreement, it achieved a notable triumph a year later by persuading the separate Protestant and Catholic taxi-drivers' unions to work together. Taxi-drivers at that time could not raise finance from the banks, and their best hope was to borrow at 60 per cent plus from informal moneylenders. ASPIRE located itself in 'neutral' territory dominated by neither of the two groups, raised finance from a consortium of four banks (Allied Irish Bank, Bank of Ireland, Ulster Bank and Northern Bank) and on-lent to both groups at 19 per cent through a new credit union, the West Belfast Taxi-Drivers' Association, established for the purpose of ensuring loan repayment. ASPIRE having lowered the cost of finance, the Association then lowered the cost of insurance by purchasing a collective insurance contract for its members. Members of this union came from both the Catholic and Protestant sides, and although free to operate where they chose, many soon found that they could increase their takings by crossing 'the line' which divides Catholic West Belfast from Protestant North and East Belfast. By doing this they opened the way for many other institutions to operate de facto (the Good Friday Agreement, establishing the intention to put an end to religious partitioning, had been signed only two years previously) on a basis of free movement which ignored sectarian divisions.

In this way, community-building through microfinance preceded other actions to overcome the religious divide, and the 'community' which was formed was a taxi-drivers' union and a credit union which, small as it was, did not confine itself within but transcended the two dominant religious groupings of Northern Ireland. The CDFI provided two things: money which enabled the taxi-drivers to overcome their financial exclusion and lower their costs; and bridging social capital, formally in the shape of the new credit union but informally also in the shape of encouragement and facilitation which gave them the idea of cooperating and helped them to get their vehicles and parts at advantageous prices. The really exciting thing, which was the fact of Protestant and Catholic taxi-drivers operating in collaboration, then occurred spontaneously rather than through institutional engineering, since once the new credit union was established both Protestants and Catholic members of it could see that the market for both of them was widened by each driver being willing to drive any client across any place in the city rather than by respecting sectarian demarcation lines. A new vision was brought into being simply by enabling market forces to operate. This of course has relevance for the problem of clashing ethnicity – or faith-based networks, to be further discussed below.

We now examine some cases in which social networks were developed by CDFIs and clients within our sample, beginning with the Glasgow business CDFI, DSL. As described in Chapter 3, DSL has accepted from the beginning a remit to assist the poorest and smallest businesses in the city – although since 2005 it has been constrained by the requirements of the Small Firms Loan Guarantee Scheme, which imposes a minimum loan size of £5,000 – and it has a higher 'impact margin' or number of poverty exits per loan, than any other respondent in our sample (Table 4.3). Throughout the city, it operates in partnership with the Regeneration Agencies (before 2008, Local Economic Development Companies),[4] and these agencies, in the case of small firms with fewer than five employees,[5] are the main channel by which know-how and moral support, and thence bridging social capital, are conveyed to clients.

We now provide three examples of social capital creation by DSL clients themselves: one (Soapy Bubbles) from the 'subsistence' end of the business CDFI spectrum, or the left-hand end of the curve on Figure 4.1 and the other two (MacVicar and TIGERS) from the right-hand, or small and medium enterprise, end.

Case Study 4 Social capital-building and survival at the subsistence level: Soapy Bubbles, Glasgow (interviewee G6)

The co-owners of the Soapy Bubbles launderette, Karen and Kim, had in the late 1990s been made redundant from the laundry for which they previously worked. One of them was previously in a violent relationship with her partner, 'losing a great deal of work through her split with him', as she emphasised. Thus, in two ways, their backs were against the wall when they decided, in 2001, to go it alone and set up their own business in partnership together. At this point, finance to establish the new enterprise was refused by all the banks to whom they applied, on the grounds that the postcode in which Soapy Bubbles is located (at the southern end of Springburn (G21), one of the poorest neighbourhoods in the country; see 'S' on Figure 5.2) had been 'red-lined' and was not eligible for small business finance. Thus their only possible recourse at the time (early 2001) was DSL, which they learned about through the local economic development company, Glasgow North. A DSL loan (£4,000) was used to buy the washing machine which is the enterprise's main asset. 'Without them [DSL] we would never have existed: it's only thanks to them that we got the chance.'[6] A supplementary loan of £3,000 was provided in 2004 and used to buy ironing equipment. The turnover of the enterprise, since then, has expanded modestly, with seasonal ups and downs ('takings are always less at the end of the month as money runs short, and when the football season stops in May, we stop')[7] to reach about £22,000 in 2010; but the managers have always managed to keep their heads, just, above water. The enterprise's cash-flow has in recent years become more stable and less risky, much helped by the award of a bulk contract from the Strathclyde Fire Service in 2008. That summer

Karen and Kim were able, for the first time since the inception of the business, to take a holiday, as they did again in 2010.

To understand the neighbourhood in which Soapy Bubbles operates, it is necessary to see it in the context of local social structure and housing policies. Soapy Bubbles occupies a unit in a single-storey set of shops in Barmulloch, two miles east of the city centre. These shops are in the shadow of the Red Road flats (a cluster of thirty-storey flat blocks erected in 1966 as a response to the problems of overcrowding and low housing quality experienced at that time), and separated from them by large patches of waste ground patrolled by numerous dogs and foxes. The Red Road flats are higher than most residential housing blocks even in the United States, and great pride was felt by the city council, which initially owned and managed them, in the path-breaking steel girder technology which brought them into being (Jacobs *et al.* 2007). Almost all of them are occupied by tenants of the Glasgow Housing Association (GHA), to which the management of the city council's housing stock was devolved in 2003, and which in turn has sought to delegate many of its local functions to local housing organisations (LHOs), which in many parts of the city have provided local residents with opportunities to become effectively involved in the governance of their housing stock (Lawson and Kearns 2010).

In Red Road, however, this kind of community participation is very weak, and the reasons for this go beyond the high levels of poverty and asset deprivation found in the neighbourhood. Not immediately after their construction, but certainly by the 1980s, the Red Road flats (as distinct from the low-rise dwellings nearby) quickly ceased to be a place where anyone chose to live if they had any alternative options open to them. The problem was compounded by increasing awareness that the asbestos used in the flats to combat fire risks posed its own health problems, and by one of the highest drug abuse and violent crime rates in the country, much encouraged by the untenanted waste ground around the flats. By 2005, the GHA had announced its intention to knock down some of the Red Road tower blocks and to rehouse about 130 of the 1,100 current tenants in low-rise dwellings nearby. In the interim, the GHA was forced to use the flats, because of their decreasing desirability, as an asylum of last resort for those who had no other refuge, such as asylum-seekers and those with a criminal record. The flats achieved notoriety through the suicide of two Russian asylum-seekers in January 2010; six clients of Scotcash and DSL live within the neighbourhood, and whereas only a quarter of clients, in the survey questionnaire, mention crime as a factor influencing their quality of life, all of these six mention not only crime, but explicitly murders, amongst the factors which worry them.[8] By any standards, this is one of the most dangerous environments in Europe; its atmosphere of communal menace and individual fragility is brilliantly conveyed by Andrea Arnold's 2006 movie, *Red Road*, which incidentally gave a transient boost to the cashflow of Soapy Bubbles, whose managers figure as extras in that film. In that year, a 'Red Road Save our Homes' campaign was mounted against the GHA's redevelopment plans, both by lobbying within the LHO and on one occasion in a specially convened protest meeting, but by contrast with other areas of the city these protests lacked any collective impetus, gradually fell apart and did not elicit any changes in policy.[9] By September 2010, demolition of the largest tower block (153/183/213 Petershill Road) had begun.

It is this fragile and threatened institutional web that Karen and Kim, in 2005, sought to reinforce by setting up a new voluntary association, the Barmulloch

Community Council. The main purpose of the association was defined by the wish of community members to cope with, once it was agreed to be a hopeless cause to prevent, the impending redevelopment of the Red Road flats, the consequent emigration of amenities as well as people – the post office and the chemist have moved out and bus services have been withdrawn – and the resulting challenge both to the individual livelihoods and collective well-being of the remaining residents. The only surviving shops now in Karen and Kim's precinct are one Chinese restaurant and one Asian-owned general store, both of which can respond to the challenge by exporting their services outside the community as take-aways, which the managers of Soapy Bubbles, unable to afford a car, cannot do.

The network established by Karen and Kim's initiative consists formally of the monthly meetings of the Barmulloch Community Council, and informally of a process of social interchange around, and mainly within, their shop, which is probably the major centre for the exchange of news, information and mutual support in Barmulloch. Karen and Kim, being trusted by most of the local residents, find that '90% of them come into the shop and talk to us' (private communication 14 August 2009), and they have invested in assets ancillary to their launderette which although privately owned are in essence community resources.[10] In particular, they have installed a payphone (a key asset; most phoneboxes in the area have been vandalised), a Marie Curie collecting box and have surrendered an entire wall of potential selling space to a comfy bench seat along one side of the shop. This bench seat, above which they have erected a bookshelf and a lending library, is the informal social hub of Barmulloch.[11] Often worries and suggestions which emerge from casual conversations in the shop find their way on to the agenda of the Community Council. They have campaigned, with variable success, against the closure of bus services, for a swimming pool, and for tenants' rights and other matters, including crime and vulnerability to crime, which the GHA LHO is not felt to be satisfactorily dealing with. Also sometimes on the agenda are financial issues such as the operations of doorstep lenders, a theme taken up further below. What is not in question is that, in an environment where most feel very vulnerable and where existing forces for social cohesion including the GHA are badly in need of supplementation, these initiatives have given local residents some shelter against that vulnerability; not only through voice, which is the formal purpose of the Community Council, but by providing a shoulder to lean on. Analytically, what is provided is mainly bonding social capital within Barmulloch; but through making linkages with other community associations, the GHA and utility providers such as the bus companies – and of course loan providers such as DSL and credit unions – it contains elements of bridging social capital as well.

Attenders at monthly meetings of the Community Council are predominantly white Scottish members of the neighbourhood, and as its population becomes more diversified, the problem of within-community fragmentation arises (Robinson 2005; see also pages 91–92), i.e. that bonding within the sub-group of threatened Barmulloch white people will be at the expense of threatened Barmulloch immigrants. Karen and Kim are well aware of these problems: 'Up here', they said, 'there's a lot of racist people – we seem to be the only white people in the whole of Barmulloch' (private communication 5 February 2008). Like DSL and Scotcash, the Barmulloch Community Council has had little success in incorporating ethnic minorities into its structures. The most successful grouping at achieving this in this postcode (G21) is probably the Glasgow North Regeneration Agency, which reports a very rapid recent increase in enquiries from, and small grants and loans made to, ethnic minorities (private communication, Will Nisbet, 18 November 2010). Most of these loans, now, are not made by DSL, which, as mentioned above now lends a minimum of £5,000, but by the agency itself or, in the case of younger entrepreneurs, by the Prince's Scottish Youth Business Trust.

We now consider the case of two DSL borrowers from Easterhouse, in the east end of Glasgow ('T' and 'M' on Figure 5.2). These are larger firms than Soapy Bubbles, and they approach the scale of medium-scale social enterprises rather than subsistence enterprises (albeit the manager of TIGERS explicitly resents his firm being described as a social enterprise!). But, like Soapy Bubbles, they were financially excluded in the sense of not being able to raise the capital they needed from commercial banks, again partly because of their neighbourhood's unfashionable postcode (G32). The level of deprivation in Easterhouse is actually higher than in Red Road if measured in terms of income level, although it is lower if measured in terms of unemployment or crime indices.

Case Study 5 TIGERS (DSL7) and MacVicar (DSL8)

These two case studies are complementary in the sense that they both create intra-community linkages, and indeed create them in and for the poorest neighbourhood in the UK, the Easterhouse area of Glasgow.[12] More than this, John Gibson and Jim MacVicar are business partners, each owning half the equity of one another's companies. Thus the social capital on which they draw consists of one another as well as the social linkages of the neighbourhoods where their businesses are located. Both obtained loans from DSL around the millennium, and between them they account for about one-third of the exits from poverty (nine out of twenty-four) recorded in our sample of DSL borrowers over the period 2007–10, as recorded in Table 4.6.

TIGERS (Training Initiatives Generating Effective Results Scotland) was initiated in 2001 by an entrepreneur who had thirty years' experience in stockbroking, with the help of a £7,500 start-up loan from DSL, alongside a small start-up grant from Scottish Enterprise. Commercial banks, at the time, were not willing to lend for start-ups without collateral and a clear business profile; without the intervention from DSL and the guarantee provided by Jim MacVicar, the company might never have been established. The company provides training services for previously unemployed sixteen to eighteen year olds. Its approach is rigorously commercial rather than 'social': 'I ask, what does the market look for in young people, and try to anticipate that.'[13] Its focus is on up-skilling workforces to be competent to undertake high-skill jobs within the regeneration areas of Glasgow (see Figure 2.3a), and the company has made its reputation in particular by doubling the completion rates of young apprentices, from 45 per cent to over 80 per cent[14] and building a reputation for reliability in them which can be seen, we later argue, as a contribution to social capital (trustworthiness) and not just as human capital. At one stage, in 2002, TIGERS took its expansion plans further, providing about twenty new jobs within a call centre, but this experiment has now been abandoned. The company has gained support from its partnership with MacVicar (q.v., below) but also from its partnership with the Glasgow East Regeneration Area, which supplies it with many of its contracts. In 2008 it became part of a multinational, having made a contract with the property management company Carillion to multiply its training courses across the whole of Scotland. Over the last four years it has made steady profits of £70,000–80,000 annually on a turnover of just over £1 million, and its debt is now minimal. Its employment has grown from twelve to twenty-three between 2008 and 2010, most of these low-income people from the Easterhouse area, and there is hope that this growth can continue in the wake of the construction boom expected to be generated by the 2014 Commonwealth Games, to be held in Glasgow and to be focused on the south-east of the city. Apart from the low-income employment and training it provides in Easterhouse, the company supports a number of other charitable causes, including Glasgow Women's Aid and a number of local football clubs. By building a reputation for trustworthiness amongst his trainees (and also indirectly by making a dent in local unemployment) TIGERS generates bonding social capital;[15] in addition to this, John Gibson also provides 'bridging social capital' by hosting, together with Jim MacVicar and the business adviser of the Glasgow East regeneration agency, meetings of entrepreneurs in the Greater Easterhouse area on the regeneration agency's premises, at which business ideas and contacts are exchanged.[16]

Jim MacVicar Printers is a long-established family business, established by the client's uncle in 1974 and taken over by him in 1985. Like TIGERS, MacVicar was unable to raise the required finance at the start from high-street banks, and secured a loan from DSL of £10,000, to finance a new printing press. Much more than his business partner, MacVicar has sought to spin off new private businesses from his core printing business in a wide range of areas (including film-making, scripts and a new magazine called *LoveLife*, a lonely hearts magazine for business executives and for people coming out of the services).

In April 2002, MacVicar's business suffered a major shock. It was burnt to the ground as the consequence of an electrical fault, suffering nearly £700,000 of damage. The insurance company, at this point, deepened the shock, refusing to pay because of incomplete paperwork (the insurance broker had failed to fill in an annual return). In spite of entreaties from his wife to give up, MacVicar had the business up and running again within three days ('a winner never quits' was his comment to a printing trade journal).[17] The first adaptation he made was a technical one: to restore service as soon as possible by drawing on savings, on emergency lines of credit and on the loyalty, otherwise trust or 'bonding social capital', between himself and his staff. 'The ingenuity of my staff is beyond belief', he commented: 'without water, phone or electricity, one employee made a roller door in three hours.'[18] 'At one period', he added, 'I worked for 36 hours without stopping.' The second adaptation he had to make was a financial one, and this time the banks were more helpful, offering bridging finance of £50,000, which was topped up with extended credit from suppliers and from DSL, who chipped in with an emergency loan of £12,000. Given that the company was inches away from dissolution at the time, this small supplement may have made all the difference. The third adaptation was in pricing strategy: the company now operates on bigger margins. And, fourth, broadening the principle of reciprocity, he supports local Catholic charity activities on a larger scale than before, judging an annual

Christmas card competition, and running the Cardinal Winning Charity Ball. Having grown steeply until the time of the fire, MacVicar's turnover has levelled off to a stable level of about £1.2 million in 2009.

As may be apparent from the above, MacVicar and Gibson are complementary in personality as well as in a financial and social capital sense, the one more extrovert and private-sector orientated, the other quieter, more risk averse and more public-sector oriented. Their interdependent efforts, a small private-sector island not quite comfortably embedded into the public-sector employment-creation efforts that dominate east Glasgow, have done much to revitalise one of the country's most depressed labour markets.

In Birmingham, our illustrations come entirely from business CDFIs, and indeed from ethnic-minority entrepreneurs. We develop the theme of community-building among ethnic minorities in the penultimate section of this chapter.

The business idea of client B2 was the highly innovative one of providing support services – home repairs, decorating, cleaning and shopping – for women within ethnic-minority communities who found it difficult to look after themselves, for example, because they were ill, disabled or victims of abuse. The entrepreneur, a trained social worker with a postgraduate qualification, sold this idea to 3Bs (Black Business in Birmingham), an NGO which as described below, moved into the CDFI business around the millennium, and received a loan of £7,500 in 2005. She is an active member of the New Jerusalem Church (which we shall encounter again later in the chapter), and although committed to operate it as a business, wished also to operate it as a social enterprise for the benefit of the disadvantaged ethnic groups she had gone into business to assist. At the outset she employed four part-time staff, a figure which at the time of writing had grown to six.

In preparing her business plan, she was mentored not by 3Bs but by an ethnic-minority NGO with a Caribbean focus (Community Roots or, as it is widely known in Birmingham, simply 'Roots'). In our extended interview, we asked her for her opinion of the service she had received from Roots. The printable part of her reply was: '[They are] the biggest insult in the world: you expect some level of support and it does not come ... it makes you doubt your own ability' (interviews, July 2006 and November 2009).

Unlike other clients of both 3B and Roots, however, she did not allow herself to be deterred by the lack of mentoring and, indeed, decided, once her business was up and running, to expand from the provision of home maintenance services into the establishment of a network of providers of such services willing to operate in partnership with social service departments. Rather than the 'social capital formation as reciprocity' that we encounter with DSL (and will encounter with Scotcash, below), this is social capital formation as compensation for a service badly provided by the voluntary sector. Her determination to consolidate her enterprise into a network of service providers was motivated, not at all by

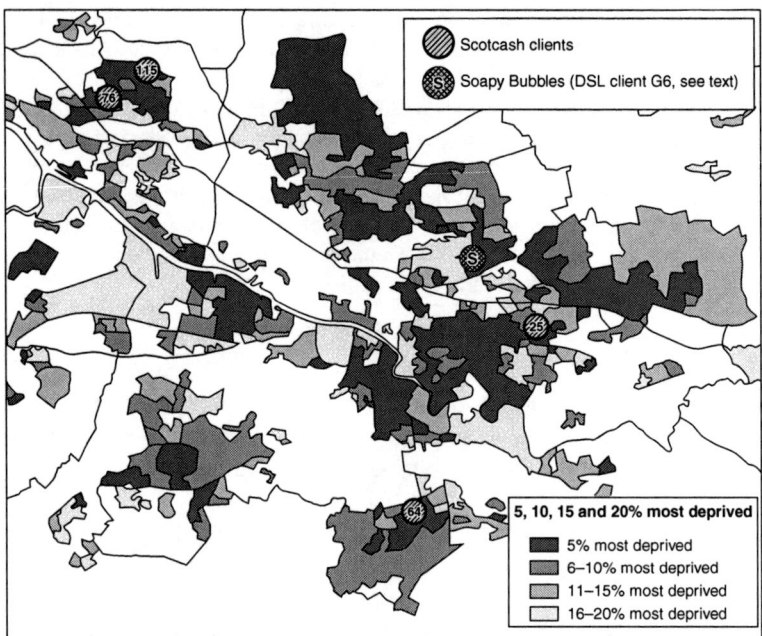

Figure 5.2 Social capital creation through CDFIs in Glasgow (source: adapted from deprivation map published by Glasgow City Council using the Scottish Index of Multiple Deprivation (SIMD). Copyright of the map original rests with the Ordnance Survey and the figure is reproduced under licence number 100018617).

Notes

Client 25 moved out of severe poverty between 2007 and 2009, from an annual (equivalised) income of £7,574 to a 2009 level of £14,564. She is a member, and has recently become the meetings organiser, of the Catholic Church in her home community, Shettleston G32. Within that community she has proposed – a suggestion not yet taken up – the holding of advice meetings under church auspices which could provide information about self-employment prospects in this high-unemployment area.

Client 64 took out her first Scotcash loan in 2007, and on their advice joined Castlemilk Credit Union a year later. In her home neighbourhood of Castlemilk (G45) has become secretary of the local parent–teacher association, and within that is collaborating with the credit union to establish programmes for young savers.

Client 76 took out a loan from Scotcash in 2007, but still has loans outstanding to National Provident. He is currently doing voluntary research and advocacy work 'for the disabled, to help get people to know what their rights are'. Having been troubled by noisy neighbours in his home neighbourhood of Drumchapel (G15), he established a residents' group when the local housing association failed to respond to complaints ('we have antisocial people straight above me. There is one chap in particular who is always causing mayhem… [we have protested, but] I am afraid the policy is not on the housing at the moment, it's because he is an alcoholic, they say you don't, he needs support because of the way he behaves. They say, leave him alone, he has got alcohol problems.') This residents' group now acts as an informal group for discussion of issues related to benefits and personal finance – through which a number of people have become clients of Scotcash and of the credit union.

Client 115 extended a network for the disabled in her home community of Drumchapel (G15). When initially established by her grandmother ten years ago it provided a meals-on-wheels service, but the client now has broadened her operation to become a point of contact for all disabled people in the neighbourhood with worries or grievances, in particular related to the benefits system. In addition she disseminates publicity for the Glasgow Credit Union which she has recently joined – and of course for Scotcash. An important motivation for her is the quality of service she has received from Scotcash.

reciprocity, but by determination that she and those for whom she felt responsible would not be pulled under by the institutional failings either of 3Bs or Community Roots – much as Soapy Bubbles had sought to compensate for the failings of the GHA LHO by setting up networks which filled the voids which the GHA had left.

Client B19, initially a client of Aston Reinvestment Trust (ART) and since 2006 also of the Black Country Reinvestment Society, is one of our few CDFI cases who is also a successful exporter (of industrial paints and chemicals): indeed, over 90 per cent of his output goes overseas, mostly to Nigeria, and his firm has a subsidiary in Lagos. Partly because of this insulation from the effects of the European credit crunch, he has withstood the recession well, and since 2008 has doubled turnover, from £800,000 in 2006 to £2 million in 2010, and expanded employment from six to eight 'core' full-time employees. During 2006 he was the caretaker-manager of Community Roots, seeking without great success to professionalise the mentoring and support services they offered to the black community, and since reverting to the role of full-time businessman he has continued to offer informal support to fellow Afro-Caribbean entrepreneurs. His contribution to network-building contains three distinct elements:

1   maintenance, as an informal support network, of advisory relationships with other Afro-Caribbean entrepreneurs within Birmingham begun when the respondent was managing director of Community Roots (q.v., bridging social capital);
2   membership of the 'Afro Business Network', an informal partnership of Afro-Caribbean manufacturers conveniently located near the intersection of the M5 and the M6 motorways just west of Birmingham city centre (bonding inter-business social capital, and transformation of a formal into an informal support network);
3   international networking, mostly within Nigeria and West Africa but with possibilities for spreading further afield in Africa (also bridging social capital).

Consumer-lending CDFIs

As discussed in our first chapter, consumer-lending CDFIs operate through a different mechanism from business-lending CDFIs. They seek to capitalise their clients not by supporting entrepreneurship, but rather by boosting their loan management capacity and their connectedness with the financial system. As a consequence, investment by consumer-lending clients in community-building operations is rarer than among business-lending CDFIs, and these operations are more of the bonding (intra-community) than of the bridging (inter-community) variety, as we shall illustrate. However, it is possible for CDFIs themselves to bridge between communities through the provision of advice and information, a function which we showed in Chapter 4 to be important for determining the rate of exit from the poverty trap. Amongst consumer CDFIs, Scotcash has shown the greatest awareness of the importance of the money advice function, and offers this service to all its clients; indeed, many clients who are refused loans are nonetheless offered advice. (Sheffield Moneyline offers money advice only to a few clients on an experimental basis, and Derby Loans delegates the money advice task to the CAB and similar agencies.) The way in which Scotcash money advisers operate is to win the confidence of their clients by achieving a financial advantage for them – for example, by illustrating to them ways of raising their entitlement to benefits, or by persuading the Provident or other doorstep lenders to ease its demands on them – and to use this trust-relationship to persuade clients that if they arrange their finances in a more rational way, this will enable them to cope better with their debts and in particular to escape from the hold of the doorstep lender. As the Scotcash money advisers emphasised to us, sometimes a meeting with a loan adviser can be the catalyst which turns the trauma of financial incapacity into a purposive approach, and make an effective vow never to get into debt again; and in other cases not. This does not always work – as one adviser commented, 'there are a few compulsive non-copers for whom bankruptcy is the best option', 'but these are a small minority'.[19] Often the fact of advisers being able to achieve some initial coup, however small, which eases financial pressure – whether getting the Provident to ease its demands, or demonstrate a client's entitlement to welfare benefits of which s/he was not aware, or in one case simply enabling a client to find a suitable house – can initiate a process of building trust-relationships which eventually brings about a fundamental change in attitudes.

We now describe four cases in which Scotcash clients were able to build social capital within their neighbourhoods. These are depicted on the Glasgow social deprivation map of Figure 5.2, together with the DSL clients previously discussed, in relation to the known locations of doorstep lenders.

We now consider some cases from the consumer-lending CDFI, Sheffield Moneyline. The main difference in its architecture from that of Scotcash is that the mentoring function is weaker – in place of Scotcash's comprehensive money advice service, there is only a skeleton in-house money advice service, provided through a research project financed by HBOS; the majority of advice clients must be referred to the local branch of the Citizens' Advice Bureau (CAB), where they often confront long waiting lists.

Notwithstanding this, we encounter some outstandingly creative cases of network formation also amongst Moneyline clients, notably the following three.

Respondent 109 took out a £600 loan from Moneyline in 2009. The rest of her story is best told in her own words:

> I had got myself quite deeply into debt before I came to Moneyline. The banks are bad enough, they used to phone me about having a loan before I'd even paid the old one off. But as for the Provident ... it's like a maze,

very easy to get into and very hard to get out of ... Unfortunately, with these people it doesn't benefit me to pay it off early. You will probably pay just as much if you do. So I struggled with them for a number of years; but I would never have got free of them if it hadn't been for Moneyline.

After that, I wanted to give something back ... but the original idea of doing something within the community originally came not from Moneyline, but from when I went to St Wilfrid's (day centre for mentally handicapped and vulnerable people). At that point I began to take control of my life. I gradually became involved in the organisation of the centre, and also started to teach photography classes for them. I also became involved as a debt management counsellor working for both them and the CAB. Having known what it is like to get into the debt trap and having benefited from them and Moneyline, I wanted to return the favour in whatever way I could ... to show people the way out of the maze.

(interview, Castle Market Building, Sheffield, 2 February 2010)

Client 126 'had to dig herself out of a very deep hole'. Her husband has gone to prison on account of rent arrears, and having mismanaged his account, had left her with debts to banks and credit-card companies of which she had had no previous awareness. In the past she had borrowed from Provident, but 'not for a right long time'.

To help clear her debts and give her a breathing space, she received a £750 loan from Moneyline in September 2007, and started studying for an Open University degree. Within this structure, she now organises meetings, in her house, of students studying on the social sciences foundation course. About nine people, as a rule, are present at these monthly meetings, which enable participants to share ideas and give them encouragement to keep going when juggling all their different responsibilities has become impossible. Two of them, it turns out, are also fellow Moneyline borrowers, and 'that turns out useful when we are discussing social exclusion and the recession' (interview, Castle Market Building, Sheffield, 3 February 2010).

Finally, client C4, an unemployed ethnic-minority client, took inspiration from his wife's experience. She was a member of a rosca (rotating savings and credit association). 'My wife sometimes saves with a group of women who put in £20 per week, and once a week one of the women gets to use the money.' He determined to emulate this model, and thus set up a rosca of his own, open to both men and women, in the front room of his house. This rosca now has thirteen members, and lends mostly for consumption, but 'for the first time last week we gave a loan to help start a business – a corner shop' (interview, Burngreave Housing Office, Sheffield, 15 February 2010).

Derby Loans (now Midlands Community Finance), rather untypically, provides both business and consumer loans. From the business side of its portfolio, we encounter the case of an ethnic-minority entrepreneur who built up a chain of retail shops, exclusively within his own community.

Case Study 6 An ethnic-minority entrepreneur: Magda Food Market, Derby

Mr A, an Iraqi from Kurdistan, arrived in Derby in 2003 with capital of under £1,000. He is educated to the equivalent of A-level standard, and speaks five languages, including Turkish, Farsi and – significantly – Polish. For four years he worked night shifts in a chicken factory, and in 2006 invested some of the savings he accumulated during that period in a restaurant which he operated in partnership with another Iraqi.

A year later he sold this restaurant, finding partnership constricting (he claimed that his partner 'resented his qualifications'), and he now operates five retail businesses as a sole trader.

Attempting to break out on his own, he attempted in early 2007 to borrow from two of the high-street banks but was unsuccessful. Eventually, later that year, he borrowed £6,000 from Derby Loans, which he used to open what was at that time a new concept – a mini-supermarket, the Magda Food Market, catering for most of the ethnic-minority communities established in the Normanton area of Derby (see Figure 2.3b) including Pakistanis, Poles, Latvians and Russians all of whom are more numerous than Kurds. This model has now been widely imitated, notably by a Nigerian entrepreneur who is also a Derby Loans client, and at the time of writing there are seven multi-ethnic mini-supermarkets in the Normanton Road alone. Mr A has now opened four further shops, all of them bought leasehold from a property dealer. His modus operandi is to buy short leases and immediately to rent them out, using the rent to fund the expansion of the business – his particular advantages within this market are his linguistic ability, his command of Derby City Council planning processes and, in particular, the language of leasehold contracts, and his awareness of where to secure cheap raw materials. He rents only to fellow Kurds – 'they are the only people I trust and, besides, they are cheaper'.

He is hugely admiring of the service he has received from Derby Loans, describing one of the managers as 'a very good man' and another as 'good and also beautiful', but his relationship with the organisation has not always been easy, on account of his reluctance to open a business account – 'he was always trying to pay his instalments out of money kept in a shoebox', as one of the managers recollected – and on account of arrears problems. He has now been elected chairman of the Kurdish community association, and has secured a grant from Derby City Council to decorate a vacant hall in Normanton and use it as a Kurdish community centre.

However, over the study period, turnover has risen from £60,000 to nearly £300,000, the number of persons employed by Mr A has risen from one to five (all of them below the poverty line before employment, and now above it). Notably through his ability to buck the recession, he has been one of the more important contributors to Derby Loans' poverty-reduction effectiveness.

Most cases of the creation of bridging social capital are from business clients. However, the following notable case comes from a personal-lending client who managed, as our Scotcash and Sheffield Moneyline cases did, to move into creative institution-building. This is the Osmaston Information Centre, which began as the initiative of a Derby Loans client in 2005.

Case Study 7 The Osmaston Information Centre

Don Parker, a retired engineer, took out a consumer loan from Derby Loans in 2004, and as a client became aware of the potential of the organisation for transferring not only money but ideas, and in particular for redressing power-relationships between providers and clients of welfare benefits – who constitute the bulk of the market for consumer loans. Having become an enthusiastic supporter of the Derby Loans' chief executive's interest in the money advice process, Mr Parker offered to develop a prototype information centre, aimed particularly at clients of doorstep lenders who were being caught in the debt trap through ignorance. He had observed a number of cases of clients unjustly losing their entitlement to benefits, often as a result of their disabilities not being appreciated (including a blind friend who had lost some his benefits as a result of failing to answer letters written to him on ordinary printed paper) or as a result of poor literacy – a problem which became rapidly worse through the 2000s with the large wave of immigrants, especially from Eastern Europe, who arrived into Derby at the time.[20] Seeing claimants' ability to achieve their benefit entitlements as an acutely political issue, in which the weakest could only achieve their rights with the help of a champion willing to help confront the bureaucracy, he expressed his motivation in combative terms – 'when someone hits you with a stick someone needs to be able to hit the buggers back',[21] and offered to act as Robin Hood on behalf of the victims. Like the managers of Soapy Bubbles (Case Study 4) he was motivated to set up a new voluntary organisation by awareness of deficiencies in the existing service providers, in this case Derby Home and the Derby City Council.

Working through his established contacts within the community in the Osmaston area of south-east Derby (DE24), which has a high concentration of council tenants heavily dependent on benefits and a high concentration of doorstep lenders (see Figure 2.3b), Mr Parker established the Osmaston Information Centre in 2005. The centre is entirely dependent on voluntary contributions and operated in 2007 on a budget of £25,000 per annum, contributed by Derby Loans, Derby Homes and Derby City Council. The centre provides free consultations with advisers, publicity on benefits and a sympathetic hearing; help is offered with filling in claim forms. The centre is open to all and not just clients of Derby Loans, although these have provided the core (probably just under half) of all the enquiries coming in to the centre. Some of the publicity relates not just to the benefits system but to credit availability and to the operations of doorstep lenders – for example, a leaflet which shows that toys bought with a loan from Shoppacheck are three-and-a-half times as expensive as the same toys bought for cash. Mr Parker has also been willing to campaign for other local causes, including training (see TIGERS, Easterhouse, Case Study 5) and the establishment of a new open space to be known as the Osmaston People's Park. In essence (and, as shown above, the centre's ambitions go quite a long way beyond this core) the Information Centre is a voluntary-sector complement to the Citizens' Advice Bureau, whose unique selling points are its location within the areas of maximum deprivation and its willingness, to a fault, to fight the cause of the underdog. As both a critic of Derby Homes and a beneficiary of its sponsorship, it has had an ambivalent relationship with the City Council, which cut off its sponsorship in 2008.

Mr Parker is now ill with cancer, and in the light of this and of the erosion of the centre's financial basis, the sustainability of the centre is currently in doubt, since there is no obvious successor or deputy to Mr Parker.

The formation of social capital networks and trust: explanatory hypotheses

These thirteen cases of 'client-driven social capital formation' all, through various channels, provided a multiplier to the impacts of CDFIs on individual clients discussed in Chapter 4. But they are very diverse, both in respect of the form of organisation which was established for the networks, and the process through which they impacted on the host community. In the first place, they filled gaps in the structure of public service provision, especially of housing and social services (Soapy Bubbles, Osmaston Information Centre, B2, Scotcash 115). Second, in association with CDFIs, they filled gaps in the structure of clients' *financial information*, typically by providing information about doorstep lenders and alternatives to them (Osmaston Information Centre, B19), but sometimes also by providing informal alternatives to them, such as rotating savings and credit associations (Sheffield C4). Third, in the case of Soapy Bubbles (Case Study 4) and Scotcash 76, they mediated between members of the community and agents who had been accused of causing trouble within it, within the explicit intention of building trust in place of conflict. The one thing which they all did was to provide a place and an informal mechanism in which members of the community could express grievances and exchange ideas, sometimes specifically on financial issues and sometimes on broader community issues. This function is closest to that highlighted in Putnam's study of Italy, in which the creation of structures which motivate free communication of ideas is the key to social capital formation. We should bear in mind, however, the fact that networks, in the context of CDFIs, do not just circulate valuable information, they also expose clients to peer pressure, after the developing-country model (Putnam 1993: 102, 113) and thereby contribute to reducing their default rates.

What motivated them to do this? This is, as Putnam notes, unexplored territory. One fascinating element in the story is that there is little evidence of these social entrepreneurs being motivated by financial gain. (Most of them, indeed, had lower incomes than the sample average and, contrary to Forrest and Kearns' finding that social capital formation is favoured by house ownership, the majority of our sample of thirteen were tenants and not house-owners.)[22] One motivation, certainly, is a kind of reciprocity, a desire to give something back to an institution which had supported them (Derby 111, Scotcash 64 and 115, Soapy Dubbles, TIGERS). But it is an indirect reciprocity, as the benefit goes to the neighbourhood and not to the CDFI; but in one case, B2, the motivation is the exact opposite – not at all a wish to reward a competent CDFI, but a determination to defy a bad one. Often direct encouragement from a CDFI manager has been crucial in getting networks established, as in the case of the Osmaston Information Centre (Derby 111), as has advice from CDFI money advisers (Scotcash 25, 64, 115). But, as discussed earlier, what has often been critical has been awareness that some service provider was unable to meet the neighbourhood's needs (Community Roots in the case of B2, Derby City Council in the case of the Osmaston Information Centre and the GHA in the case of Soapy

Bubbles) coupled with, and this is the thing which really distinguishes these thirteen cases from the rest of the sample, the willingness to leap into the breach. Possession of a 'rational approach to problem-solving', as discussed in the previous chapter, was certainly advantageous in this regard;[23] but to make or even extend a network requires more than rationality, it also requires individual enterprise applied in a social context.

As we saw earlier, the neighbourhoods literature has a tendency to prioritise the construction of bridging social capital, in which networks are extended outside the parent neighbourhood, over bonding social capital, in which they are consolidated. This kind of enterprise was commoner amongst CDFIs themselves and their business clients (TIGERS, MacVicar, Soapy Bubbles) though there does exist the impressive counter-example of the Osmaston Information Centre, which was bridging social capital set up by a consumer-lending client of Derby Loans. As emphasised above, social capital creation often does not consist simply of the creation of an oasis of sociability within a relational desert but often, rather, of the attempted replacement of one kind of social tie by another. The particularly relevant case for the purposes of our discussion is that where a new network sought to attack the dependence of clients on a doorstep lender – in other words to replace a vertical and hierarchical one-to-one dependence relationship between moneylender and client (Leyshon *et al.* 2006) with a lateral and more democratic associational relationship between client and client. The power held by loan sharks derives from them having few or no community resources to fall back on – they are a form of *negative* bridging social capital, as they undercut the ability of clients to make lateral bridges with the rest of the community by asserting the primacy of the vertical bond of dependence with the doorstep lender. The explicit intention of Soapy Bubbles (DSL 6), Scotcash 64, Sheffield 109, Sheffield C4 and Derby 111, was to make lateral bridges of this sort. Neighbourhood coordination groups of this kind, if they are able to hold together, thus have political as well as economic significance: they give the client a counterpoise against intimidation by the moneylender, or simply their power to crush their ability to save.[24] Simply by reducing the doorstep borrower's perception of herself as isolated and dependent, they empower her.

What enables informal social networks to hold together, in face of scarce resources, self-doubt and, sometimes, hostility from government and rival networks? One factor, of course, as in the case of CDFIs themselves, is the individual charisma and organisational ability of the organisers. Another factor was thus described by Putnam in his analysis of Italy:

> In the civic regions of Italy, by contrast to Naples, social trust has long been a key ingredient in the ethos that has sustained economic dynamism and government performance. Cooperation is often required – between legislature and executive, between workers and managers, among political parties, between the government and private groups, among small firms, and so on. Yet explicit 'contracting' and 'monitoring' in such cases is often costly or impossible, and third-party enforcement. Trust lubricates cooperation. The

Table 5.1 Instances of social capital creation and possible causal factors

Client cases	Social capital creation[a]			Causal factors					
	Bridging[1]	Bonding[1]		Policy		Client's			Attitude measures and risks
				Financial support received from CDFI and support agencies	Advice received from CDFI and support agencies	Income band	Assets/housing tenure	'Rational'[2]	'Social'[2]
Business-lending CDFIs									
DSL clients (provided mentoring support in association with Regeneration Agencies)									
DSL6 (Case Study 4)	Formation of community council and intermediation through it with service providers	Interactions between network members within shop (note: mainly within white community)		DSL loans (total value c. £7,000) within excluded neighbourhood	Minor, through Glasgow North Regeneration Agency	<£15,000	No car; house from council	N.A.	N.A.
DSL7/8 (Case Study 5)	Skill development in low-income communities, establishing reputation for trustworthiness amongst employees	Both clients: Creation of entrepreneur groups in association with Glasgow East Regeneration Agency (Note also: both clients also able to support one another)		DSL loans (total value c. £30,000) within excluded neighbourhood	TIGERS: establishment of linkage with Glasgow East Regeneration Agency, which provides contracts	>£25,000	House and car owners	N.A.	N.A.
Birmingham clients (B2: mentoring support provided until 2009 through Community Roots NGO, B19: mentoring support provided through Birmingham Enterprise)									
B2	Provision of home maintenance services to disabled women	Solidarity meetings organised between clients		3Bs loan £7,500	Received advice from Community Roots (for comments on which, see Appendix)	>£25,000	Owns car and holds mortgage.	N.A.	N.A.
B19	Provision of technical support services to Afro-Caribbean entrepreneurs (formal 2005–06 in the shape of chairmanship of Community Roots, informal at other times)	Co-organiser of Afro-Caribbean industrial estate, Oldbury		ART loan £25,000	Received technical advice through Business Link/Community Roots, later became, as general manager of Community Roots, a provider of advice	>£25,000	Owns car and holds mortgage	2.4	1.9

Consumer-lending CDFIs

Scotcash (mentoring and money advice provided through specialist advisers within CDFI to all requesting it; sometimes in association with provision of loans, more often not)

Scotcash25	—	Organiser of Catholic church meetings	No loan	Received Scotcash advice	2007: <£10,000 2009: >£15,000	No car; house from council	1.75	2
Scotcash64	—		Loan £800, also saver with credit union	Received Scotcash advice	2007: <£10,000 2009: >£10,000	No car; house from council	2.4	2.1
Scotcash76	—	Established residents' group when the local housing association failed to reply to complaints	No loan	Received Scotcash advice	2009: >£10,000	No car; house from council	1.5	1.4
Scotcash115	—	Extended meals on wheels network for disabled established by her grandmother, also disseminates publicity	Loan £400	No advice	2009: >£20,000	Car owner; house from council	N.A.	N.A.
Derby Loans (provides mentoring services through referral to CAB and other advice agencies)								
Derby111	Establishment of neighbourhood advice service, especially related to benefits	—	—	Received substantial moral and technical support from Derby Loans chief executive	£10,000–£15,000	—	N.A.	N.A.
Yorkshire Moneyline, Sheffield (provides mentoring services to a few clients directly, through HBOS project; otherwise through referral to CAB and other advice agencies)								
Sheffield109	Provided informal debt advice	Extended teaching provision within	Loan £400	Received no mentoring	<£10,000	—	—	—
Sheffield126	—	Established Open University students' solidarity group	Loan £600	Received no mentoring	£10,000–£15,000	—	—	—
Sheffield C4	—	Establishment of rotating savings and credit association	No loan	Received no mentoring	£10,000–£15,000	—	—	—

Notes

1 *Bonding* social capital is the establishment of social networks within the neighbourhood or wider community. *Bridging* social capital is the establishment of social networks which cross neighbourhood boundaries and/or establish links between service recipients (in this case principally clients) and service providers.

2 '*Rational*' coping strategy is defined in Table 4.4.

greater the level of trust within a community, the greater the likelihood of cooperation. And cooperation itself breeds trust. The steady accumulation of social capital is a crucial part of the story behind the virtuous circles of civic Italy.

(1993: 170–171)

Of course, Putnam is concerned here with more formal organisations, and with a far longer timescale, than ours. But as in Putnam's northern Italian business associations and church choirs, so in our own community councils, information centres and neighbourhood clusters, it is intergroup trust holds together the organisation and lowers the cost of doing business. Intragroup trust and awareness of group interdependence, it will be remembered from Chapter 1, is also the 'goldfish bowl' which, especially in a developing-country context, enables members of microfinance groups to monitor each other's behaviour and protect groups' financial discipline.

Finally, informal groups such as the ones we have described are sustained by voluntary labour. Of those listed in Table 5.1, only the Osmaston Information Centre and the Catholic Church (Scotcash 25) have a budget. Without volunteers, they would all have rapidly fallen apart. Together with mutual trust and organisational charisma, they provide the dynamic which holds networks together and enables some of them to grow.

In Table 5.2, we make use of data on trust and volunteering from our whole sample – not just the thirteen 'network creators' described above. Unsurprisingly, the level of trust, on our measure,[25] is higher among network members, and especially among network creators, than among non-members. However, and more puzzlingly, it is not significantly different between richer and poorer people, nor between the more and the less educated. How then can it be motivated?

We find some clues towards the answer from the lower part of Table 5.2. As illustrated there, those with 'rational' rather than 'emotional' responses to crisis – in other words those who replied to the questionnaire that they would make a proactive and analytical response to a financial shock, rather than hope for the problem to go away and for others to solve it – were more likely to trust others. So were clients who had received money advice and so, finally, were the small group of twenty-eight individuals who had escaped from financial dependence on doorstep lenders during the period of the 2007–09 recession. The last two of these factors were also significantly associated with a higher likelihood of volunteering.

What causal judgment underlies these behavioural differences? In our judgment, all of the characteristics associated in Table 5.2 with higher trust are associated with a *shift from a **passive** to a **proactive** attitude to personal relationship*. Those who are untrusting often have negative interpersonal experience which deprives them of the perception that that they can make choices, whether specifically in the field of debt management or more broadly in the construction of social networks. Trust and volunteering, in other words, jointly derive from an experience and from policy actions[26] which make individuals believe that they can change the world, in their own and others' interest, by social action. The results of this are exemplified by the thirteen cases of social action in Table 5.1, and they supply benefits additional to the individual-level impacts described in the previous chapter. Of course, social networks overlap and may conflict with one another, and so it is not just a question of adding up the cohesive forces within individual neighbourhood groups, but rather of trying to understand when individual networks are mutually conflictive and when they are supportive. One area in which this is particularly relevant is ethnic minorities – which, of course, are a particular target group for British CDFIs – and in the next section we focus on network-building among the minority-ethnic groups of Birmingham.

Microfinance and community-building in ethnic-minority communities

Members of ethnic minorities are amongst the poorest people in the UK; a higher proportion of them than of the population as a whole live in inner-city areas and in rented accommodation, such that they lack the equity required to get loans from banks (Deakins *et al.* 1995), and thus they are at particular risk of being forced into sub-prime credit markets even before issues of discrimination are considered. In addition, they are currently underrepresented in lending by CDFIs: for example, about 6–7 per cent of the population of Glasgow are from ethnic minorities, but less than 1 per cent of Scotcash borrowers are from ethnic minorities; the neighbourhood of Normanton, in Derby, has a 20 per cent ethnic-minority population but less than 5 per cent of Derby Loans clients are from ethnic minorities. Since ethnic minorities have a higher than average propensity to be socially and, on this evidence, also financially excluded, it is relevant to ask how CDFIs can best adapt their product to make it accessible to the needs of ethnic minorities, and thereby how to maximise its impact, not only on individuals but on the community networks that are the focus of this chapter.

Our analysis of community-building amongst ethnic minorities focuses on Birmingham and its surrounding area. Within the city of Birmingham, about 32 per cent of the population is from a black and minority ethnic (BME) community, which is about double the percentage for the UK as a whole, and in excess of the BME share for any other large city in Britain except Leicester (Advantage West Midlands 2008: Table 3; Cangiano 2010: Figure 1; Johnston *et al.* 2002: Table 1). The largest constituent populations within the ethnic-minority population in Birmingham are Pakistani (11 per cent), Afro-Caribbean (6 per cent) and Indian (5.9 per cent). In Figure 5.3 we show the level of multiple deprivation across the wards of the city, and on to this we superimpose the locations of our interviewees; it will be observed that several of the interviewees are concentrated in areas of high social deprivation which also have high concentrations of specific ethnic minorities, such as Sparkbrook, B9 (mainly Pakistani) and Handsworth, B20 (mixed Afro-Caribbean and Indian). We have also superimposed the locations of known doorstep lenders and of churches involved in providing social and technical support to borrowers, both of which will be important to our subsequent argument.

Table 5.2 Volunteering, trust and community-building

Client category	Trust score, 2009[1]	Volunteering score[2]
All clients	1.68	1.11
(n = 366)	(0.70)	(0.91)
Network creators[3]	2.29***	0.91
(n = 13)	(0.61)	(0.83)
Others	1.59***	1.01
(n = 351)	(0.70)	(0.92)
Network members[4]	1.90*	0.98**
(n = 82)	(0.60)	(0.85)
Others	1.74	0.69
(n = 138)	(0.72)	(0.94)
Business and mixed lenders	1.59	0.68
(n = 59)	(0.64)	(0.82)
Consumer lenders	1.70	1.16
(n = 303)	(0.71)	(0.92)
Poor (equivalised hh income <£12,500)	1.66	0.76
(n = 88)	(0.68)	(0.93)
Nonpoor (equivalised hh income >£12,500)	1.73	0.62
(n = 94)	(0.64)	(0.81)
Education A-level or better	1.66	1.18
(n = 86)	(0.66)	(0.86)
Education GCSE or less	1.72	1.07
(n = 266)	(0.73)	(0.93)
'Rational' response to crisis[5]	1.75*	0.70*
	(0.62)	(0.85)

	'Irrational' response to crisis[5]	
Received loan advice between 2007 and 2009	1.59	0.93
	(0.61)	(1.05)
(n = 66)	2.15**	0.87**
	(0.62)	(0.82)
Received no loan advice between 2007 and 2009	1.79	0.65
	(0.75)	(0.88)
Exited from dependence on National Provident or other doorstep lender between 2007 and 2009	2.04**	1.19**
	(0.63)	(0.82)
(n = 28)		
Remained dependent on National Provident or other doorstep lender between 2007 and 2009	1.64	0.73
	(0.62)	(0.91)
(n = 60)		
Control group	1.71	1.11
	(0.77)	(0.92)

Sources: Table 5.1; Surveys, 2007–10, questions 70–72 (volunteering) and 74 (trust). Data are summarised in Appendix 1 and the full data array is online, available at: www.poverty.group.shef.ac.uk.

Notes

*** Denotes difference between sample means (of this row and the row below) significant at 1% level, ** denotes significance at 5% level, * denotes significance at 1% level.

1 *Trust indicator* is the average score of respondents to question 70, 'Do you have family or friends whom you would trust in the event of a serious personal problem?' on the scale: 1 = No, there is no one I would trust; 2 = There are a very few people I would trust; 3 = There are several people I would trust.

2 *Volunteering indicator* is response to question 70, 'Do you do any sort of voluntary work?', coded 2 = regularly, 1 = intermittently, 0 = never.

3 *Network creators* are the thirteen 'instances of social capital creation' listed in Table 5.1.

4 *Network members* are those reporting that they belong to one or more clubs, social organisations or affinity groups.

5 *'Rational' coping strategy* is defined in Table 4.4.

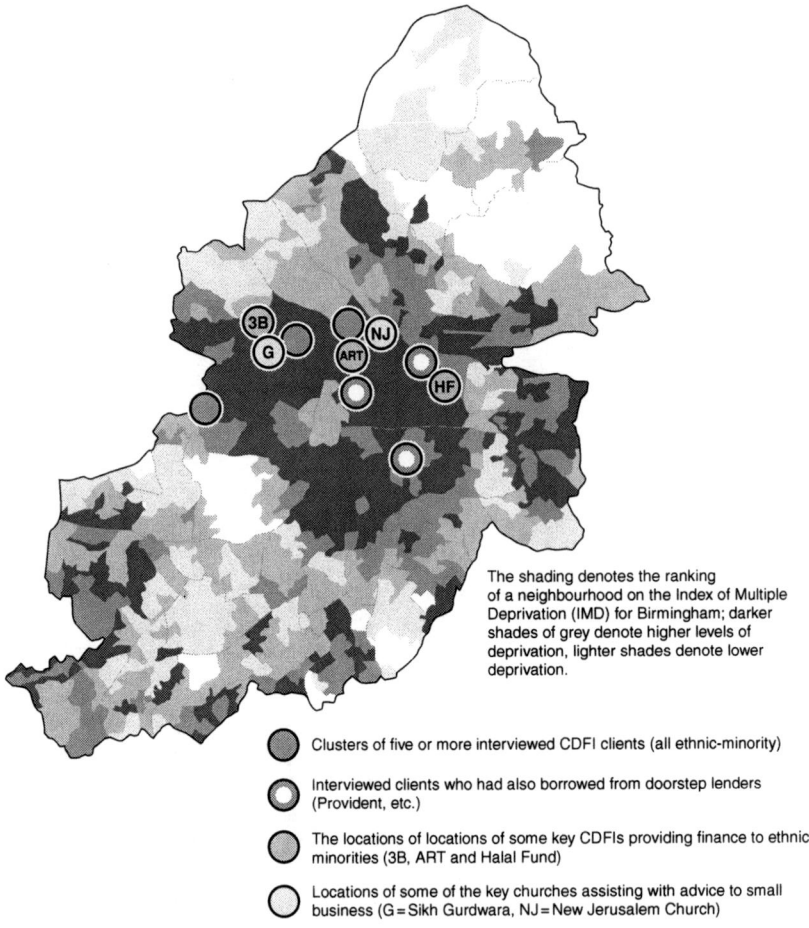

The shading denotes the ranking of a neighbourhood on the Index of Multiple Deprivation (IMD) for Birmingham; darker shades of grey denote higher levels of deprivation, lighter shades denote lower deprivation.

⬤ Clusters of five or more interviewed CDFI clients (all ethnic-minority)

◉ Interviewed clients who had also borrowed from doorstep lenders (Provident, etc.)

⬤ The locations of locations of some key CDFIs providing finance to ethnic minorities (3B, ART and Halal Fund)

◯ Locations of some of the key churches assisting with advice to small business (G = Sikh Gurdwara, NJ = New Jerusalem Church)

Figure 5.3 Birmingham 2007–09: CDFI lending to BMEs in relation to deprivation indicators (source: adapted from deprivation map published by Birmingham City
Council. Copyright of the map original rests with the Ordnance Survey and
the figure is reproduced under licence number 100018617).

Within the large literature which examines the particular needs of ethnic
minorities in the context of urban regeneration, Oc and Tiesdell (1999), Smallbone *et al.* (2003) and Fraser (2006), in particular, focus on the specific requirements of small business finance (the literature on personal finance for ethnic
minorities is much smaller). Oc and Tiesdell emphasise that many of the problems faced by BME small businesses are not specific to ethnic minorities but are
the problems of inner-city small business in general, including lack of manage-
rial resources, inability to access the market and availability of finance; writ
large because ethnic-minority businesses are concentrated in highly competitive

sectors with high failure rates (Smallbone *et al.* 2003). But some problems are specific to some members of ethnic-minority communities, including difficulties in breaking out of ethnic-minority markets, English-language ability and, for Muslim clients, the availability of Sharia-compliant, interest-free loan packages. The potential for specifically ethnic discrimination (adding to the discrimination that very possibly still exists on grounds of gender and postcode, see Case Study 4) inevitably enters the discussion, although Fraser notes (2006: 14) that 'a review of the evidence in Bank of England (1999) found no evidence of [racial] discrimination by finance providers, [even though] a *perception* of unfair treatment by finance providers [persists]'. Both these studies emphasise that the needs of different ethnic minorities are extremely diverse, and also that across most (not all) ethnic minorities, low levels of income paradoxically coexist with high levels of human and, as discussed in the previous section, social capital. Table 5.3, using the data from our questionnaire survey of all four cities, suggests that participation in social networks – a positive factor, as we saw in our last chapter, in facilitating exit from poverty – was significantly higher among ethnic-minority populations than among our sample as a whole. The organisations to which ethnic minorities attached themselves also had a different composition from that found in the population as a whole. In the population as a whole, the organisations which people joined are mainly secular, whereas amongst ethnic minorities and especially those of the Pakistani, Afro-Caribbean and Indian Sikh populations, they are more often religious. As we shall see, this provides an important clue to the way in which social capital-building can occur amongst ethnic-minority populations.

We now examine what kinds of financial institutions have been successful at meeting the needs of low-income ethnic-minority communities in the Birmingham area, and how they have achieved this success. We begin with the cluster of three Birmingham institutions listed in Table 2.1: Aston Reinvestment Trust (ART), whose lending is 40 per cent BME, and Black Business Birmingham (3Bs) and Halal Fund, both of whose portfolios are 100 per cent BME.

These are very diverse institutions, both in their architecture and their outcomes. ART, established in 1993, is one of the pioneers of community development finance. It is a 'reinvestment trust' – non-profit with a commitment to reinvest funds in the Birmingham community. Having initially attempted to support all kinds of financially excluded business, including ethnic-minority business at the start-up stage, it moved into larger small business and small enterprise, and now only supports businesses within the £10,000–£50,000 range; however, it maintains a commitment to lend to start-ups. Technical support is provided by a range of sources, but for ethnic minorities specialist support is provided by Birmingham Enterprise which, as we shall see, provides access to a variety of ethnic-minority networks. Like many businesses in the West Midlands, ART was badly hit by the 2007–09 recession.[27] However, it was able to benefit from deficit spending policies adopted by Birmingham City Council and by Advantage West Midlands in a bid to buck that recession, and by the middle of 2009 was announcing a record (£1.2 million) amount of funds available to

Table 5.3 CDFI members: membership of social groups among ethnic minorities and the sample as a whole, 2009

	Ethnic minorities (n = 65)	Non-ethnic minorities (n = 301)	Total sample population (n = 366)
Member of any social group	35 (53.8%)***	78 (19.8%)***	113 (26.8%)
Type of organisation:			
Community group or social club	14 (20.2%)*	52 (13.3%)*	66 (15.3%)
Sports club	6 (8.7%)*	14 (3.6%)*	20 (4.5%)
School group (PTA, etc.)	0	6 (1.5%)	6 (1.1%)
Religious organisation	23 (35.3%)***	21 (5.3%)***	44 (12.0%)
Political party	2 (2.9%)	1 (0.3%)	3 (0.8%)
Other social group	9 (12.8%)	51 (16.9%)	60 (16.3%)

Source: questionnaire survey, 2007–09, questions 45, 49 and 50.

Notes
*** Denotes difference between ethnic minority and non-ethnic minority percentage significant at 1% level, ** denotes difference significant at 5% level, * denotes difference significant at 1% level.

lend out. A further benefit of the recession, in the view of the chief executive, was that it 'brought us a better quality of BME entrepreneur'.[28] There was a shake-out, in other words, and we examine the consequences for those at the bottom of the heap further on.

3Bs, as Black Business in Birmingham is now universally known, has functioned as a voluntary community organisation, which has existed in partnership with Birmingham City Council since the mid 1980s, and has served as something of an icon symbolising the council's commitment to the black self-employed. In 2000, 3Bs moved from the city centre to a new industrial estate in Handsworth, one of the poorest neighbourhoods in Birmingham, the '3Bs village', of which it is the owner and landlord; a number of small BME businesses rent units within this complex. In 2001, backed by £4 million grant finance from Birmingham City Council, the government Phoenix Fund and Advantage West Midlands, the local regional development authority, it took the decision to move into microfinance, offering business loans 'for start-ups to a maximum of £10,000 and existing businesses to a maximum of £25,000'[29] – thereby aiming at a smaller average size of business than that targeted by ART. Between 2000 and 2008 it offered some 350 microfinance loans, with a modal size of £6,000–£8,000, mostly to Afro-Caribbeans but some to other ethnic minorities. Most of this money never came back – according to 3Bs' own estimate the recovery rate over this period was a mere 15 per cent.[30] Reasons for this disaster include the following:

1   Lack of entrepreneurial experience. Neither the general manager nor any of the seven loans staff employed by 3Bs had experience of running a business. For this reason, there was nobody in the company able to advise clients either on technology or on how to position themselves within the market, and 3Bs saddled itself with a high proportion of what one of their managers characterised as 'hairdressers'. These are what Chapter 4 called 'lifestyle businesses': low-tech service sector firms with little propensity to transmit their skills and ideas to the rest of the community or to advance the sector's competitiveness – and a low proportion of exporters and high-tech businesses. As a further consequence of the management's lack of technical skills, the crucial function of loan advice and mentoring was not performed in-house, but rather was subcontracted to the Birmingham ethnic-minority NGO Community Roots, widely known as 'Roots'.

2   Lack of financial and, crucially, credit control capacity. Overdue loans were not chased,[31] and once it was known that they were not being chased word got round that, in words echoed by seven out of our eight 3Bs client interviewees, 'the loan could be seen as a grant and not a loan', thus giving everyone an incentive to cancel their direct debits on the grounds that no penalty would be attached to this.

3   The indulgence of sponsors and, specifically, the Birmingham City Council. For many years the Council's support of the innovative 3Bs concept (there had to our knowledge been no previous black-only services companies in

the country before) represented, in the council's eyes, one of the showpieces which represented what was most enlightened about its ethnic-minority policies. The relationship between the council and 3Bs had for many years been one of mutual admiration, pride and in the case of many individuals, personal friendship, rather than objective appraisal of outcomes, and when 3Bs launched into microfinance operations, that cosiness continued. Indeed the City Council, like Pygmalion, fell in love with its own creation (or rather creations – the remark applies equally well to Community Roots), and remained blind to its faults even when those were transparent both to CDFIs and to clients. It was only because of this that from 2003 through 2007 3Bs was able to lobby, from a position of near bankruptcy, for further funds rather than being put under pressure to become financially competitive. Indeed, there is no evidence that the City Council even asked for any information about 3Bs' arrears position until 2007, by which time 3Bs had made seven years' worth of loans and recession was on the horizon; true, the critical position on the loan portfolio was masked by healthy earnings from rentals on units in the '3Bs village', but this cross-subsidisation is evident in the profit and loss account. Within a year 3Bs' lending operation had been shut down; but the long delay illustrates the broader point about governance. The City Council was simply too close to 3Bs. There was an absence, on the board, of persons able and willing to ask awkward questions.[32]

4   Community Roots – to whom the critical task of writing business plans and making loan proposals 'investment-ready' for 3Bs to finance – was simply not up to the job. We have already heard the testimony of one of 3Bs' clients on this issue (client B2, quoted on p. 99), and other CDFI managers have claimed that 'there was no point in even looking at a loan proposal backed by a business plan from Roots'.[33] Innumerable 3Bs clients, on asking the organisation for help in getting a business up and running, were provided with faulty business plans and advice which the organisation did not tell them were lacking; and when as a consequence they were not able to afford loan repayments, they were, as mentioned above, seldom pressed to repay nor were their personal guarantees drawn on. Once again, part of the problem lay with the City Council's soft budget constraint and associated relationship of mutual admiration with what it saw as an innovative spearhead of pro-black development initiative, and two observers, one a successful ex-client of 3Bs and the other a CDFI manager, suggested in only slightly differing words that 'often it was difficult to tell where the dividing line was between 3Bs, Community Roots and the City Council; they seemed basically to be part of the same organisation'.[34] Another part of the problem, as with 3Bs, lay with Roots' failure to see that the market in which ethnic minorities should expect to trade had moved beyond 'hairdressers', was increasingly being judged by the quality of what it could deliver rather than by the volume of its activities in support of the ethnic-minority communities, and that it needed skilled advisers to help the organisation achieve this

metamorphosis. The Community Roots Foundation itself went bankrupt in 2009; 3Bs still functions but only as a trading estate.

The Halal Fund offers a completely different architecture. By contrast with 3Bs, it is highly private-sector oriented, and indeed the only part of its funding or governance that is from the public sector is a small grant from Advantage West Midlands. Its main financing (around £0.5 million) is from the Islamic Bank, with further support from a Pakistani-owned supermarket, Pakfoods, in whose premises the Halal Fund office is located. Since its foundation in 2005, the Halal Fund has lent exclusively to ethnic-minority clients, mainly Muslims from the Indian sub-continent, with a particular concern to provide financial products which fit within the Halal brand, such as Sharia loans.[35] Literally and metaphorically, it finances very few 'hairdressers', and indeed is concerned to back winners, especially in the technological sense. Its main innovation is in its response to a problem identified by Birmingham Enterprise, 'the real void is not finance – it is building up to that finance';[36] which, of course, was the void into which 3Bs fell. Technical support (human capital) was organised for the client by the Halal Fund – mainly informally by inserting Fund clients into international networks which helped them to find niche markets, to develop their product and to market it, but also formally through the establishment of a training college known as the Halal Academy. But in addition to this, what the Fund referred to as 'hand-holding' was also needed: 'we had a team of people in the company which facilitated and stayed with the client from beginning to end until the business was "afloat" ':[37] as illustrated by Case Study 8.

Case Study 8 Construction of mentoring networks: Cabsafe, Birmingham

In 2006, the Halal Fund lent £25,000 to client B17, a taxicab proofing company. The company was established by six directors who are also investors. The client, for twenty years a Jaguar Land Rover employee and a member of the lender's extended family, had designed a new form of security screen for taxicabs. The fact that many taxi-drivers, during a recession in which unemployment and anti-social behaviour increased, were looking for additional protection for their cabs did no harm to the company's cause.

According to the client, the lender provided:

1   Core finance, coupled with access to financial networks especially in Pakistan (the country of origin of both borrower and lender) which made it easier to raise the additional finance required. (Notably, access to Sharia finance was not an important issue for this company; Sharia finance was offered, but was in the end not accepted, because it was not financially advantageous to the firm.)

2   Technical support in the highly specialised area of motor vehicle security-proofing. Halal's advisers were able to suggest modifications to the design of

> the cab and in particular suggested the replacement of a British design for the screen separating driver and passenger with a screen of Chinese design which was both cheaper and more powerful.
>
> 3   'Hand-holding', in the shape of encouragement to keep going, especially in the hard early years when the firm was just starting and initial market trends were not good. 'They encouraged us to trust that the basic idea was good and that, given the basic modifications which Halal were suggesting, would eventually come good.'[38]
>
> 4   Basic advice on how to build up the business plan: 'Halal grounded us in terms of business strategy: it moved us from a survival orientation to a profit and loss orientation' as the managing director put it.
>
> The company has grown through the recession years 2006–09 from a turnover of £20,000 to a turnover of £70,000 and is projected to rise to over £120,000 in 2010. The changes which the company has made to achieve them are not really architectural, but technical and psychological; they were facilitated by a trust between lender and client which was lacking in most cases we examined of the 3Bs–Community Roots–client triangle. The client told us: 'We became involved with them, not because of any specific product or idea they had to offer us but because they provided an advisory and support service of a kind which a high street bank cannot.'[39]

Between them, these modes of support provide what we have previously described as *bridging social capital*, which incorporates socially excluded members of communities in networks which link them with their markets and with those that supply finance and know-how. The Fund's willingness to act as a translator for its clients has, on other projects (not B17 whose managers' English is excellent) helped to reinforce the bridge,[40] and has prompted investment in various new bridge-building projects including an after-hours English language teaching venture, to be further discussed below. Often, the nodal point of these networks was located in the country from which the client had immigrated – typically, in the Halal Fund's case, Pakistan or Bangladesh. The Halal Fund has always complained of being under-capitalised, and has made loans to only a small number of clients (thirty-five over five years), but with a reasonable, if not exciting, recovery rate (*c.*75 per cent, i.e. 25 per cent default). It is now financially independent and has no need to raise funds from the markets.

Other financial organisations have now joined the market for fair-priced finance in the region, and Table 5.4 presents a panorama of the main players in the microfinance sector in Birmingham and the West Midlands (now grouped together as a 'Fair Finance Consortium'), for all of whom ethnic minorities are an important part of the market. To the three organisations just described, we add: the Black Country Reinvestment Society (BCRS), a not-for-profit cooperative operating essentially the same business-lending model as ART across the eastern part of the West Midlands; two organisations,

Arrow Fund and Prince's Trust, both focussing on very small loans and in the case of Prince's Trust specifically on young people;[41] Derby Loans (Midlands Community Finance) which as related in Chapter 3 has recently extended its business lending activities into the West Midlands area; and two consumer lenders, Coventry and Warwickshire Reinvestment Trust and Street UK. From this list emerges a peculiarity of the structure of microfinance in the region: it is heavily slanted towards business lending, even though across Britain as a whole personal (consumer) loans have since the mid 2000s been the main locus of growth. Of the nine institutions involved in the Fair Finance Consortium, all began as business lenders, and the only two which also offer consumer loans, Street UK and the Coventry and Warwickshire Reinvestment Trust, became involved in this only because they were offered a slice of the DWP Growth Fund (q.v., Chapter 1) for this purpose. Anomalous as it may seem in the perspective of financial exclusion nationally, this pro-business slant has a certain logic from the point of view of promoting the interests of ethnic-minority communities, in some of which (notably Pakistanis, Bangladeshis and Chinese)[42] the self-employed are a much higher proportion than in the population as a whole. However, there is a danger attached to this slant, which the remainder of this chapter explores: the combination of a race to secure safe high-income borrowers among many business CDFIs (very evident in ART, BCRS and Halal Fund) with inadequate provision of personal loans may combine with residual ethnic and postcode discrimination to leave the poorest members of ethnic minorities at best with no escape from exploitation by doorstep lenders and at worst financially disenfranchised.

In this and the previous chapter, we have found evidence of a two-way linkage from bonding and bridging social capital networks to the performance of individual CDFI clients and vice versa, and we now apply this framework to the cases listed in Table 5.4. As we have already seen simply within Birmingham, the reasons why people become engaged in community-building activities are multiple, and some of them are common between ethnic-minority groups and other people, including *reciprocity*, the desire to return and extend to others a favour initially provided by the CDFI (B19 for an ethnic-minority example), *compensation*, the desire to fill a gap in public or NGO provision of public services (B2) and *emulation*, the desire to copy or adapt to another neighbourhood a successful model already working somewhere else (Sheffield C4).

In the following respects, however, the nature of social capital-building among Birmingham ethnic minorities was different from the process as it has been described for the target population as a whole.

1 *Culture-specific financial products and technical support.* Amongst ethnic minorities the ability of CDFIs to converse and construct business plans in the client's own language, in the longer term to provide facilities for teaching that language[43] and to devise financial products (in particular interest free) with which the client feels comfortable have been important

Table 5.4 Ethnic-minority microfinance and community-building in Birmingham and the Black Country

	Business lenders					Domestic lenders	
	Black Business in Birmingham (3Bs)	*Halal Fund*	*Aston Reinvestment Trust (ART)*	*Black Country Reinvestment Society*	*Arrow Fund*	*Street UK*	*Coventry and Warwickshire Reinvestment Society*
Type	Business lender	Business lender	Business and social enterprise lender	Business and social enterprise lender	Business lender (focus on start-ups and microbusiness)	Initially business lending; since 2006, almost entirely consumer loans	Business lending plus, since 2006, some consumer loans
Size (portfolio/ loans)	300 loans 2000–06, £5,000–£20,000	35 loans 2005–10, £5,000–£25,000	438 loans since 1997, £10,000–£50,000	180 loans 2006–10, £10,000–£50,000	Small business loans £1,000–£7,500	Personal: c.1,800 loans 2009, average size £640	Business: c. 60 loans/year Personal: c. 700 loans/year
% ethnic minority clients	100	100	41	14	49	?35	15
Distinctive design features	Financially integrated with 3Bs village, rents of which now sustain the organisation	Regional networks – connect people in same area and same clan; equity; Sharia loans	Cooperative model; some partnerships with Halal/BCRS	Cooperative model (more or less as per ART)	Partnership with Lloyds Bank, which makes and guarantees the loan	Expansionist consumer lender; operates also in Walsall and Salford and supplies 'back-office' services to many CDFIs	Only organisation in region to offer both business and personal loans; cooperative model, in partnership with credit union
Arrears rate 2009	Lending terminated 2006 (average arrears 2000–06: 85%)	c.25%	31%	c.28%	–	9%	23%

Financing	Birmingham City Council; Advantage West Midlands	Advantage West Midlands; Islamic Bank	Birmingham City Council; Advantage West Midlands; European Regional Development Fund	Various West Midlands local authorities; Advantage West Midlands; European Regional Development Fund	Birmingham Chamber of Commerce; Lloyds Bank	DWP Growth Fund; West Midlands Housing Consortium	DWP Growth Fund; Advantage West Midlands; C and W credit union
Technical support: CDFI inhouse	None	In-house staff provide moral support and links to established marketing and technical networks	Mostly subcontracted to Business Link and to Birmingham Enterprise, q.v.	None	In-house consultants	None	None
Technical support – voluntary and state sector	2005–09, Community Roots (now defunct) Since 2009, mainly churches, esp. New Jerusalem Church	Business Link; Advantage West Midlands	Business Link; especially for ethnic minorities, Birmingham Enterprise, with its own links to churches	Business Link; 2006–09, Windrush Foundation (now defunct)	–	Citizens' Advice Bureaux; also national debt assistance charity	Citizens' Advice Bureaux; Amazon Initiatives; Faith and Communities Trust 2006
Technical support – private and supranational sector	None	Pakfoods; Islamic Bank	European Regional Development Bank	European Regional Development Bank	Lloyds Bank	–	–
Informal sources of social capital	Networks established by clients (see Table 5.1)	Pakistani roscas (Case Study 9)	Networks established by clients (see Table 5.1)	Networks established by clients	–	–	–

among particular ethnic-minority groups and in particular among Pakistanis and Bangladeshis in enabling the CDFI to provide the necessary pre-investment support for borrowers. We have observed the importance of these factors in building a brand identity for the Halal Fund, in particular.

2   *The role of the churches.* As noted above (Table 5.3), participation in community groupings is higher among ethnic minorities, as a totality, than amongst the white population (within our sample, more than twice as high) and within those communities, participation in churches and religious institutions is far more important among ethnic minorities than amongst the population as a whole. In Birmingham, the role of the churches has been particularly important in providing support for those Afro-Caribbean clients bereft by the failure and demise of 3Bs and Community Roots. When those institutions closed, clients were told to go to one of three places: the George Street Church (to which the director of Community Roots, on the dissolution of that institution, has attached himself); to St Andrews Centre on Grove Lane in Handsworth; or to the New Jerusalem Church in Aston. All of these were Christian churches with an Afro-Caribbean clientele but an inclusive ethos which saw business support and networking activities as synergistic with their own desire to expand their congregation;[44] and all of them played a part in setting back on their feet as entrepreneurs clients of 3Bs and of Community Roots who had been abandoned by their parent institutions (including our own interviewees B2, B5 and B18). The New Jerusalem Church – which occupies premises in the same industrial estate as ART and Birmingham Enterprise – has also been highly active in organising such contacts, and has achieved a valuable tie-up with Birmingham Enterprise, for whom it has organised a number of training meetings and networking events.[45] It has recently (December 2010) become a borrower directly from ART. An additional merit of these institutions, from the point of view of CDFIs, is that once clients are incorporated into regular church attendance, the combination of affiliation to a religious institution and extended family provides a powerful basis for peer pressure to deter rebellion against institutional norms which the CDFI also desires to enforce – default on debt in particular.

   More broadly, the Central Gurdwara in Handsworth Road and various mosques have been active in organising networking meetings respectively for the Sikh and Muslim communities of Birmingham.[16]

3   *Roscas and other 'clubs for the financially excluded'.* Another counterpoise against institutional gaps which ethnic minorities create for themselves consists of the many 'savings clubs' – such as the Sheffield rotating savings and credit association examined in Table 5.1 – which since long ago have provided a survival strategy for those denied access to state or private institutions of social protection.[47] Another illustration from Sparkbrook – the region of Birmingham with the second highest level of social deprivation indicators – is provided by Case Study 9.

Case Study 9 The Roscas (rotating savings and credit associations) of Sparkbrook

A *rotating savings and credit association* (or rosca) is an institution which collects small instalments of money on a regular basis and lends the total proceeds out as a 'pot' to one member of the group, thereby enabling the beneficiaries to afford lumpy consumer or capital goods they could not otherwise have afforded. They exist on all continents and many, as mentioned above, have deep historical roots. They vary greatly in their institutional design – in relation to, for example, their size, their social mix, their links with other institutions and their operating rules, in particular their criteria for determining who should receive the payout.

Within simply the low-income area of Sparkbrook, which is poorly supplied with fair-priced nonbank credit and as a result thickly populated by doorstep lenders (see Figure 5.3), seven roscas are known to operate, within which the South Asian and specifically the Pakistani population is dominant. In one with which we are familiar on Ladypool Road, B16, there are sixty-five members, all Pakistani, each of whom put in £20 per week. The rosca operates on a cash-only basis; it has no bank account, no legal existence and indeed no name. It is known simply by the address of the lady who acts as secretary of the rosca. The rosca is of mixed membership in which males predominate, but is run by women. From the pool thus generated, loans are allocated to members by a bidding process which in the event of any competition is settled by a democratic vote (other allocation mechanisms are possible and found within Birmingham; see Besley *et al.* (1993) for a review of the possibilities). There is of course no collateral guaranteeing repayment of the loan and, as in the solidarity groups of the Grameen Bank of Bangladesh (q.v., Chapter 1), mutual trust between the members of the group, backed by their ability to apply peer pressure if required, is the substitute for collateral – lacking physical assets, members pledge their social connections (Putnam 1993: 168). In a majority of cases (as in the case of CDFI loans) the proceeds of the loan pot are used to satisfy consumption requirements such as holidays, furniture and white goods, but in about a quarter of cases in this rosca they have been used to finance new businesses and associated capital goods; for example, a restaurant, a mobile phone retailer and repair shop, and the vans used by each of them for their businesses.

In all of these cases, of course, as with the Kurdish mutual-support group observed in Case Study 6 above, what is created is solidarity within an ethnic group and neighbourhood – in all of these cases Pakistani – at possible risk to cohesion across the wider community. At the same time it can be emphasised that in Sparkbrook, a low-income community from which high-street banks have absented themselves, roscas such as these represent one of the few options which is unambiguously pro-poor and pro-egalitarian. We take up the theme again in the final section of the chapter.

4   *The human–social capital intersection.* Our discussion has shown that there is a gap in the provision, not so much of finance, but of technical support for

the transition from subsistence to entrepreneurship. This gap is bad every-where because CDFIs are moving upmarket and neglecting subsistence enterprises in need of small amounts of money. It affects ethnic minorities, on average, more severely than white people, in a small way because of lin-guistic problems, but this is by no means the root cause – indeed, it is among Afro-Caribbean communities in Birmingham, where linguistic problems are almost absent, that the greatest problems of 'lack of investment-readiness' are apparent.

Through our case studies (summarised in Table 5.4 and Case Studies 6, 8 and 9) we have observed the ways in which Halal Fund, ART (through Birmingham Enterprise) and Arrow Fund, in particular, have struggled with the problem of filling this hole. As indicated on pp. 119–120 this is classic 'bridging social capital' – a role which combines the functions of knowledge transfer and moral support (or, as the Halal Fund calls it, 'hand-holding'). Given that Arrow Fund is about to disappear and that the Halal Fund, itself very small, is searching for new pastures, it is clear that the hole is one which is still badly in need of filling.

As we have seen earlier (Table 5.1) bridging social capital can be created not only by CDFIs, but also by selected clients to whom they lend. Table 5.5 gives details of the ethnic-minority clients who created social networks within the Fair Finance Consortium region. Our particular interest is in understanding how these precious voluntary networks were constructed and how they may have contrib-uted to raising their members' productivity. In the final column, we speculate concerning the ability of the network to assist the process of exit from the pov-erty trap.

The big message from Table 5.5 is that, as in the non-ethnic-minority case, there is a substantial potential for the creation of social capital networks by clients of CDFIs, which adds a multiplier to what the microfinance organisation itself is able to achieve. Clients reported a diversity of motives for wishing to establish networks, ranging from expressions of gratitude for the inspirational influence of the CDFI (B19 and Derby 74–79) to determination to compensate for the CDFI's incompetence (B2) and extension of a commercial network into an ethnically specific network (Derby 84). In all cases except B22, the social capital-building which took place consisted of bonding *within* a specific ethnic-minority community rather than any attempt to cross the inter-ethnic divide. In cases B2 and Derby 74–79, membership of religious organisations is important both in bonding the ethnic group together and in providing training. The training provided for these improvised groups, and the social bonds within the groups themselves, help to fill the severe gap which we have identified in the market for making small business proposals 'investment-ready'. In the two Derby (Mid-lands Community Finance) cases only, most members of the group were low income and on benefits and membership of the informal network contributes to members' exit from poverty.

A final problem remains. This is that given that the structure of microfinance provision in Birmingham is slanted towards businesses and that within this

Table 5.5 Ethnic minority cases: social capital development and its possible causes

Initiator (organisation to which affiliated in brackets)	Type of network	Apparent motivation for network	Social capital input (any crossing of ethnic boundaries?)	Human capital input	Ability to assist transition out of poverty?
B2 (3Bs)	Homecare providers' group	Frustration with low level of support being provided by Community Roots (q.v.)	Formation of network for liaison with social services, mainly confined to Afro-Caribbean community	No formal link; but most members are also members of New Jerusalem Church, providing social solidarity through this route	Minor; beneficiaries mostly above poverty line
B19 (ART)	Informal advisory network (leader is established African industrialist)	Preservation of links originating with organiser's interim directorship of Community Roots (q.v.)	Moral support, mainly confined to Afro-Caribbean community	Business planning advice	Minor; beneficiaries mostly above poverty line
B22 (BCRS)	Informal advisory network	Solidarity group (established Afro-Caribbean IT specialist)	Moral support, going beyond Afro-Caribbean community	Business planning advice	Minor; beneficiaries mostly above poverty line
Derby84 (see Case Study 6)	Kurdish community association	Extension of this into other fields (e.g. visas, mobile phones, travel bureaux); conversion of commercial network into political leadership	Moral support and extension of labour market contacts, confined to Kurdish community	None	Significant: two employees exited from poverty during time period specified
Derby74–79: 'Zimbabwean group'	Zimbabwean community association	Some 'reciprocity' (gratitude for link with Derby Loans)	Moral support and extension of labour market contacts, confined to Africans	Technical support linked with church (cf. B 2)	Significant: three members of group exited from poverty during time period specified

Source: questionnaire survey, 2007–09. Further details of poverty exits in final column are provided in Appendix.

structure the business providers themselves are moving up-market, there is little provision for the ethnic-minority borrower at the bottom end of the market – for example, a person depending on subsistence benefits, struggling with large debts and in need of an emergency subsistence loan in order to cope in the short term. In London, such a person can go to Fair Finance; in Sheffield, to Moneyline or to the Sheffield Credit Union; in Glasgow to Scotcash. But in Birmingham, they face a desert – Street UK, offering around 1,800 loans a year within the city, is the only CDFI offering a fair-priced alternative to the doorstep moneylender or pawnbroker. This makes all the more important what roscas and other informal institutions – including the loose-knit informal networks described in Table 5.5 – are able to construct.

Conclusion

Our purpose has been to understand the contribution which CDFIs can make to the building of neighbourhoods and communities. A part of this contribution is economic, and illustrated by the close association revealed in Chapter 4 between membership of affinity groups and exit from poverty. But another part is social and political: we have argued that livelier and more extensive *lateral* social networks enable more effective self-expression by individuals – and in particular weaken the *vertical* dependence of the client on the doorstep lender. This potentially creates a more favourable climate for the political process to operate in a democratic way at local level, and also to a climate in which social tensions can be eased and the threat of crime reduced;[48] but often, community-building within neighbourhoods is confined to specific neighbourhoods and specific ethnic groups, and may be at the expense of social cohesion amongst other neighbourhoods and ethnic groups.

Nobody suggests that building social networks is a quick or easy thing to do. Putnam's study of Italy draws attention to the fact that the differences in patterns of social linkage to which he draws attention had roots which go back a long time: 'People in Bologna and Bari, in Florence and Palermo, have followed contrasting logics of communal life for a millennium and more' (1993: 182). These ancestral cultural traditions are important in determining social cohesion in Glasgow and Birmingham also, but that does not preclude more short-term institutional initiatives, including CDFIs, from seeking to make them work in a more open and equitable way. The initiatives described in this chapter can be visualised as short-term initiatives in support of making (local) democracy work, and specifically in support of making financial inclusion work, on the premise that the social bonds by which the client is surrounded are as important as individual personality or institutional design in achieving long-term exit from poverty. In general, they are of two kinds: actions by CDFIs or their partner agencies, which often have the role of providing access to advice, technical or moral support within a neighbourhood, and actions by clients, which also do this but more often reinforce social bonds within that neighbourhood.

The kind of technical and moral support which microfinance clients require to make their borrowing effective is much disputed, and there are some very distinguished voices, including the general manager of the Grameen Bank of Bangladesh, who insist that it is not needed at all, on the grounds that 'clients are the best judge of how to run their own business and should not be interfered with'.[49] Our argument for believing that mentoring is important is based on the evidence accumulated through this book that for fragile start-up businesses, and for a majority of personal-lending CDFIs, exit from poverty requires the creation of assets, and loans on their own will not create durable assets. We have reviewed a number of models of provision of mentoring (Table 5.1), in a majority of which the mentoring function is bought in from an external supplier, but there are several cases, notably Scotcash and ELM, of outstanding in-house provision of mentoring support. What happens when mentoring fails is most graphically illustrated by the case of the ethnic-minority lender 3Bs, where the service provider and the mentor each passed the parcel of responsibility for client support to the other, and the end result was that the best part of 300 small businesses, and the jobs dependent on them, collapsed. More positively, in the cases where assets have been created and the client has made the transition from subsistence to a savings account, this has typically not been done by giving the client a loan and leaving her to her own devices, but rather by incorporating her into a support network which can both sustain her and impose financial discipline on her.

Our other contribution has been to document the process by which clients of CDFIs create their own networks, and thereby contribute to the process of community-building. These 'mini-networks' are often inspired by CDFI leadership and thereby extend CDFIs' work of plugging gaps in state structures – in particular the provision of facilities by local housing offices, as in the case of Soapy Bubbles (Case Study 4) and local benefit offices, as in the case of the Osmaston Information Centre (Case Study 7). However, in some cases they are motivated by indignation at the incompetence of the CDFI itself, and plug gaps – in the CDFI's own provision, sometimes with assistance from other agencies such as the Birmingham churches (Table 5.1: client B2). Such mini-networks have often been able to create additional social capital, and sometimes additional financial capital as well (e.g. the Sparkbrook roscas, Case Study 9) at neighbourhood level; in this way they move informally from the characteristic CDFI mode of operation, which lends to individual clients, towards the modus operandi of developing-country microfinance, which is more often buttressed by peer pressure within groups. These mini-networks, indeed, can be seen as an unofficial substitute for collateral.

We suggest that these mini-networks could benefit from being reinforced – even within those organisations, such as Scotcash, where financial discipline is excellent. Our suggestion is that CDFIs could consider convening 'local support groups' of existing clients in areas where they are highly concentrated (as illustrated, for example, by the red circles on Figures 5.2 and 5.3). These groups could meet in a local housing office, at a credit union collection point or in a local regeneration office, and would initially be led by a loan office or money adviser but if the idea catches on could become self-sustaining after a meeting or two. This would have the following functions. First, mutual support: once the group are known to one another as near neighbours with the same purpose, i.e. financial self-improvement, they may be the better motivated to help one another; for example, by each boosting the other's morale when the other is down. Second, this may help sustain and even improve the CDFI's repayment rate, partly because mutual support can persuade members to carry on, in every sense, rather than give up, and partly because the fact of being in a network makes everyone more transparent and less willing to default 'in public'. Third, the networks could become a useful channel for new financial products promoted both by the CDFI and by other agencies (for example credit unions) – and, especially in the case of business CDFIs, for exchanging ideas about products and technologies.[50] Fourth, the networks, if successful, could grow and thereby supply the CDFI with new members.[51] Finally, they could also act as focus groups and supply the lender with *group* feedback, as well as the individual feedback already supplied directly to the CDFI. In addition, where a solidarity group is ready-made, as in the case of the Sparkbrook roscas, the CDFI could simply lend to it directly, thereby augmenting its asset-creating potential.

A main message from both this and the preceding chapter is that CDFIs do not operate alone and that their effectiveness is not determined only by the qualities of their staff and structures. In the next chapter we take this idea further. We develop the theme that in Britain, by contrast with much of the developing world, the function of microfinance institutions is to provide social protection within the context of a welfare system which already exists, albeit it is being radically reformed, and which both constrains and stimulates what CDFIs are able to achieve. We now examine the implications of this for the way in which CDFIs operate.

6 Fiscal impacts

Introduction

In industrialised countries, social protection is typically achieved by making cash grants, rather than loans, to low-income groups. However, as budgets have come under pressure, welfare providers have naturally looked for ways of providing it in a more cost-effective way. One approach to this is potentially through providing welfare through microfinance loans, rather than grants. For example, if loans to financially excluded small businesses reduce unemployment over the long term, then the repayment of those loans can enable economies to be made on state welfare payments. This will help achieve 'welfare ends by market means'– a key aim of, in particular, the Anglo-Saxon democracies over the last thirty years (Taylor-Gooby *et al*. 2004). Of course this depends on lending to the poor being feasible and expandable; but as we saw in Chapter 1, microfinance has been able to grow fast across most of the developing world (Hulme and Mosley 1996; Armendariz de Aghion and Morduch 2005; Hermes and Lensink 2007) and now makes a contribution to welfare in most industrialised countries. The most recent overview of the microcredit sector in the European Union records that in 2009, 432 microfinance institutions in twenty-eight European countries provided some 135,000 micro-loans, worth €1.3 billion, aimed at the relief of poverty (Jayo *et al*. 2010: 17). The fiscal impact of this new form of welfare has never been investigated; in this chapter we examine it with a particular focus on its poverty impact.

Until the early 2000s most microfinance programmes in industrialised countries took the form of *business CDFIs*: loan funds for the promotion of small businesses excluded from access to high-street finance, typically operated by non-profit organisations and financed by a mixture of NGO, central government,[1] local government and private capital, with contributions also from international organisations such as the European Social Fund. This way of organising microfinance in industrialised countries then, as related in Chapter 1, came to be supplemented in 2001 by a new form of CDFI, the *consumer CDFI*, which has no parallel in developing countries. The objective of consumer CDFIs is to ease the debt problems of low-income people who are financially excluded, i.e. unable to borrow from banks, and as a consequence find themselves open to exploitation by loan sharks and doorstep lenders at very high rates of interest.[2] Most of the beneficiaries from this new kind of CDFI (unlike beneficiaries from business CDFIs) are not in work of any sort and are dependent on welfare benefits for their livelihood; in consequence, the budgetary implications of this new kind of CDFI can be expected to be very different from the consequences of business CDFIs.

What fiscal impact has this new form of welfare provision had overall? Initially, it was expected that business-lending CDFIs would enable a switch from unemployment to self-employment and thereby reduce public spending on welfare benefits (United Kingdom, Social Exclusion Unit 2000) and there is some evidence that this in fact occurred: for example, Mosley and Steel (2004: 728), using back-of-an envelope methods, calculated that through loans by CDFIs in 2000–02 '21900 individuals exited from unemployment as a consequence of microfinance lending over the period 2000–02 (saving an estimated £0.3 million within the sample or £178 million on the national social security budget)'. However, even in the case of business CDFIs, the relationship between microfinance spending and welfare spending is more complex than a mere switch from an income pattern based on benefits to an income pattern based on self-employment. In many cases, as we shall document, the shift from unemployment to self-employment which CDFIs were seeking to facilitate could not have occurred without an expansion of the new welfare-into-work benefit, working families' tax credit (later working tax credit), first introduced in 1999: thus it would not have been possible to expand CDFIs without first *expanding* welfare benefits. It is not, in other words, a question of simple crowding-in or crowding-out of state welfare spending by CDFIs, but rather a more complex pattern of interaction.

In this chapter, we establish, in the next section, a simple picture of the inter-relationships between the growth of different kinds of CDFI and different kinds of welfare expenditures, with a view to understanding how the advent of CDFIs has influenced the level and pattern of welfare benefits expenditure. The model is matched against data for 2007–09 for a sample of CDFI beneficiaries in our four cities.

Policy towards CDFIs and welfare benefits, and their interrelationship

Three key principles guiding the evolution of the UK welfare system since the late 1990s (Brewer *et al.* 2002) have been *compatibility with active labour-market policies, fiscally efficient redistribution* and *asset-based welfare policy.* Active labour-market ('work-first') welfare policies are fiscal policies which increase the incentive to seek work and thus the flexibility of the economy, with a view to maximising competitiveness and reducing unemployment. Fiscally efficient redistribution is the targeting of welfare on those most in need, an approach adopted since the 1970s in all industrialised countries but especially in the market-oriented welfare states of North America and northern Europe

(Taylor-Gooby *et al.* 2004) in the context of a desire to bring public expenditure under control, and currently being pursued with renewed vigour by the new (2010) coalition government. Asset-based welfare policy consists of measures to build up not only the income but also the assets of the worst off, deriving in part from an awareness that poverty has a tendency to persist over long periods and, as we saw in Chapter 1, across generations.

In Table 6.1 we present a chronology of modifications to the welfare system introduced from the late 1990s to the present, encompassing the 2007–09 period on which our survey is focussed.

The first two measures in the table, *New Deal* and *Working Families'* (now Working) *tax credit*, were both aimed at the active labour-markets objective. New Deal was a selective employment subsidy aimed sequentially at various target groups (young people, long-term unemployed, lone parents, disabled people, ethnic minorities, over fifties and, eventually, as discussed in Chapter 5, communities), made available to unemployed people in the stated categories on the condition of them accepting a period of training aimed at enabling the trainee to access higher-skill labour markets. A number of business CDFIs (see Table 4.3) took on New Deal employees. Working tax credit (WTC) was a welfare payment provided in the form of a tax credit only to those low-income households working in excess of the 'National Insurance limit' of fifteen hours per week; initially it was provided only to households with children, but this requirement was waived after 2003. In order to remove the obstacle that many single parents were staying out of the labour market because they could not afford the costs of childcare, the credit contains a generous (currently up to £300 a week) childcare allowance.[3] As related in some of our case-studies in Chapters 4 and 5, WTC has been very important in keeping some business CDFI clients afloat. Some benefits (e.g. income support and jobseekers' allowance) disappear when a person moves from unemployment into work,[4] deterring them from taking up or remaining in self-employment, and the fact that WTC is contingent on work has been important in providing a counterpoise. The threshold for WTC was raised in 2008, and then the basic rate of credit was raised by 1.5 per cent above the rate of inflation in early 2010, with a proviso that this was a one-off to counter the crisis, not to be repeated and indeed to be clawed back somewhat in 2011. A further element in active labour-market policy since the 1980s, finally, has been the continuation of unemployment benefit in the form of *jobseekers' allowance*, an allowance which is only claimable for a limited period after the claimant becomes unemployed and which is no longer income related.

Fiscally efficient redistribution has, since the 1970s, been pursued by both Labour and Conservative governments through the route of making most benefits income related, in particular, council tax benefit, housing benefit and incapacity benefit – in fact all benefits except child benefit and maternity benefit – with the objective of relating them to need. A child tax credit was introduced in 2003, following the approach of the WTC: all subsequent increases in benefits for children have been directed towards the (income-linked) child tax credit rather than towards the (fixed and universal) child allowance, which has served as a vehicle

Table 6.1 Amendments to the benefits system and their rationale, late 1990s to 2010

Date	New measures	Reforms and amendments	Objective
1998	New Deal	Initially announced as New Deals for Young People and for Long-Term Unemployed; New Deals for Lone Parents, for Disabled, for Ethnic Minorities and for Communities subsequently added to programme.	Payroll subsidy for categories of unemployed named, conditional on acceptance of training programme.
1999	Working families' tax credit	Converted to working tax credit, 2003. Threshold increased, 2008. Basic level increased by 1.5% above inflation; to rise by 1.5% below inflation in April 2011.	Encourage movement from welfare benefits into work by confining benefit to working households. Prior to 2003, available to households with children only.
2003	Employment tax credit Child tax credit	Increased by £50 above average earnings, April 2008 and April 2009.	Provides income-related support to main carer (and thus makes a part of support for children income related).
	Pension credit	Replaced Minimum Income Guarantee.	
2004		Pathways to Work programme (DWP).	Encourages new claimants of incapacity benefit to move into paid work, in return for additional benefits.
2005	Child tax credit supplement (baby element)	Increased by £150 above average earnings, April 2008; by a further £208, June 2010, to take effect April 2012.	The first element of 'asset-based welfare policy' to be implemented: selectively increases benefits available to young children below the age of two.
2008		Child benefit supplement (disability element).	Selectively increases benefits available to children with disabilities.
2010 (October)	Council tax benefit to be terminated from April 2013	To be replaced by grants to local authorities.	Devolution of power from centre.
	Incapacity benefit to be replaced by Employment and Support Allowance (ESA)	Child benefits to be frozen for three years from April 2011, and removed from higher-rate taxpayers. Housing benefit capped and time-limited; disability living allowance subjected to medical tests.	Tougher means test: contributory ESA will now only last a year unless judged very disabled.

Source: HM Treasury; Institute for Fiscal Studies; Child Poverty Action Group (online, available at: www.cpag.org.uk/publications).

towards making the benefits system increasingly need related. The DWP's Pathways to Work programme attempted in 2004 to strengthen this linkage for incapacity benefit, by providing increased levels of benefit to new claimants in return for increased obligations to seek work (Adam *et al.* 2006). In 2010, in the context of a widespread programme of expenditure cuts by the new coalition government, incapacity benefit was abolished and replaced with a new Employment and Support Allowance (ESA), contingent on a low income or on the making of national insurance contributions; for those making national insurance contributions, ESA payments will end after a year except for claimants judged 'very disabled'. Thus less-disabled ESA recipients and recipients with savings will lose. Finally, as part of the same package of reforms the child benefit nettle was grasped. From January 2013, it will be removed from households containing a higher-rate taxpayer; thus the whole of the welfare system which relates to children is now to be means tested. In addition, the government has at the time of writing announced its intention (United Kingdom, DWP 2010) of rationalising most benefits into a single 'universal credit', blending together the housing-related, disability-related, income-related and now asset-related elements in welfare policy;[5] we discuss this further below.

Finally, *asset-based welfare policy* represents the confluence of several different strands of thinking. One of them derives from the awareness of Sen (1982) that many forms of poverty including its most extreme form, famine and malnutrition, do not derive from deficiency of income itself but from deficiency of entitlements to income, in particular lack of physical, human and social assets. Another strand derives from an American initiative to deal with the problem of intergenerational transmission of poverty, exemplified in the work of Sherraden (1991), who argued that having assets and engaging in the process of saving could be associated with a range of beneficial effects, including household stability, risk-taking, participation in education and improved health. Asset-based policies are also in operation or under discussion in Australia, Canada, Singapore and Sweden (Emmerson and Wakefield 2001: 4). In principle, asset-based policies can be used to encourage the acquisition of any kind of resource, including adult education, unemployment insurance, support for families and health insurance, but in Britain the approach has been applied exclusively to the acquisition of financial assets by the worse off. The Labour government, in April 2001, announced a consultation on 'policies designed to increase rates of saving and asset-ownership, both among the lower-income households of today, and in generations of families to come' (United Kingdom, HM Treasury 2001; Emmerson and Wakefield 2001: 1). To date, the idea has entered UK social policy only through the medium of a supplement of £500 to child tax credit for each child below the age of two, known at the time of its introduction in 2005 as a 'baby bond', which combines an asset-based approach with a focus on children and child poverty. Both as chancellor and as prime minister, Gordon Brown made a personal commitment to the abolition of child poverty within a generation, and both child tax credit and this supplement to it were explicitly linked to that objective. However both the commitment and the policy instrument have now become bipartisan: a Child Poverty Act was passed in 2010, making the achievement of the 2020 target for eradicating child poverty legally binding (Joyce *et al.* 2010: 2). Later the same year, the newly elected coalition government raised the 'baby supplement' by £208 per annum as a contribution towards this objective.

In addition the government initiated discussions in 2001, and throughout the second half of the 2000s solicited the interest of CDFIs and banks in membership of a *Savings Gateway*, which is a savings account for those on lower incomes. The intention was that government would match individuals' contributions fifty/fifty to provide an incentive for account holders to place funds in these accounts. In the end the Savings Gateway never reached the statute book, and was abolished by the coalition government in the summer of 2010, but it remains an important marker for future policy initiatives, and we return to this theme in the next chapter.

As business CDFIs came to be complemented by consumer CDFIs, so the focus of government support for CDFI initiatives moved from financially excluded small businesses to financially excluded consumers. From 1999 to 2003, the Department of Trade and Industry (now the Department of Business, Innovation and Skills, BIS) provided seed-corn finance for business-lending CDFIs through its Phoenix Fund, but this was terminated in 2003, although some funding of business CDFIs continued to be provided through regional development authorities (RDAs). The following year, 2004, the Treasury report on *Promoting Financial Inclusion* (United Kingdom, HM Treasury 2004) identified the rapid growth of debt among low-income people with no access to high-street finance as a factor aggravating not only inequality but also financial instability, and recommended the establishment of government support for small loans to the financially excluded consumers, through what became known as the *Growth Fund*, through CDFIs and credit unions. The Growth Fund came to be administered, from 2006 on, by the Department of Work and Pensions (DWP); indeed, for the first time the department responsible for providing government subsidy to CDFIs was now also the organisation principally responsible for administering the welfare benefits regime. The Growth Fund was increased by degrees during the period of the 'credit crunch' to reach a level of £100 million by 2009. However, this instrument of state subsidy for microfinance is to be terminated: it has been announced that the Growth Fund will end in November 2011, and no replacement is in sight. Moreover, the RDAs, which finance much of the budget of business CDFIs, are themselves to be terminated in 2012. Thus CDFIs face a funding and a viability crisis, and we discuss possible responses to this in the next chapter.

From our earlier discussion, it can be seen that CDFIs support all of the main thrusts of modern welfare policy described above. Both business and personal CDFIs, like government, aim at fiscally efficient redistribution; indeed, most of them go further than any branch of the state welfare system, and profess the objective of becoming financially sustainable in the sense of directly paying for themselves out of user charges (i.e. repayments of interest and capital on loans).[6] Business CDFIs, in particular, seek to support the functioning of open labour markets by facilitating transfers from unemployment into self-employment. Finally, CDFIs aspire to be an even more asset-based form of welfare policy than any based on fiscal transfers. As we recall from Chapter 4, business CDFIs typically finance the acquisition of physical assets and therefore contain an in-built incentive to accumulate capital, but personal-finance CDFIs are typically used to finance consumption goods such as Christmas presents and holidays, and therefore whether assets are accumulated will typically depend on the initiative of individual CDFIs. As the cases of ELM and Scotcash make clear, if incentives to save are present and are responded to, the impact on the likelihood of exit from poverty was dramatic (Tables 4.9 and 4.10).

The question now for discussion is how these two forms of welfare relate to one another, and could be enabled to relate better. The following four relationships, at least, appear to be potentially crucial.

1   *If CDFI beneficiaries move from unemployment into work, and/or their income or that of their employees/dependents moves above the threshold for the payment of income support, and expenditure on welfare benefits is to that extent reduced.* This is the classical channel by which it was originally hoped that business CDFIs would 'substitute' for government benefits. The rate at which this can be done depends on the rate at which business CDFIs can expand their lending, and on the rate at which their clients and their employees transfer themselves and their employees from unemployment into employment. We call this effect 'benefit crowding-out'; the effect is 'positive', in the sense that expansion of CDFIs reduces expenditure on state benefits, and it can be expected to be more significant in the case of business CDFIs since they typically create employment (even if only for themselves as entrepreneurs) whereas as consumer CDFIs do not.

2   *If a CDFI client depends on welfare benefits in order to repay a loan, this is likely to increase state benefits expenditure, because the cost of loan repayment is an increased certain claim on income, payment of which the client will not wish to put at risk by incurring the costs and risks of searching within the labour market.* In other words, anyone who takes a new CDFI loan becomes more motivated to search for new ways of securing and extending their benefit entitlements, since that person loses her line of credit if she or he cannot keep up repayments.[7] We call this the *pinning-in effect* – getting a loan pins you into protecting the benefit entitlements required to repay it, in proportion as you fear the risks associated with the alternative strategy of trying to move off benefits into work.[8] The pinning-in effect is negative, in the sense that it increases claims on the benefit system. It is likely to be more significant in the case of consumer CDFIs than of business CDFIs, because the clients of consumer CDFIs depend much more heavily on income from welfare than do the clients of business CDFIs (see Table 4.4).

The argument so far is portrayed by Figure 6.1 in terms of the textbook income–leisure choice diagram, in which state welfare payments are split into two parts: a fixed element which is not income dependent, depicted as the vertical part of the income–leisure frontier in the diagram, and a flexible element which depends on hours worked and on income from non-labour sources. When business CDFIs are expanded, this increases the possibilities for unemployed people to shift from unemployment into self-employment, which alters the income-possibility frontier from A to B on the diagram, and this shift by entrepreneurs and their employees reduces dependence on welfare benefits (notably jobseekers' allowance and income support) – portrayed as the shift from (1) to (2) on Figure 6.1. The expansion of consumer CDFIs, by contrast, causes a different kind of change in people's opportunities. Unlike business CDFIs, it brings about no change in their ability to generate income from work; however, it does bring about a change in their expenditure patterns, since it requires them to devote a share of their income to debt repayment to the CDFI – which if lost will deepen their exclusion from financial markets, as if they default on their CDFI loan they will lose the lifeline of access to low-cost credit. We visualise that this fear will make them more risk averse – a change which we interpret as a steepening of their income–leisure curves, from C to D on Figure 6.1. If clients of consumer CDFIs do indeed react in this way, then the ending of their financial exclusion will make them more, and not less, dependent on welfare benefits – a move represented as a shift from point (3) to point (4) on the diagram.

The movement from point (1) to point (2) in the diagram is the crowding-out effect, in which increased CDFI activity reduces the spend on benefits; the

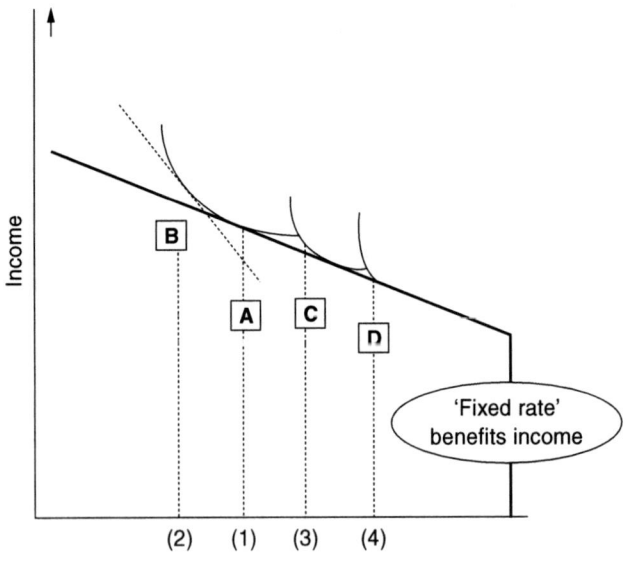

Figure 6.1 The crowding-out and pinning-in effects in business and consumer CDFIs.

movement from point (3) to point (4) is the pinning-in effect, in which increased CDFI activity increases the overall spend on benefits. According to our argument we are more likely to observe the first effect among business CDFIs and the second among consumer CDFIs, but it should be remembered that clients of both institutions derive income from a number of sources, and the suggested directions of effect shown in the diagram are simply hypotheses which will be examined in the next section.

Before we do this, there are other interrelationships to be examined.

3 *Some welfare benefits are needed by CDFI clients in order to achieve the transition from unemployment into self-employment.* This is the case where a particular form of welfare benefit – typically working tax credit, but also including various forms of New Deal expenditure – provides the beneficiary with the subsistence required to keep an income-generating activity going while it grows to viability. If and only if the business succeeds, this can be viewed as a purely temporary subsidy. This case is contingent on operating an income-generating activity and therefore more typical of business CDFIs.

This effect is prima facie 'negative' – in other words this linkage detracts from effect (1) above and inflicts a net cost on the exchequer, although it can reasonably be seen as an infant-industry activity designed to reduce the costs on the exchequer in the long term.

4 *Some CDFIs act as an indirect vehicle for promoting the acquisition of assets by the poor, and thereby contribute to the growth of personal income over the long term – and thence the reduction in the long term of dependence on benefits.* This linkage is different from the others because it is long term and not immediate. As institutions not directly regulated by the Financial Services Authority, CDFIs are not authorised to accept deposits. However, they frequently act as a highly effective motivational force to encourage their clients to save with banks, mutuals or credit unions, and through this intermediation convert direct action against financial exclusion into broader anti-poverty action, which over the long term reduces dependence on benefits:[9] de facto, they pursue asset-based welfare policy through their own channels. As we shall discover in the next section, there is wide inter-institutional variation in the effectiveness with which this kind of intermediation is done. In principle this impact can be achieved by any CDFI, but in practice those most active in this field have been personal lending CDFIs. Personal lending CDFIs also vary very much between themselves (Chapter 3): some commit themselves to making sure every client opens a savings account with a bank, credit union or mutual and thereby practise a very asset-based approach; others take a much more short-term perspective and focus simply on developing their loan business.

This impact is prima facie 'orthodox' or 'positive' – in other words the expansion of this form of CDFI activity yields a fiscal saving to the exchequer.

These interlinkages are summarised in Table 6.2.

Table 6.2 Likely interlinkages between CDFIs and state welfare benefits

Effect	Presumed impact on benefits	Types of CDFI affected	Types of state welfare benefit affected	Likely factors influencing magnitude of impact
1 'Crowding out' – CDFI removes access barriers to capital market for self-employed, thereby creates self-employment and derived jobs, reducing need for benefit payments	Net reduction in benefits expenditure	Mainly business CDFIs	Benefits related to the level of employment or income – Jobseekers' Allowance, also Income Support as income rises above the threshold	Success rate/growth rate/labour intensity of CDFI-supported enterprises; locality of CDFI investment (in high-unemployment area or otherwise); management/ entrepreneurship within CDFI
2 'Institutional transfer' – CDFIs act as the gateway for promoting for more self-funding forms of welfare, including saving, pensions etc.	Reduction in benefits expenditure	Potentially all CDFIs; in practice, a few evangelistic personal lenders	All benefits	Institutional mechanisms for promoting savings (on Savings Gateway model); personal commitment of CDFI staff and ability to form collaborative relationships with bank staff
3 'Infant industry support' – state benefits provide temporary assistance which helps CDFIs or clients supported by them to establish themselves	Increase in benefits expenditure	Both – business CDFIs through Phoenix Fund and their clients through, especially, working tax credit	Especially working tax credit	Income growth in supported CDFIs
4 'Pinning-in effect' – once benefits come to be required to repay CDFI loans	Increase in benefits expenditure	Consumer loans	All (but anecdotally, especially Housing Benefit, Disability Living Allowance and Incapacity Benefit)[1]	Risk aversion Other sources of income (client and other household members)

Note
1 Now converted into Employment and Support Allowance (ESA) – see Table 6.1.

In what follows we examine the changes in benefits use by CDFI clients across a sample of institutions between 2007 and 2009 and seek thereby to test the hypotheses set out above. We shall be concerned to find out not only what kind of CDFIs have the most 'favourable' impact on benefits, but also what kinds of benefits used by CDFIs appear to increase and decrease most over the period, and whether there are any implications of this for welfare policy.

Impact of the welfare system on CDFIs

Table 6.3 gives details of aggregate expenditure on state welfare benefits in 2007 and 2009 for each of our business and personal CDFIs, in relation to their respective control groups. In line with the hypothesis set out above, our business CDFIs have a tendency to reduce the level of welfare benefits, achieving an average saving on benefits of £603 per client (or about £0.11 per £1 lent), but our personal CDFIs have a tendency to increase spending on welfare benefits, by an average of £566 (or about £0.93 per £1 lent; consumer CDFIs on average give smaller loans). We infer that this is because in business CDFIs, in which most income is from employment or self-employment, what we have described as the crowding-out effect dominates over the pinning-in effect, whereas in personal-lending CDFIs the net effect is the opposite. Whereas the fiscal effect across different clients is fairly homogeneous in personal-lending CDFIs (i.e. most clients increase their uptake of welfare benefits between 2007 and 2009), in business CDFIs it is highly clustered: more than half of the £603 per capita saving on welfare benefits derives from the *employees* of just eight enterprises (B5, G1, G2, G6, G7, G8, D4 and D15), which expanded their recruitment from low-income areas, such as Drumchapel, Easterhouse (Glasgow), Allenton and Normanton (Derby), with the consequence that expenditure on jobseekers' allowance and income support, in particular, no longer had to be paid. This 'negative pinning-in' effect, in which welfare benefit payments increase among consumer-CDFI clients, is even greater in the personal loan sample than it is in the control group.

We now consider the uptake of benefits by CDFI clients within particular categories. The categories are based on the Child Poverty Action Group (CPAG) typology of 'low-income based' (income support and jobseekers' allowance), 'child related' (child allowance and child tax credit), 'health and disability related' (disability living allowance, incapacity benefit and carer's allowance), 'housing-related' and other. However, the working tax credit has been placed within the 'low-income based' category, as it is indeed based on the level of household incomes from work: as we shall see, it occupies a key role in poverty exit strategies.

Among clients of consumer-lending institutions, it will be observed that there are particularly big increases in consumption of income support, housing benefit and child-related benefits (child benefit and child tax credit). Among clients of business-lending institutions, although the overall trend is towards a reduction in benefits use, there is a substantial increase in the uptake of Working Tax Credit.

Table 6.3 Business and consumer-lending operations: estimated fiscal impacts

Institutions	Total expenditure on welfare benefits 2007				Total expenditure on welfare benefits 2009				Change in total benefit usage 2007–09	
	Borrower sample		Control group		Borrower sample		Control group			
	Total income from benefits (£/annum)	% of total income	Total income from benefit	% of total income	Total income from benefits	% of total income	Total income from benefit	% of total income	Change (£ per capita)	Change in dependence over two-year period
Business-lending clients										
1 DSL										
Clients (n=28)	2,820	10	8,507	67	2,344	8	8,296	69	−476	−15.2
Employees (n=12)	3,400	31	8,507	67	1,200	9	8,296	69	−183	−1.4
2 Derby Loans										
Business clients (n=22)	2,409	8	6,059	71	1,775	6	7,111	56	−634	−35.2
Employees (n=9)	4,600	38	6,059	71	2,650	20	7,111	56	−1,950	−15.0
3 'Birmingham cluster' (n=21)	4,850	29	−	−	5,772	29	−	−	922	+6.8
Employees (n=10)	6,400	56	−	−	5,100	41	−	−	−1,300	−9.6
4 Business lending:										
Total	4,079	29	7,283	69	3,140	18	7,703	62	−603	−11.1
(excluding employees)	3,359	16	7,283	69	3,297	15	7,703	62	−555	−21.6
(excluding Birmingham)	2,614	9	7,283	69	2,059	7	7,703	62	−810	−16.5
Personal-lending client										
5 Scotcash (n=126)	7,134	64	8,507	67	7,334	62	8,296	69	+200	+1.8
6 Derby Loans (personal clients) (n=75)	6,727	63	6,059	71	7,900	71	7,111	56	+1,173	+10.6
7 Moneyline Yorkshire (Sheffield) (n=127)	9,083	84	5,461	67	9,410	87	5,500	47	+327	+3.0
8 Personal lending total	7,648	70	6,675	68	8,214	73	6,969	57	+566	+8.0
9 Control groups total	−	−	6,675	−	−	−	6,969	−	+294	+2.2

Source: surveys 2007–09, questions 57 (benefits), 50 and 55 (household income).

Thinking about the relationship between CDFIs and the state welfare system inevitably prompts us to think about the interrelationship of the two modalities in dealing with the objective to which they are both committed, namely the reduction of poverty. The key question which needs to be answered is what combination of the two instruments reduces poverty, overall and within particular city environments, most effectively. As a first step towards this, we have divided all the clients within the sample, exactly as in Table 4.7, into four categories

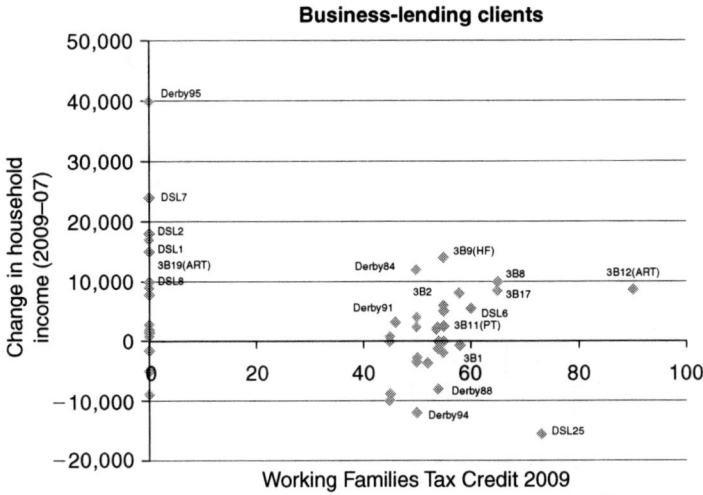

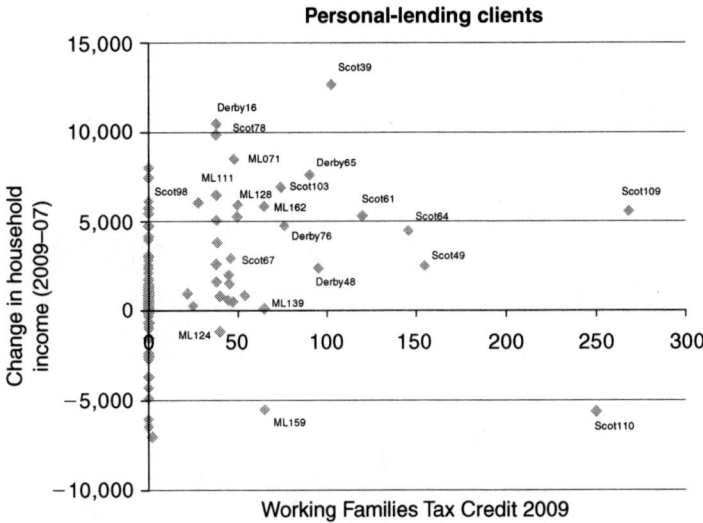

Figure 6.2 Scatters of working tax credit in relation to change in income, 2007–09 (source: surveys, 2007 and 2009).

Table 6.4 Sample institutions: value of benefits per capita, CDFI clients, 2007 and 2009

Types of benefit:	Target group:											
	1 Low-income based			2 Children		3 Disability			4 Housing		5 Other[1]	Total (1 to 5)
	General		Working households									
	Income support	Jobseeker's allowance	Working tax credit	Child benefit	Child tax credit	Disability living allowance	Incapacity benefit	Carer's allowance	Housing credit	Council tax credit		
Business-lending institutions (clients + employees)												
DSL (n=40)												
2009	164	50	733	339	177	265	22	27	194	209	164	1,772
2007	622	239	684	328	165	254	16	24	177	165	146	3,110
Derby Loans; business clients (n=31)												
2009	137	102	756	166	124	175	16	27	14	12	246	2,212
2007	486	403	702	150	111	187	22	38	12	10	288	3,504
'Birmingham cluster' (n=22)												
2009	178	200	1,456	1,144	850	178	320	0	410	68	632	5,436
2007	158	412	1,092	936	922	164	345	150	369	55	1,023	5,625
All business lending institutions:												
2009	159	117	981	549	383	206	19	15	206	96	347	3,078
2007	422	351	826	471	399	201	27	70	186	76	485	3,514
Change 2007–09:												
£ per capita	−263	−244	155	78	−16	5	−8	−55	20	20	−138	−433
As % of 2007 income[2]	−1.0	−1.0	0.6	0.3	−0.1	0.0	0.0	−0.2	0.1	0.1	−0.5	−1.7

Personal lending institutions

Scotcash												
2009	1,802	634	1,040	670	546	371	250	405	966	650	0	7,334
2007	1,655	557	898	564	549	501	315	450	856	589	200	7,134
Derby Loans (personal clients)												
2009	1,685	401	681	814	778	321	535	381	877	863	565	7,900
2007	1,349	352	667	651	619	240	540	342	780	724	463	6,727
Sheffield Moneyline												
2009	2,496	216	362	1,303	1,404	648	449	197	555	649	1,131	9,410
2007	2,029	68	145	1,040	1,124	230	161	71	1,289	274	2,431	9,083
All personal lending institutions:												
2009	1,994	417	694	929	836	446	411	327	799	720	565	8,214
2007	1,677	325	570	918	764	323	233	287	975	529	871	7,648
Change 2007–09:												
£ per capita	317	92	124	11	72	123	178	40	−176	191	−306	566
As % of 2007 income (note 2)	0.3	0.1	0.1	0.0	0.1	0.1	0.2	0.0	−0.2	0.2	−0.3	0.5

Sources: surveys 2007–09, questions 57 (benefits), 50 and 55 (household income).

Notes
1 'Other' includes jobseeker's allowance, sickness benefit, maternity benefit, pension credit.
2 Change in benefits is expressed as a proportion of 2007 income levels as recorded in Table 4.1 (£24,700 for business and £10,813 for personal-lending clients).

according to their poverty dynamics – those who emerged from poverty (using the standard Plimsoll line of 60 per cent of median income before housing costs) over the two-year period 2007–09, those who fell into poverty, those who remained poor and those who were never poor.[10]

The two parts of Table 6.5 present a comparison of the first three of these poverty trajectories (we disregard for this purpose those who never fell into poverty over the period) separately for business and consumer lending institutions. The objective is to see what patterns of benefit use are associated with exit from poverty.

The main finding from the two parts of Table 6.5 is that Working Tax Credit (WTC) occupies an important strategic role in the process of escape from poverty for clients of both types of CDFI. Amongst business CDFIs, a number of small-business respondents to our survey – notably client DSL6 (Case Study 4), Derby84 (Case Study 2b) and B9 testified that they would not have been able to subsist and at the same time run a business if WTC had not provided them with a breathing space whilst they built up their market – and enabled them to cope with shocks to that market. This role of WTC as a survival strategy for small subsistence businesses is illustrated in the upper part of Figure 6.2.

What is perhaps more surprising is that WTC has also been important in enabling some personal-loan clients to make the transition out of poverty. The scatterplot linking acceptance of WTC with change in income for personal-lending clients looks quite different from that for business-lending clients (lower part of Figure 6.2) – most clients are clustered around the bottom left-hand corner, the 'poverty trap' situation in which there are no or minimal earnings from work and, as a consequence, no eligibility for WTC. However, some clients (such as, in Figure 6.2, Scotcash39, 49, 61 and 98, Moneyline 71, 111 and 128) did make the leap into employment or more rarely self-employment, thereby received the additional bonus of WTC (with no sacrifice of benefits, except income support and jobseekers' allowance) and thereby exited from poverty. (Scotcash 39 we recall in addition from Chapter 5 as a client who built up social networks.) This correlation is, indeed, at its most dramatic in Glasgow, where two-thirds of the escapers from poverty and none of those who fell into poverty drew WTC. We have encountered no other types of welfare benefit (as illustrated by Table 6.5) which had this strategic role in encouraging poor people to accept the risks associated with moving into work.[11] Thus, even for personal-lending clients, WTC has been complementary with microfinance in enabling an escape from the poverty trap.

We illustrate this more formally in Table 6.6. This is simply the poverty-trap model introduced in Table 4.9, with a term representing use of WTC introduced into the income equation. Thus in this new formulation we now visualise income as being determined (within the framework of our existing poverty-trap model) by the level of WTC as well as savings and the various 'disturbances' – in particular health and demographic shocks – which can also propel households into and out of poverty. Within this framework, we find that WTC is a significant influence on the change in income (third column of Table 6.6) – in other words,

Table 6.5a Poverty trends 2007–09, in relation to CDFI loan and uptake of specific benefits: (6.5a) Business CDFIs (DSL, Derby Loans business lending and 'Birmingham cluster'); (6.5b) Personal-lending CDFIs (Scotcash, Yorkshire Moneyline and Derby Loans consumer lending)

	Per capita annual income from state benefits, 2009, by type of benefit expenditure (£/annum)								
	Types of benefit							*Total annual benefits*	*Benefits/ loan value*
	1 Income related	*Of which: working families' tax credit*	*2 Child related*	*Of which: child tax credit*	*3 Disability related*	*4 related*	*5 Other*[1]		
Risers out of poverty (N=13+13)									
2009	894	871	571	80	0	214	0	1,679	0.26
2007	1,798	578	555	66	0	179	0	2,532	0.46
% change	−51	−34	+3	+21	0	+19	0	−34	
Fallers into poverty (N=13+3)									
2009	985	680	199	0	0	550	0	1,734	0.39
2007	1,231	639	186	0	0	467	0	1,884	0.34
% change	−20	+6	−7	0	0	+17	0	−8	
Stayed poor (n=32+9)									
2009	964	650	364	146	375	458	104	2,265	0.36
2007	1,554	652	344	138	354	434	88	2,774	0.50
% change	−38	0	+6	+6	+6	+5	+18	−19	

Sources: surveys 2007–09, questions 57 (benefits), 50 and 55 (household income) and xx (labour income).

Note
1 'Other' includes jobseeker's allowance, sickness benefit, maternity benefit, pension credit.

Table 6.5b Poverty trends 2007–09, in relation to CDFI loan and uptake of specific benefits: (6.5a) Business CDFIs (DSL, Derby Loans business lending and 'Birmingham cluster'); (6.5b) Personal-lending CDFIs (Scotcash, Yorkshire Moneyline and Derby Loans consumer lending)

Per capita annual income from state benefits, 2009, by type of benefit expenditure (£/annum)

	Type of benefit:							*Total annual benefits*	*Benefits/ loan value*
	1 Income related:	*Of which: working families' tax credit*	*2 Child related:*	*Of which: child tax credit*	*3 Disability related*	*4 Housing related*	*5 Other*[1]		
Risers out of poverty (n=46)									
2009	3,900	2,426	2,600	1,196	780	802	936	9,018	14.0
2007	3,601	2,344	2,444	889	701	771	821	8,338	13.0
% change	+3	+3	+6	+34	+11	+4	+14		
Fallers into poverty (n=34)									
2009	2,777	265	2,345	1,456	1,213	1,645	778	8,751	13.6
2007	2,449	250	2,255	1,202	1,105	1,255	734	7,798	12.1
% change	+11	+6	+4	+21	+10	+31	+6		
Stayed poor (n=170)									
2009	2,626	756	2,652	1,300	1,612	2,364	560	9,814	15.3
2007	2,441	666	2,501	1,106	1,487	2,079	501	9,009	14.1
% change	+8	+13	+6	+17	+8	+8	+11		

Sources: surveys 2007–09, questions 57 (benefits), 50 and 55 (household income) and 48–53 (labour income).

Note
1 'Other' includes jobseeker's allowance, sickness benefit, maternity benefit, pension credit.

it is a component of the welfare system which, in the midst of present cuts and reforms, needs at all costs to stay in position if CDFIs are to play their role effectively.

Implications and conclusions

Our aim here has been to sketch out the observable linkages between CDFIs and the system of state welfare benefits. We find that the form of CDFI which has grown fastest and attracted most government support in recent years, the personal-lending CDFI, appears in the short term not to reduce but rather to increase the level of state welfare spending, by contrast with the model which gave CDFIs their initial impetus, the business-lending CDFI; however, long-term effects are important as well as short-term effects, and increasing some forms of benefit in the short term holds out of reducing them over the long term. In this context, analysis of poverty dynamics in both business- and consumer-lending CDFIs suggests that the form of state benefit most intimately associated with the process of escape from poverty is WTC, and indeed that WTC (Table 6.6) has played a measurable role in helping UK microfinance clients (personal as well as business) escape from poverty in all the inner-city regions that we study. In this important sense, as well as in the sense of providing the majority of the income flow out of which personal-lending CDFIs make their repayments, the welfare system is highly complementary with the operations of CDFIs.

At a time (end 2010) when the UK government, in common with many governments, has announced sharp reductions in welfare benefits as a contribution to a process of reducing the fiscal deficit, it is important to see that there are ways of doing this that can be achieved without obviously poverty-increasing consequences. One particularly direct way of doing this is to place more weight on to the shoulders of business-oriented CDFIs, which create employment in low-income areas and thereby reduce public expenditure on income support and jobseekers' allowances. However, this idea is of limited applicability, because the number of financially excluded individuals who can be made into bankable entrepreneurs is, on the evidence of Chapter 4, quite small. There is scope also, we believe, for a broader view of the link between CDFIs and the state welfare system, in which personal-lending CDFIs, which in the short term increase benefit dependence and benefits expenditure, over the long term, if they are properly designed, create 'relational capital' which, over the long term, helps to construct social networks and increases the likelihood of entry into well-paid jobs (as illustrated in Chapter 5), thus reducing long-term dependence on benefits. In other words, personal-lending CDFIs, like the welfare system, could be made more asset based than they are. We have not attempted to quantify these potential long-term effects here, but they need to be looked at if we are to construct a cost-effective and joined-up welfare system.

Although some of the welfare reforms to be implemented by the coalition government have been precisely specified, seeking to take the process of 'fiscally efficient redistribution' one step further by extending it to child and disability

Table 6.6 Working tax credit in a model of exit from poverty (estimation method: 3SLS).

| Dependent variable
Regression coefficients on independent variables	Loan size[1]	Change in income 2007–09[2]	Change in saving 2007–09[3]
Constant	580.8
(0.76)	700.4
(1.41)	−56.8
(0.29)
Instruments for loan size (participation in CDFI)			
Index of multiple deprivation[4]	−445.3
(2.24)		
Equivalised household income, 2009[2]	0.18***
(7.84)		
Causal influences on exit from poverty			
Change in saving 2007–09[2]		3.21***
(12.01)	
Educational qualifications[5]		125.1
(0.51)	
Change in working tax credit receipts[6]		21.7*
(2.16)	
Demographic shock dummy[7]		1,497.6*
(1.70)	
Causal influences on saving			
'Termination of borrowing from doorstep lender' dummy[8]			227.3
(0.84)
Received loan advice[9]			1,202.1***
(3.80)
Number of observations	119	119	119
'R2'	0.38	0.08	0.10
Hansen-Sargan overidentification statistic	0.70		

Source: questionnaire survey 2007–09, available from www.poverty.group.shef.ac.uk.

Notes

Figures in parentheses below coefficients are Student's t-statistics: *** represents significance of a coefficient at the 1% level, ** at the 5% level and * at the 10% level.

Variable definitions:

1 *Loan size* is the value in £ of all CDFI credits received by the client between 2007 and 2009. If loan size is 0, the implication is that the respondent was turned down for a loan and received only loan advice during these periods.

2 *Change in income 2007–09* is equivalised to compensate for variations in demands on the respondent's income. For details of the formula used, see Table 4.3, Note 1, and for further notes on this approach see Institute for Fiscal Studies (Brewer *et al.* 2009).

3 *Change in saving 2007–09* is self-reported savings in cash and kind in the seven categories 'bank or building society deposits', 'credit union deposits', 'Christmas club or similar run by a local shop', 'informal deposits with work colleagues, friends or the committee system', 'putting money by in a jar or envelope', 'asking a relative or friends to save or look after money for you', 'lending money to friends or family as a way or saving' and 'savings deposited with a lender, e.g. credit card lender or catalogue lender such as BrightHouse', see question 15 of questionnaire surveys 2007 and 2009.

4 *Index of multiple deprivation* is a measure of deprivation according to indices such as income, asset ownership, house condition, crime, unemployment and educational standards, originally standardised by the Office of the Deputy Prime Minister and now collected by city councils and by the Scottish and Welsh governments and displayed on those authorities' websites (for the Glasgow data used here, see online, available at: www.scotland.gov.uk/simd2006). In the four cities for which we present data, we rank the respondent's postcode in one of five descending categories of deprivation according to the values the index of multiple deprivation (IMD) for that area, as follows:

	Glasgow	Sheffield	Derby	Birmingham
5 *(most deprived category)*	G32–34	S5	DE23	B20
4	G5, G21, G40	S2, S4	DE24	B9
3	G22, G31, G45	S3	DE21–22	B18
2	G15, G51–G53	S8, S13	DE1 (part)	B11
1 *(least deprived category)*	All other postcodes	All other postcodes	All other postcodes	All other postcodes

5 *Educational qualifications*: responses are coded according to the five-point scale: 0, no qualifications; 2, GCSE, O-levels or equivalent; 3, A-levels, Scottish Highers or equivalent; 3.5, other further education or vocational qualification; 4, university degree.

6 *Working tax credit* is change in weekly receipts of working tax credit between 2007 and 2009.

7 *Demographic dummy*: takes the value −1 in the case of a demographic event with negative implications for the respondent's income or assets, e.g. divorce from death or a partner, or birth of a third or subsequent child; +1 in the case of an event with positive implications for the respondent's income or assets, e.g. marriage, getting employment after a period of unemployment, or movement from part-time to full-time; and 0 in all other cases.

8 *Termination of borrowing from doorstep lender*: takes the value 1 if respondent moved, between 2007 and 2009, from borrowing from a high-cost lender (pawnbroker, doorstep lender such as National Provident or Greenwoods, or loan shark; see question 19 of survey questionnaire) to no borrowing from such sources; takes the value −1 if respondent increased her borrowing from these sources between 2007 and 2009; and takes the value 0 in all other cases.

9 *Received loan advice*: takes the value 1 if the respondent received advice on managing money during the period 2007–09, whether from the lending institution itself or from an external agency such as the Citizens' Advice Bureau; 0 otherwise.

benefit (see Table 6.1 and, for more detail, Brewer 2010), other elements in this process remain on the drawing board. One particularly interesting strand is the Department of Work and Pensions' proposed Universal Credit (United Kingdom, DWP 2010). This credit, to be introduced from 2013–14 on new claims if approved by parliament, is

> an integrated working-age credit that will provide a basic allowance with additional elements for children, disability, housing and caring. It will support people both in and out of work, replacing Working Tax Credit, Child Tax Credit, Housing Benefit, Income Support, income-based Jobseekers' Allowance and income-related Employment and Support Allowance
>
> (United Kingdom, DWP 2010: 3)

In the light of the previous discussion, what is important is that the incentives to work and invest within the existing system (and in particular WTC) should be protected and strengthened.[12] In the text of the White Paper, although the stated intentions of the reform are impressively progressive (for example, 'we expect that as many as 350,000 children and 500,000 working age adults could be moved out of poverty by these changes'),[13] there is little which enlightens us about whether this is likely to happen. It is notable that stronger sanctions are to be applied to unemployed people who refuse offers of work, and that anyone with a child over one – rather than seven as at present – will be expected to turn up regularly to a jobcentre, but it is far from clear whether these measures, aiming to move the able-bodied more rapidly off income support and jobseekers' allowance, compensate for the putative disappearance of WTC. Focussing on CDFIs, our intuition is that it is business-lending CDFIs which are likely to be more disadvantaged by the planned introduction of the Universal Credit. As we have seen, it is the (small-scale 'subsistence' or 'lifestyle') businesses which, of all CDFI clients, are the most dependent on WTC, and it is also this type of CDFI which, in our judgment, is most vulnerable to cuts in government spending. This takes us to the issue of how, and if so in what shape, CDFIs can weather the expected austerity of the next few years. This is the theme of our final chapter.

7 Where next?

The impact of CDFIs: summary of argument

Over the last three years, from 2007 to 2010, the people and institutions in this book have certainly been subject to the ancient Chinese curse of 'living in interesting times'. They have experienced, in that time, a global financial crisis, the deepest recession since the 1930s and, arising from both of these, a programme of cuts in public expenditure – focussed, as we discussed in the last chapter, on welfare budgets. Ideally, CDFIs should be well positioned to provide a counterpoise to this, by supplying social protection in the form of loans rather than grants. But CDFIs themselves also are in peril – since from early 2011 onwards they will lose the two main sources of state subsidy which have sustained their growth up to this point: the DWP Growth Fund and the regional development authorities (RDAs), both of which are scheduled to terminate in 2012.[1] In the light of what we have learned in this book, are they worth preserving? In which case, can they preserved, and if so how?

Our argument is that they are worth preserving – because they offer a form of social protection which is cost effective and which potentially provides a financial route out of the poverty trap – but that there is a grave risk that many of them, given their current vulnerability, will not survive. The rationale for their existence is that they overcome a market failure, which is the inability of many people to borrow even though they have potentially bankable projects. In all the institutions which we have analysed (Chapter 4), the average increase in income between 2007 and 2009 in the CDFIs we surveyed was in excess of that in the control group; significantly so in the case of Scotcash, DSL and Derby Loans business loans. In these institutions, the availability of CDFI credit helped to provide low-income people with a buffer against recession. It did this in the short term by enabling clients to borrow and thereby afford additional consumption goods, but in the longer term especially among business CDFIs by increasing their assets, and in some cases also (Chapter 5) by developing social and business networks within the community. We examined in some detail the factors which distinguish successful from unsuccessful clients, including membership of social networks, availability of loan advice, ability to escape from dependence on doorstep money-lenders and finally (Chapter 6) the pattern of welfare benefits received.

In spite of all this, CDFIs have underperformed even in relation to reasonable expectations of what they could deliver. Under UK conditions, nobody could expect microfinance institutions to grow as fast as the Grameen Bank of Bangladesh, or to reduce poverty by anything like the rate which they have achieved. On the other hand, in the much richer country which Britain is, it would have been reasonable to expect arrears to be kept well below 10 per cent, as has occurred across the whole of the developing world. It would also have been reasonable to expect most if not all microfinance clients to open and maintain savings accounts, as has occurred across the whole of the developing world. In Britain, neither of these things has happened (Chapters 3 and 4). In Chapter 3, we ascribed variations in CDFI performance to three factors – their strategic assets and in particular their reputation and competitiveness in the market; the 'architecture' of their relationships with sponsors, clients and suppliers; and their incentive structures and policies towards good performance. All of these factors are partly under the control of CDFIs themselves and partly under the control of external agencies. We look now at these two dimensions of control, the internal and the external, in sequence.

What CDFIs need to do

Let us begin where developing-country microfinance began. The great achievement of the founding fathers of microfinance was to work out a technology for controlling default rates – generally to less than 5 per cent – even though borrowers were too poor to be able to provide collateral. This technology of cost control was the key change in incentive structures that then made the microfinance industry able to grow and reduce poverty rapidly. In Britain, however, with the exception of Scotcash, whose default rate is around 4 per cent, microfinance institutions in industrialised countries including the UK have not been able to emulate this achievement.[2] This is the single most important fault in the design of CDFIs, and their survival depends on it being rectified. Industrialised countries have generally preferred to lend to individuals rather than groups,[3] such that formal peer-pressure methods are not available. Once that decision is taken, three approaches to deterring default are left – rigorous screening out of bad risks at appraisal (possibly coupled, as in Scotcash, with money advice as a consolation prize); 'progressive lending', i.e. always start with a very small loan as a way of minimising risks and getting to know the borrower, and then scale up for borrowers with a good record; and, unromantic but essential, follow up all overdue accounts by telephone the day the loan goes overdue.[4] Scotcash, the star performer, and ELM, which learned in 2010 that it needed to balance its excellent growth performance with a parallel effort on loan recovery, do all of these. The 'poor performers' in our sample do none. With state subsidies disappearing rapidly, they cannot last long unless radically reformed.

Once this gaping hole in the ship's hull is mended (not yet true of the majority of CDFIs), we can begin to think where the boat might sail. Again, we can take inspiration from what is happening in the developing world. There, we notice that microfinance institutions, in the spirit of letting themselves be led by what the customer wants, are diversifying their financial products, and in particular are shifting from simply providing loans to also providing savings, insurance and, in some cases, more complex products such as credit cards, leasing and equity. From a CDFI perspective the most important of these is savings, which we have observed (Chapter 4), are tightly linked with exit from poverty. Motivating savings deposits by demotivated poor people is not easy, as we discussed there, and the solution requires particular ingenuity in the current context, because CDFIs are not empowered to take deposits, and the main instrument by which the previous government planned to motivate savings amongst low-income groups, the Savings Gateway, has been abolished by the coalition government. The problem is not one that can be solved by CDFIs alone, and we discuss it further below.

Finally, there is the contested issue of what else CDFIs need to do to be effective, apart from lend money and get it back safely. One answer to this question, favoured for example by the director of Grameen Bank, Muhammad Yunus, is 'nothing'.[5] However, in our view the balance of evidence suggests that something in the way of mentoring is needed, especially for more vulnerable clients (small business start-ups plus nearly all personal clients). As we have seen (Chapter 4) the presence or absence of effective mentoring marks, as a rule, the difference between successful and unsuccessful clients, both business and personal, and it is also strongly related with the emergence of social networks which diffuse the impact of CDFIs. This was most dramatically demonstrated in our case study of ethnic-minority clients in the West Midlands (Chapter 5), where there was almost a case-by-case association between good mentoring and good individual performance: the effective lending institutions were the ones which were supported by effective mentoring institutions, and the collapsed lending institution was the one where mentoring services broke down. In the West Midlands, and indeed generally across UK CDFIs, mentoring has been outsourced to external specialists, and we discuss these cases in detail below; but in Scotcash, it has been done in-house, and has been a spectacular success (Chapter 3, Case Study 1). Because most mentoring has been done externally, we now discuss it, as part of a broader review of the factors that lie outside the compass of the individual CDFI.

What other institutions need to (and are able to) do: the institutional and policy context

Much of the impact of CDFIs is not determined by CDFIs themselves. Banks and other financial institutions, advice providers and the multiple tiers of government, in particular, all have a bearing on their effectiveness. These institutions constitute the 'external architecture' of CDFIs, and we now bring this into the centre of the stage. We shall not examine every aspect of this external architecture, but three critical components of it – the taking of savings deposits, money advice and sponsorship.

Savings

CDFIs are not regulated institutions and therefore not authorised to collect savings deposits, and therefore if they wish to promote savings they must do this in partnership with another body. This can be a bank, a building society or a credit union. The most successful model of savings mobilisation, in our judgment, is the ELM model (Case Study 3) in which clients who have loan accounts with ELM are invited by loan officers to put a part, typically 20 per cent, of their monthly direct debit into a savings account with HBOS, and the other 80 per cent into repayment of their loan instalment. Scotcash and Sheffield Moneyline operate in partnership with credit unions rather than banks, and promote savings in a more permissive way – in these institutions the borrower opts in, if she chooses, to make a savings deposit with the credit union, whereas under the ELM system,[6] the borrower must opt out, if she so chooses, from a recommendation by the lender to make a savings deposit with HBOS. Derby Loans (Midlands Community Finance) does not currently put pressure on clients to save, although it is currently negotiating for trusted partner status with the Royal Bank of Scotland.[7] Most low-income people find saving extremely difficult (Chapter 4), which is not surprising since both the television and their children subject them to continuous pressures to spend the little money they have, whereas nobody puts them under pressure to save or even explains to them how they might achieve that. Hence the attraction of the ELM system, which provides a counter-pressure and at the same time an explanatory story which convinces the client from personal experience that saving is a good idea and shows them how it can be done. The proof is in the results – ELM has been able to mobilise savings one-for-one with lending, a pound saved by clients for every pound lent, which no other CDFI has been able to emulate. And the ability to save, of course, as Chapter 4 showed, is the gateway to exit from the poverty trap.

Money advice

What the financially excluded lack is not only access to financial institutions; it is also access to information and ideas. The information that is required varies between the two types of CDFI. Clients of business-lending CDFIs often require highly technical information about technologies and markets, whereas clients of personal-lending CDFIs are more in need of information about how to manage their debts. Both types of clients often require social contact and moral support also. We have referred to these advice functions collectively as *mentoring*. With the exception of the business lender Halal Fund, Birmingham (see Chapter 5) and the personal lender Scotcash (see in particular Case Study 1 in Chapter 3) this vital mentoring function is typically provided not in-house by staff of the CDFI but by another institution, as part of the CDFI's external architecture. For both business and personal CDFIs, there exists an agency which offers these support services in a countrywide network; in the case of business CDFIs, this is Business

Link (in Scotland, the Business Gateway) and in the case of personal-lending CDFIs, this is the national network of Citizens' Advice Bureaux. However, alternative providers of these mentoring services also exist, and often, our research suggests, it is the alternative which provides the best-practice solution.

In Glasgow, advice to small businesses receiving finance from DSL was initially, through the first half of the 2000s, subcontracted to Local Economic Development Companies (LEDCs, now known as Regeneration Agencies), one of which was located in each of the seven main low-income areas of the city. These agencies took responsibility for the mentoring of small loans to start-up clients, with the intention that as and when the client's company achieved lift-off, it would graduate to the Business Gateway, or to the banks. Because this advice was in general technically excellent, because it provided moral as well as technical support and not least because it was free, this model has in past years been crucial to the survival and growth of DSL clients (see Case Studies 2b, 4 and 5) and much of the remarkable poverty reduction achievement reported for Glasgow in Table 4.6 is owing to this support. However, although the support continued to be forthcoming, fewer and fewer DSL clients availed themselves of it. This is because DSL, in common with ART and the Black Country Reinvestment Society (BCRS) in the West Midlands, had moved up-market after 2006 in pursuit of sustainability, and now provided only larger loans (always more than £5,000 and averaging just over £10,000). This territory was outwith the scope of the LEDCs, and DSL clients were now referred to the Business Gateway for technical support, which they had to pay for. In other words, financially excluded individuals contemplating starting a new business now (after 2007–08) had less access both to microfinance and to associated support services, because the microfinance organisations were no longer willing to bear the risk of supporting them, and the support companies without a CDFI to partner them were less effective. In Birmingham also, the upper end of the small business sector is well provided for: an outside contracting company, Birmingham Enterprise, has been successful in providing specialised mentoring support to ART clients, notably the ethnic-minority clients discussed in Chapter 5, in the same way as the LEDCs (Regeneration Agencies) formerly did for DSL clients in Glasgow; they moreover are not subject to an upper limit on the size of company they support, as the Regeneration Agencies are in Glasgow. The void afflicting the more vulnerable end of the small-business sector, however, persists in every city.

In the case of personal-lending institutions, the problem looks simpler, because the increasingly technical support which small businesses require is not a big issue. Rather, clients of personal CDFIs are faced with the problem of coping with often mountainous debts, and the big issue is to be able to cope with them in a way which leaves them better off in the long term. To do this, they need advice and social support, ideally before the problem becomes desperate. As we have seen in Chapter 4, clients who received money advice, within our sample, were more likely to increase their savings and thus to escape from the poverty trap,[8] and the question of how to provide such advice effectively is therefore central to the question of how to make CDFIs work better.

In Britain, money advice to people with debt problems is seldom (with important exceptions to be discussed below) provided by CDFIs themselves or by charities (New Philanthropy Capital 2009: 30), and the main organisation offering such advice is the national network of Citizens' Advice Bureaux (CABs). CAB staff are very diverse, however, with some highly professional staff who combine accountancy, legal, counselling and sometimes banking skills, and a large band of volunteers qualified to offer little more than sympathy. In addition, they are overburdened: within our sample, there are cases, notably in Blackburn and Sheffield, of debt-distressed CDFI clients who sought CAB advice and were told there was a three-month waiting list for an appointment.[9] The Treasury's financial inclusion initiative, as we have seen, put debt advice high on its list of priorities, and its Financial Action Plan 2008–11 set the target that 'all adults should have access to "high-quality money guidance"' (United Kingdom, HM Treasury 2007: 36). In pursuit of this objective, the government in 2006 augmented its own network of money advisers to provide face-to-face advice,[10] and established a National Debtline run by the Money Advice Trust, which provides a telephone counselling service. In 2010, the Financial Inclusion Task Force reported that 'government intervention through the financial inclusion fund has successfully delivered a significant increase in the debt advice available to the most vulnerable' (United Kingdom, HM Treasury 2010: 4). However, the taskforce provided no evidence to support this statement, and the government's intervention has certainly gone above some clients' heads: not one of the 320 personal-lending clients whom we interviewed recalled having heard of either the Financial Inclusion Fund or the National Debtline advice services.

Thus there remains a problem of matching the supply of money advice to the need for it, and, together with the problems of credit control and savings mobilisation, this is the biggest constraint on the effectiveness of personal CDFIs. Scotcash, as we have seen (Case Study 1) provides an exemplar of how to deal with the problem: it has established its own money advice service.[11] This service is highly professionalised, quickly available on demand and imaginative (like the East Lancs Moneyline savings advice service) in the persuasion strategies with which it wins the confidence of advisees.[12] These qualities have contributed to enabling a larger number of Scotcash clients than of Derby Loans or Sheffield Moneyline clients to buck the recession.[13] However, and this is a crux, they have only been made available because Scotcash, buttressed by the combined resources of Glasgow City Council, the Glasgow Housing Association and the Royal Bank of Scotland, has been able to finance high-quality money advisers. Derby Loans and Sheffield Moneyline, operating on a shoestring and now hit by cuts in sponsorship, cannot afford to provide an in-house money advice service,[14] even though they are perfectly well aware that it would make their financial services more effective, because they would derive no short-term return from it. This is what is known as a *public goods problem* – more and better money advice would be good for all financially vulnerable people, but it is not being made available by several of the CDFIs who are in the best position to target such assistance because they cannot risk bankrupting themselves by providing a service from which they would derive no immediate financial return. Public goods problems, of course, are traditionally for central government to resolve; and in the past, this is precisely what government has attempted to do with debt advice through the Financial Inclusion Fund. But in the present political environment, when the Financial Inclusion Fund is being wound up and is planned to terminate in 2011, this approach offers no help. This throws us immediately up against the third and most immediately urgent element in the external architectures of CDFIs – how in the current climate they can possibly fund themselves, and thereby survive?

Even before the 2007–09 recession, as described in Chapter 1, CDFIs were taking part willy-nilly in a contest in which the more successful, such as ELM, Street UK and DSL, were able to transcend the boundaries of the community which initially provided them with their bedrock and the less successful, such as 3Bs, Ethnic Mutual, and Blackpool and Salford Moneylines, have either perished or been absorbed by the more successful. With the recession and with the impending disappearance of the government Financial Inclusion Fund, Growth Fund and RDAs, the contest has become more savage. We have already described some of the survival strategies which CDFIs have used to protect themselves in face of this predicament: product diversification (additional financial products such as housing, as in South Coast Moneyline, or 'back-office services' as in Street UK), raising interest rates in the unregulated part of the market (Sheffield Moneyline), reduction of risks by moving up-market (ART, Black Country Reinvestment Society and DSL) and of course cost-cutting, a key element in which is getting arrears under control. But only a handful of successful practitioners of these strategies are currently able, without raising additional money to compensate the cuts in government funding, to keep going. What can the others do?

If they are extremely lucky and gifted at fund-raising, they can raise resources from commercial banks (as Scotcash have), from the European Regional Development Fund (as ART and DSL have) or from private foundations (as Aspire and Sheffield Moneyline did; but never on a scale rivalling what has been achieved in the United States, which is one reason why UK CDFIs broadly find themselves in a worse current predicament than American ones).[15] Of these options, commercial banks might appear to be a good bet, as there is a natural synergy between them in the cause of invading sub-prime credit markets and taking market share away from highly profitable corporations such as National Provident. However, with the extremely important exception of the ELM/HBOS and Scotcash/RBS partnerships, this potential synergy has not really materialised,[16] and the risk aversion engendered by the credit crunch (which of course was born within sub-prime credit markets) is unlikely to make things better in the short term.[17] This leaves CDFIs, in our judgment, with only one serious alternative fund-raising option – but an important one.

This is the funding option represented by local authorities, and in particular local authority housing departments; plus quasi-autonomous housing associations and corporations. (Several local authorities, such as the Glasgow City Council in its establishment of the Glasgow Housing Association, have recently passed over from the first status to the second, thereby giving them more entrepreneurial autonomy.) The housing departments of local authorities provided the original impetus for the setting up of many personal-finance CDFIs, and in a number of cases, e.g. South Coast Moneyline, ELM, Scotcash, even Derby Loans, much of their core finance also. Such support is rational, since a large component of the financial problems of housing authorities (and of their tenants) consists of rent arrears, and relieving debt problems by lending into those arrears is something which CDFIs are well qualified to do. There, therefore, seems to be a case for CDFIs to seek, as a coping strategy in present conditions, to derive a larger proportion of their funding from housing authorities and corporations. Greater linkage with this market might then lead them in turn towards new and imaginative financial products – for example, the community development bank Shorebank (formally South Shore Bank) in the United States has recently by this means become 'far and away the largest multifamily lender to neighbourhoods more than 80 per cent minority' (New Economics Foundation 2008). There is particular inspiration here, of course, for the funding of CDFIs' lending to ethnic minorities (Chapter 5).

Thus in all of the three territories which we have identified as crucial for the effectiveness and survival of CDFIs – savings, advice and fundraising – there is a need for that majority of CDFIs which are currently not using best practice to move towards it, and in each of these cases they can take inspiration from the best practice which we have attempted to identify in Table 7.1. Of course, every city and community has its own unique traditions, institutions and politics, and so it is not a question of simply photocopying and adopting the best practices we have described, but rather of grafting what is usable within the best-practice model into the parent rootstock. This sort of hybridisation is not easy when the plant is immature – but without it, many promising plants will die.

CDFIs constitute one of the outstanding ideas in social protection of the last fifteen years. Not only have they assisted many inner-city people to escape from poverty, but they have done so in a way which, unlike conventional welfare benefits, enables at least a part of that service to be provided on a self-financing basis. Especially in times of recession, like those studied in this book, they provide a valuable adjunct to the welfare state, and indeed a means by which that welfare state potentially can reform itself and become more 'joined-up'. But CDFIs, still in an experimental and vulnerable state, are far short of realising that potential. One measure of the gap between hope and fulfilment is the difference between the two million and more low-income people who currently hold unfair-price loans from doorstep lenders and the 20,000 or so who hold fair-price loans from CDFIs. But another, more worrying measure of this gap is the gap in public awareness – signalled by the fact that in the most recent social protection White Paper, on Universal Credit (United Kingdom, DWP 2010), CDFIs, indeed every kind of credit except for the government's Social Fund, is not even mentioned.

As CDFIs have evolved they have changed out of recognition, and they have been forced to become creative, which in many cases has involved a severing of

Table 7.1 Supporting institutions and the efficiency of CDFIs

Service	Best practice	Special features of best practice	Lessons for other CDFIs – next steps needed
Deposit-taking	'Bridge schemes' (e.g. ELM–HBOS partnership, or in principle RBS Trusted Partner status) with positive encouragement to all CDFI clients to save with the partner institution	'Imaginative pressure' from CDFI staff (e.g. ELM, Case Study 3)	Recreation of Savings Gateway by other means
Advice providers			
For business clients	Free-of-charge mentoring, combining technical and moral support	Halal Fund: network-making input Glasgow East Regeneration Agency: formation of entrepreneur groups	
For personal clients	Professionalisation, and making available to lowest income groups, of CAB-type money advice services (whether in-house or outsourced)	'Scotcash model' (free professional advice available to all clients); willingness of advisers to go beyond the immediate budgeting problem (e.g. to negotiate directly with doorstep lenders and to provide advice on benefit entitlements); screening out of high-risk clients into advice	Use of advice as a complement to lending, not a substitute for it
Sponsors	Increasing use of banks and (especially) housing authorities as funding agencies		Possible development of new housing-related financial products (e.g. home improvement loans, multi-family mortgages)

contact with models of microfinance practised in other parts of the world. The 'personal-lending CDFI' is a new species, unknown in the developing world. But although it has had the merits, in relation to the traditional business-lending model, of being able to grow faster and of reaching out to poorer people than business CDFIs, it suffers in many cases from still unresolved problems, including in many cases, not all, an inability to build the social and human capital of their clients, or even to control their arrears. Urgent learning from the best practices presented in Table 7.1 is necessary if such CDFIs are to be able to do the best for their clients, or even, in some cases, survive.

The mere fact that many CDFIs are currently insecure and vulnerable should not in itself be taken as threatening for the future. Many institutions, including many microfinance institutions in developing countries which are now pillars of their domestic economies, at around the age of fifteen which represents the age of the oldest UK CDFIs, were likewise very vulnerable, and required the shock of a crisis to achieve 'best practice' and impel them towards their current shape (Hulme and Mosley 1996: Ch. 9).[18] Hirschman's 'Principle of the Hiding Hand' (Hirschman 1963) reminds us that many organisations and projects, even if they underpredicted the problems which they were to encounter, also underpredicted the creativity which would enable them to find a way around those problems. But to be creative, one needs a vision; and to have a vision, one needs, amongst other things, information about the range of things that are achievable. One of the strengths of CDFIs is the range of pathways by which they can potentially contribute to individual and social well-being, as we have tried to illustrate; and about these pathways, especially in an industrialised-country context, there is still very little information. Through this book we hope to have made a contribution to providing the information that will help such institutions realise their own visions of what is possible.

Appendix

Transitions into and out of poverty, 2007–09

One of our major purposes has been to understand the process of exit from poverty, what CDFIs are able to contribute to this process and what institutions or policies may be required for CDFIs to be effective in particular localities. In Table 4.7 we divided our sample into the categories: exited from poverty between 2007 and 2009 (forty cases); entered into poverty between 2007 and 2009 (twenty-nine cases); stayed poor (130 cases); and stayed nonpoor (44 cases). In order better to understand the process of exit from poverty, we focus in this Appendix on the sixty-nine cases who either escaped from poverty or fell into poverty, setting the other cases aside. We provide a quantitative picture, for each of the sixty-nine cases, of the main factors which, according to the analysis of Chapters 4 and 5, influenced poverty dynamics (attitudinal variables, relationships with doorstep moneylenders, receipt of money advice, savings, labour-market events, health shocks and demographic shocks) and set this alongside any qualitative evidence emerging from the intensive interviews.

Business Loans

'Birmingham cluster' (3Bs, Halal Fund and ART)

Table A.1 'Birmingham cluster' (3Bs, Halal Fund and ART)

	Transitions out of poverty (3 cases)			Into poverty (4 cases; but only 3 recorded here)		
Index No.	B2 (3Bs)	B9 (Halal Fund)	B12 (ART)	B1 (3Bs)	B5 (3Bs)	B18 (ART)
Loan size	£7,500	£5,000 – Bank £2,800 – Halal £8,000 – family and friends	£2,500	£7,000	£5,000?	£10,000
Ethnicity	Afro-Caribbean	Pakistani	Pakistani	Afro-Caribbean	Afro-Caribbean	Afro-Caribbean
Household type	Married, 2 children	Married, 2 children (reunited after period of separation)	Single, no children	Single, no children	Single, 5 children	Single, no children
Business type and location	Home maintenance services, Bordesley Green B9	Food retailing, B2	Training and recruitment company, Tyseley, B11	Wedding dress designer, Vyse Street, Hockley	Community bookstore, Handsworth B20	Afro baby clothes, Kings Norton, B30
Income 2009	£22,142	£25,000	£16,750	£8,710	£10,875	£3,343
Income 2007	£14,000	£11,000	£8,040	£9,380	£9,352	£4,020
Income from benefits 2009	0	0	0	0	£6,750	£2,500
Savings:						
Savings value (£) 2009	6,000	12,000	6,000	1,500	500	250
Savings value (£) 2007	2,000	−2,000	0	0	1,000	0
Financially excluded?	Yes	No	No	No	No	Yes
Contact with home credit 2007–09	None	None	None	None	£1,000 loan, repaid at £76/month	Yes – FLM provided credit, guaranteed through grandmother
Assets:						
Own house	Yes	Yes	Yes	No	No	No
Own car	Yes	Yes	Yes	Yes	No	No
Business turnover	£120,000	£70,000	£36,000	£12,000	£18,500	£3,000
Number of employees	4	2	1	0	0	0
Human capital:						
Highest educational level	Degree (Social Work, UCE)	NVQs and Diploma in Business from FE college	Degree	O-levels	GCSEs	Degree

Undertook training between 2007 and 2009?	–	–	–	Attended local college last year but 'didn't like it, it was a waste of time' Community Roots (see qualitative notes below)
Loan advice from CDFI, CAB or other agency/business mentoring?	–	Community Roots (see qualitative notes below)	–	–
Labour market:				
Self or partner entered labour market, or increased work hours?	No	No	Still works as care worker (2–4 nights a week) – shuts the business down while working outside the Jewellery Quarter	No
Labour market earnings, 2009	0	0	£9,000	0
Demographic shocks	None	None	None	–
Health shocks	None	None	None	Accident, damaged foot 2009
Health-seeking behaviour:				
Smoking	Always smoked	Recently stopped	Never smoked	Never smoked
Alcohol intake	25 units/week	None	None	Minor, 5 units/week
Fruit and vegetable consumption	Increased	Increased	–	Increased
Increased exercise?				
vigorous	No	No	No	A little
moderate	No	Yes	No	A little
walking	Yes	No	No	Every day
Community membership	Yes – Chamber of Commerce member	No business associations – 'I only meet with others in the locality if I am buying or selling something'.	Yes – Jewellery Quarter Association (see qualitative remarks)	Yes – Peace Movement

continued

Table A.1 continued

	Transitions out of poverty (3 cases)	Into poverty (4 cases; but only 3 recorded here)		
Community leadership	The client's company is a quasi-social service for people who have been victims of domestic abuse. She sees the job as 'a mission' (her words)			No ('but I'd love to")
Qualitative remarks – summary	On Community Roots: 'the biggest insult in the world: you expect some level of support and it does not come … it makes you doubt your own ability'. On setting up a business: 'there are too many bureaucratic hoops and loops to go through and if you miss one of them, they can close your business'. 'I do not wish to borrow from Halal Fund in future – they take too much time and lend very small amounts. The one merit of borrowing from them was that I was able to negotiate in my own language'. £8000 'top-up' borrowing from family and friends (with whom continues to save on regular basis).	'It is a shame that I was not able to borrow enough at the start-up stage. This kept my business underdeveloped. CDFIs are not really geared up to support start-up businesses. They seem to be confused about their role. When my father died recently I used the family 'Death Committee' for funeral expenses. It is organised on the basis of clan. We have some 180 members who contribute yearly some £30 per person. This committee pays up for all funeral expenses'.	Financially excluded by Natwest because of County Court Judgement. She herself turned down 3Bs first time 'because they were too rude' but tried a second time. Still works as care worker (2–4 nights a week) – shuts the business down while working outside the Jewellery Quarter. Attempts to meet monthly with people in Jewellery Quarter – lots of designers there. Will become a member of the British Bridal Association. She is committed to the business – doing your own business is something you do from the heart and somehow helps you cope with problems better'. But the market has changed – 'businesses like Pronuptia don't make their own bridal clothes; there are not so many design workers around the Jewellery Quarter now. Rich clients are not coming now – trade has shrunk, and I will close if trade doesn't pick up'.	Not happy with 3B because of lack of training courses. Had to go to Community Roots for training courses – was passed on to them. They helped me to do business plans.	Discovered ART through New Jerusalem Church, just near ART, which, every week, holds an evening where those interested in starting businesses pray together and talk together. These evenings helped me in drawing up my business plan. By contrast, with Business Link I kept going around in circles and kept banging my head against a wall – they sent me for business planning to a person in Harborne who told me what I already know and wanted to charge me £200 for it, then when I complained told me to go and sit in the British Library and find out what I needed Family support – grandmother guaranteed loan, cousin helps make curtains and cushions. I'm now a happier person; knowing that I've got my life in my hands is – I can't put words on it. For years I've dreamed of having my own business and now that I have I know it's going to be a true blessing.

Derby Loans business loans

Table A.2 Derby Loans business loans

	Out of poverty (3 cases)			Into poverty (2 cases)	
Index No.	82	84	95	92	90
Loan	£4,000	£7,500	£10,000	–	£2,500
Ethnicity	White British	Kurdish	White British	Chinese	White British
Household type	Single female, 1 child	Married, children	Married, no children	Single, no children	Single, no children
Business type and location	Photographic studio	Mini-market operation; trading in shop leases	Mobile phone communications	Food shop	Pie maker and retailer
Income 2009	£18,500	£35,000	£100,000	£14,394	£7,640
Income 2007	£10,000	£22,000	£60,000	£13,146	£7,640
Income from benefits 2009	£7,000	£5,600	0	£3,200	£6,000
Savings:					
Savings value (£) 2009	1,500	3,000	2,000	100	0
Savings value (£) 2007	0	1,500	10,000	0	0
Financially excluded?	Yes	Yes	Yes	Yes	Yes
Contact with home credit 2007–09	No	No	No	No	No
Assets:					
Own house	No	Yes	Yes	Yes	Yes
Own car	Yes	Yes	Yes	No	No
Business turnover £/annum	1,500	60,000	928,000	N.A.	N.A.
Number of employees	0	4	8	0	0
of which: low income	0	2	1	0	0
Human capital:					
Highest educational level	A-levels	Overseas A-level Equivalent	A-levels	A-levels	None
Undertook training between 2007 and 2009?	No	No	No	HND	IT qualifications
Loan advice from CDFI, CAB or other agency/ business mentoring?	No	No	No	No	No

continued

Table A.2 continued

	Out of poverty (3 cases)			Into poverty (2 cases)	
Labour market:					
Self or partner entered labour market, or increased work hours?	Yes	No	No	No	No
Labour market earnings 2009 (£/annum)	10,000	0	0	0	0
Demographic shocks	None	None	None	Suicide 2009	None
Health shocks	2 operations, 2010	None	None	Suicide 2009	None
Health-seeking behaviour:					
Smoking	Yes	Yes	No	No	Yes
Alcohol intake (units/week)	5	0	10	0	0
Fruit and vegetable consumption	Moderate	None	Moderate	Above average	Moderate
Increased exercise?					
vigorous	No	No	No	No	No
moderate	No	Yes	Yes	No	No
walking	No	No	No	No	No
Community membership and informal support	None	Chair, Kurdish Community Association	Member, Derby Chamber of Commerce and Derby 500 (manufacturers' association)	None	None
Community leadership	None	Chair, Kurdish Community Association	Initiating role in both associations	None	None
Deakin Coping Scale measure	1.3	1.6	1.8	0.8	0.9
Qualitative remarks – summary	Detailed profile as Case Study 2b	Detailed profile as Case Study 6	Detailed profile as Case Study 2a	–	–

Developing Strathclyde Ltd (DSL)

Table A.3 Developing Strathclyde Ltd (DSL)

Transitions out of poverty (6 cases)
(Note: in all cases except G6 and G24 the transition out of poverty is made not by the entrepreneur but by employees of the entrepreneur; see Employment below.)

Index No.	G 1 (Laplace)	G 2 (Commands)	G 4 (Clever Clogs)	G 6 (Soapy Bubbles; Case Study 4)	G 7 (Tigers; Case Study 5)	G 8 (Case Study 5)
Loan	£20,000 equity stake	£5,000 (paid off)	£20,000 (paid off)	£6,000 (2001) £3,000 (2004)	£7,500	£20,000, 2001 plus supplement, 2004
Ethnicity	White British	White British	White British	White British	White British	White British
Household type	Married, children	Married, 4 daughters	Married, 2 children	1 partner single; the other divorced, 2 children	Married, 2 children	Married, 3 children
Business type and location	Limited company, electronic engineering, Drumchapel G15	Limited company, mail order, Drumchapel G15	Nursery, Springburn G21	Partnership, shop/launderette, Springburn G21	Limited company, training services, Easterhouse G32	Limited company, printer, Easterhouse G32
Income 2009	>£50,000	£45,000	£40,000	£18,000	£45,000	£45,000
Income 2007	>£35,000	£30,000	£30,000	£13,000	£45,000	£40,000
Income from benefits 2009	0	0	0	£7,500	0	£2,000
Savings:						
Savings value (£) 2009	10,000	4,000	5,000	1,000	12,000	10,000
Savings value (£) 2007	5,000	2,000	2,000	0	10,000	5,000
Financially excluded?	Yes	Yes	Yes	Yes	Yes	Yes
Contact with home credit 2007–09	No	No	No	No	No	No
Assets:						
Own house	Yes	Yes	Yes	No	Yes	Yes
Own car	Yes	Yes	Yes	No	Yes	Yes
Business turnover (£)	5m	950k	270k	18k	986k	820k
Number of employees	40	25	16	0	24	22
of which: low income	16	18	6	0	16	14

continued

Table A.3 continued

Transitions out of poverty (6 cases)
(Note: in all cases except G6 and G24 the transition out of poverty is made not by the entrepreneur but by employees of the entrepreneur; see Employment below.)

Human capital:						
Highest educational level	Degree	Highers	Highers	GCSE	Highers	Highers
Undertook training between 2007 and 2009?	–	–	Yes	–	–	No
Loan advice from CDFI, CAB or other agency/business mentoring?	No	Mentoring (Drum Opps.)	Mentoring (Glasgow North)	Mentoring (Glasgow North)	No	Technical support (see Case Study 2b)
Labour market:						
Self or partner entered labour market, or increased work hours?	No	No	No	No	No	No
Labour market earnings 2009	–	–	–	–	–	–
Demographic shocks	–	–	Entrepreneur's children born, 2003–05.	–	–	–
Community membership and informal support	–	Informal support from family and friends crucial when entrepreneur 'was ready to throw the towel in' during recession.	Needed to borrow heavily within the family to deal with a downturn in 2004–05.	Established and run Barmulloch Community Council.	Sponsor of local football teams. Note mutual support: entrepreneur sits on the board of enterprise G8, q.v.	Substantial investment in locality and in Catholic charities. Note mutual support: entrepreneur sits on the board of enterprise G7, q.v.
Community leadership	–	–	–	See detailed profile in Case Study 4	See detailed profile in Case Study 5	See detailed profile in Case Study 5
Qualitative remarks – summary	–	–	–	See detailed profile in Case Study 4	See detailed profile in Case Study 5	–

Table A.4 Developing Strathclyde Ltd (DSL)

Into poverty (4 cases)

	G17 (Mactag)	G18 (Egobots)	G19 (Fressh)	G25 (Soul Therapies)
Index No.	G17 (Mactag)	G18 (Egobots)	G19 (Fressh)	G25 (Soul Therapies)
Loan	£20,000	£25,000	£10,000	£4,000
Ethnicity	White British	White British	White British	White British
Household type	Married, children	Divorced, no children	Single females, no children	Single female, no children
Business type and location	Limited company, manufacturer of Highlandwear, Bridgeton G40	IT, constructor of 'virtual identities', West End G12	Partnership, fresh food retailer, Hyndland G12	Sole trader, beauty therapist, City Centre G1
Income 2009	£15000	£11,000	£10,000	£5,000
Income 2007	£35,000	£15,000	£15,000	£18,000
Income from benefits 2009	£5,000	£0	£7,500	£4,500
Savings:				
Savings value (£) 2009	0	0	0	0
Savings value (£) 2007	2,000	0	500	1,000
Financially excluded?	No	Yes	Yes	Yes
Contact with home credit 2007–09	No	No	No	No
Assets:				
Own house	Yes	No	No	No
Own car	Yes	Yes	Yes	No
Business turnover (£)	500k	5k	27k	20k
Number of employees	23	0	0	0
of which: low income	10	0	0	0
Human capital:				
Highest educational level	Degree(MA)	Highers	Highers	Highers
Undertook training between 2007 and 2009?	No	No	No	Yes – HND (night school)
Loan advice from CDFI, CAB or other agency/ business mentoring?	No	No	No	Yes – (Business Link)

continued

Table A.4 continued

	Into poverty (4 cases)		
Labour market:			
Self or partner entered labour market, or increased work hours?	No	No	Yes (2009)
Labour market earnings 2009	No	No	£11,000
Demographic shocks	See non-demographic shocks under 'Qualitative remarks' below.	Divorce, 2007	See non-demographic shocks under 'Qualitative remarks' below.
Community membership and informal support	None	None	Friends sponsored launch events – and helped her find work when company collapsed.
Community leadership	None	None	None
Qualitative remarks – summary	See Case Study 2c. In 2007–08 recession, entrepreneur's overdraft was suddenly cut from £50,000 to £5,000, and combined with the collapse of the market and the overexpansion of the workforce this turned out to be uncopable with.	Company wound up in 2008 due to partners' inability to service debts.	Company wound up in 2009: proximate cause was refusal of entrepreneur's landlady to continue to grant her office space amidst a climate of worsening personal relations.

Personal loans

Table A.5 Scotcash

Out of poverty (14 cases; 10 recorded here)

Index No.	6	23	25	39	49	64	78	93	98	103
Ethnicity	White UK	White UK	White UK	White UK	White UK	White UK	White UK	White UK	White UK	White UK
Household type	Female, married, 2 children, G21	Male, divorced, Lambhill G26	Female, married, 2 children, G32	—	Female, married, 2 children, G15	Female, partnered with 2 children, Carnwadric G46	Female, partnered, no children, G21	Single male, lives with mother and stepfather, Nitshill G53	Female, same sex relationship, G33	Male, single, G31
Income 2009	£12,785	£18,000	£7,475	£23,100	£13,500	£12,500	£10,000	£13,000	£16,000	£16,201
Income 2007	£8,950	£9,000	£14,564	£10,450	£11,000	£4,000	£12,500	£8,000	£11,000	£9,350
Savings: Initiated savings with bank, credit union or other financial institution during 2007–09?	—	Yes – joined Glasgow Credit Union, 2007	—	—	—	Yes – joined Castlemilk Credit Union, 2007	—	Yes – bank deposit account opened, savings have gone from 0 to £500 over loan period	—	—
Savings value (£) 2009	200	150	250	250	100	250	150	500	300	500
Savings value (£) 2007	0	0	0	0	0	0	0	0	0	0
Exit from home credit into fair-priced borrowing?	—	Yes – large debt to IC Loans at 138% now paid off	—	—	—	No	—	Partially – loan from IC Loans at 180%, £1,000 in 2007, outstanding amount reduced to £500 by 2009	—	—

continued

Table A.5 continued

Out of poverty (14 cases; 10 recorded here)

Human capital:										
Highest educational level	No quals	No quals	No quals	GCSE	No quals	GCSE	No quals	GCSE	No quals	No quals
Undertook training between 2007 and 2009?	No	Yes (City and Guilds Engineering)	Yes	No	Yes	No	Yes – part-time (City and Guilds engineering)	Yes	Yes	Yes
Loan advice from CDFI, CAB or other agency?	–	–	–	–	–	–	–	–	–	–
Labour market:										
Self or partner entered labour market, or increased work hours?		Yes – made redundant but gained new job			Yes		Yes – has begun to work as scaffolder			
Labour market earnings 2009	–	–	–	–	–	–	–	–	–	–
Health-seeking behaviour:										
Stopped smoking?	–	Never smoked	–	–	Never smoked	–	Partially: smoking halved but not stopped	–	–	–
Reduced alcohol intake?	–	Unchanged alcohol intake	–	–	No alcohol – 'My father was an alcoholic, that has determined me that I will never drink anything'	–	No – unchanged alcohol intake	–	–	–
Increased fruit and vegetable consumption?	–	No	–	–	Yes	–	Yes	–	–	–
Increased exercise?										
vigorous	–	No	–	–	Yes	–	Yes	–	–	–
moderate	–	Yes	–	–	No	–	Yes	–	–	–
walking	–	Yes	–	–	Yes	–	No	–	–	–

Community membership	–	Yes	–	Yes – member of school PTA	No	–
Community leadership	–	Yes – member of children's panel	–	Yes – youth groups	No	–
Qualitative remarks – summary	Husband recently became ill: this imposed a shock and the application to Scotcash is an attempt to recover from this. Heavily trapped by previous loans from Provident etc. Got a job which has helped raise income, but large arrears continue in spite of her best efforts.	We have no debt so more peace of mind. Also we had just moved so did the house up. Also we decided after paying off our Scotcash loan that we would not borrow again, especially from Provident; now we save up if we want anything.	–	–	–	–

Derby Loans

Table A.6 Derby Loans

	Out of poverty (9 cases; 5 listed here)					Into poverty (5 cases; 3 listed here)		
Index No.	16	56	61	62	21	55	59	60
Ethnicity	White British	White British	White British	White British	–	White British	White British	White British
Household type	Single female, 2 children, recently divorced	Female, married, 1 child	Male, married, no children?	Single female, 3? children, no labour income	Female, married, 2 children	Male, widowed, lives with children	Single female, lives alone	Single male, lives alone
Income 2009	£23,000	£16,500	£13,500	£13,000	£13,000	£5,500	£8,500	£6,500
Income 2007	£11,000	£8,000	£9,000	£11,000	£5,500	£13,000	£8,000	£6,000
Financial exclusion?	Yes	Yes	No	Yes	Yes	Yes	Yes	Yes
Savings:								
Initiated savings with bank, credit union or other financial institution during 2007–09?	Yes	Yes	No	Yes	No	No	No	No
Savings value (£) 2009	1,000	500	300	500	1,000	0	0	0
Savings value (£) 2007	0	200	0	50	0	0	0	200
Exit from home credit into fair-priced borrowing?	Yes	Never borrowed from doorstep lenders	Home credit borrower at loan outset (2007) and still – see qualitative remarks	Yes	Never used home credit	Always used Marshall Ward catalogue, indebtedness now getting worse	No home credit	Indebtedness to home credit lenders getting worse
Human capital:								
Highest educational level	NVQ	GCSE	GCSE	GCSE	GCSE (Uni drop-out)	GCSE	GCSE	None
Undertook training between 2007 and 2009?	Yes (computer course Derby University)	No	No	No	Computer course	Yes (working with disabled children)	NVQ social care	None
Loan advice from CDFI, CAB or other agency?	Yes	No	No	No	Yes	No	None	N.A.

continued

Labour market:								
Self or partner entered labour market, or increased work hours?	Yes	No	No	No	Yes	No; lost job between 2007 and 2009	N.A.	N.A.
Labour market earnings 2009	£12,000 (Capita)	£6,000	0	0	£8,000 (care assistant)	0	N.A.	N.A.
Income from benefits (2009)	0	£6,500	£13,500	£13,000	£6,000	£5,600	£5,500	£5,450
Demographic shocks	–	–	–	–	–	Lost partner last year, 'and this has led to huge financial problems'	–	–
Self-reported health and health shocks	–	–	–	–	–	Depression	–	–
Health-seeking behaviour:								
Smoking	Never	20/day (2007) down to 0 (2009)	Always	Yes (2009)		20/day (2007) up to 40/day (2009)		
Alcohol intake (units/week)	N.A.	None	15	0	N.A.	0	0	10
Fruit and vegetable consumption?	N.A.	A little	A little	0	N.A.	0	A little	A little
Exercise?								
vigorous	A little	None	Above aerage	N.A.	N.A.	None	None	None
moderate	A little	A little	Moderate	None	N.A.	None	Moderate	None
walking	Average	Above average	Average	A little	N.A.	No	A little	None
Community membership	No	Yes – religious organisation	No	Yes – drama groups	No	No	No	No
Community leadership	No	Volunteer – in Age Concern charity shop and residential home	No	No	No	Reduced – used to work 5–10 hours per week for Barnardos, but now no longer do	No	No
Deakin Coping Scale measure	N.A.	1.00	2.22	3.4	N.A.	1.08	1.53	2.75

Table A.6 continued

	Out of poverty (9 cases; 5 listed here)		Into poverty (5 cases; 3 listed here)	
Qualitative remarks – summary	I took a computer course when the children were little at FE college – the best thing I did. I then worked at Uni (at that time, Derby College of HE). I recently split up with my partner. He left me with big debts and a black-listed property which I couldn't sell. I also had £200 borrowed from Provident and £550 from Greenwoods. I now have a job (with Capita Group) and it's full-time, double income! The Provident loan is now paid back and I am now able to save. Entrepreneurial – wants to go into catering.	Although on a consumer loan, embarked on *self*-employment. Generous, extroverted and outgoing. Chronic sick (40 years old) – rose out of poverty through an increase in benefits (began to receive carer's allowance). 'I stopped saving when I started looking after my wife'. Brighthouse borrower, still. The loan made a difference – to clear debt and have a breathing space. I am still saving, but not as I used to due to increased responsibilities. I currently have two loans of £500 from Provident and Shoppacheckers. On each, I pay £63 per month in interest rate charges. I do not intend to borrow from such sources in the future. Derby Loans helped me pay off a large debt I had been struggling to pay, it's helped me out a great deal.	I started a job in April and am now saving quite a lot. The loan gave me and my son a wicked Christmas, lots of nice photos to look back on.	–	–

Yorkshire Moneyline (Sheffield)

Table A.7 Yorkshire Moneyline (Sheffield)

	Out of poverty (5 cases)				
Index No.	109	110	111	125	126
Ethnicity	White British	White British	White British	White British	White British
Household type	Single female, 1 child	Single female, 2 children	Single female, no children	Married female, 2 children	Divorced female, 0 children
Income 2009	£12,500	£12,500	£10,000	£15,000	£8,500
Income 2007	£9,000	£7,000	£7,000	£7,500	£12,500
Financial exclusion?	Yes	Yes	Yes	Yes	Yes
Savings:					
Initiated savings with bank, credit union or other financial institution during 2007–09?	Yes – with credit union	Yes – with credit union	No	No	No
Savings value (£) 2009	50	300	0	0	0
Savings value (£) 2007	0	0	0	0	250
Exit from home credit into fair-priced borrowing?	Yes – formerly a Provident borrower	No home credit	Yes – previous loans with Shoppacheck and Brighthouse (inherited from daughter), drew down savings to get rid of debts	Yes – previous loans with Shoppacheck, interest cost £20/ week, now paid off	Persisting home credit debts
Human capital:					
Highest educational level	No quals	No quals	GCSEs	NVQs	NVQs
Undertook training between 2007 and 2009?	No	No	No	No	No
Loan advice from CDFI, CAB or other agency?	None	None	Yes	Yes – from within Moneyline (HBOS scheme)	No
Labour market:					
Self or partner entered labour market, or increased work hours?	No	No	No	Yes – got part-time work as dinner lady	No – separation during year (see qualitative remarks)

continued

Table A.7 continued

	Out of poverty (5 cases)				
Labour market earnings 2009	0	0	0	–	–
Income from benefits (2009)	£10,500	£10,000	£9,000	£8,900	£8,500
Demographic shocks	–	–	–	–	Yes – split from ex-partner who had a period in prison, also mismanaged her bank account leaving her with debts
Self-reported health and health shocks	Good	Excellent	–	Good	Depression (getting worse)
Health-seeking behaviour:					
Smoking	Always smoked, but wants to give up	10/day consistently	–	Yes	Always smoked
Alcohol intake	Moderate	Low	No data	Moderate	Moderate
Fruit and vegetable consumption?	Moderate	Moderate	No data	3+ a day, increased since 2007	No data
Exercise?					
vigorous	No	No	No data	Yes	No
moderate	Yes, increasing	Yes	–	Yes	No
walking	Yes	Yes	–	Yes	No
Community membership	Yes – see qualitative remarks	Yes, playgroup member	No	Yes – football coaching	–
Community leadership	No	No	No	No	No
Deakin Coping Scale measure	1.7	2.28	2.3	0.88	0.75
Qualitative remarks – summary	It all changed for me when I went to St Wilfrid's Centre (for mentally ill and vulnerable people). It made me realise there are other people worse off than me, and the importance of being able to give as well as take.	On Moneyline: 'The service is absolutely brilliant. If you wanted a loan from elsewhere you'd be paying massive amounts whereas here you pay peanuts.'	It helped me have a bigger Christmas than usual.	With other debt companies I can manage them better, it opened my eyes to all that. They used to come to the door, I didn't realise the interest rate.	Diploma in Foundation Studies, Sheffield. Joint bank account was mismanaged by my ex-partner. I had a fire last year (May 2009), and lost everything because of having no house insurance.

Table A.8 Yorkshire Moneyline (Sheffield)

	Into poverty (7 cases)						
Index No.	103	107	108	113	117	118	122
Ethnicity	White British	White British	White British	White British	White British	White British	White British
Household type	Single female, 2 children	Single female, 1 child	Single female, 3 children	Single female, 2 children	Single male	Single female, 2 children, lives with parents	Single male
Income 2009	£11,000	£6,800	£8,000	£10,500	£6,000	£10,500	£8,500
Income 2007	£11,000	£6,000	£8,000	£10,000	£8,000	£10,000	£7,500
Financial exclusion?	Yes	Yes	Yes	Yes	Yes – continually in prison (see qualitative evidence)	Yes	Yes
Savings:							
Initiated savings with bank, credit union or other financial institution during 2007–09?	Yes, with credit	Yes, with credit union	No	No	No	Yes	Yes
Savings value (£) 2009	20	50	0	0	0	0	200 (saving up for new motorbike)
Savings value (£) 2007	0	0	0	0	–	500	100
Exit from home credit into fair-priced borrowing?	No home credit	Remains on home credit	No home credit	Still on home credit, increasing indebtedness since 2007	No home credit	Still trapped in home credit through daughter's debts as well as her own – see qualitative evidence	Still on home credit, increasing indebtedness since 2007

continued

Table A.7 continued

	Into poverty (7 cases)						
Human capital:							
Highest educational level	GCSEs	GCSEs	None	None	GCSEs	GCSEs	GCSEs
Undertook training between 2007 and 2009?	No	N.A.	NEBOSH Diploma	No	No	No	Yes
Loan advice from CDFI, CAB or other agency?	Yes	No	Yes	No	No	No	No
Labour market:							
Self or partner entered labour market, or increased work hours?	No	No	No	Yes	Yes	No	No
Labour market earnings 2009 (£/annum)	0	0	0	9,000	6,000	0	0
Income from benefits (2009)	£11,500	£6,000	N.A.	£4,500	£6,000	0	£6,600
Demographic shocks	None	None	N.A.	None	None	This client inherited debts to National Provident, value about £1,000, through her daughter. Over the survey period, her savings reduced from £500 to 0 for this reason.	None

						Serious illness
Self-reported health and health shocks	None	N.A.	None	None	None	Serious illness
Health-seeking behaviour:						
Smoking	Yes	N.A.	Yes	Yes	Yes	Yes
Alcohol intake (units/10 week)	10	N.A.	6	0	0	10
Fruit and vegetable consumption?	None	N.A.	Moderate	Moderate	None	Moderate
Exercise?						
vigorous	None	N.A.	Small	None	N.A.	None
moderate	None	N.A.	None	None	None	None
walking	N.A.	N.A.	Above average	Small	None	Above average
Community membership	No	No	No	No	No	Yes
Community leadership	No	No	No	No	No	No
Deakin Coping Scale measure	2.1	1.3	0.76	0.66	N.A.	1.6
Qualitative remarks – summary	Moneyline helped me out when I needed money to help me and my son live and be fed and watered. They help me out a lot when I'm struggling – I feel I'm beginning to acquire a reputation for dependability.	I think as you get older you realise that you do need to be cautious with money, especially when you get your own family in case any problems should arise, e.g. household maintenance. We'd been homeless for quite some time, so the loan helped extremely well, as without it I wouldn't have been able to carpet my home.	–	He'd spent most of his life in prison, so he hadn't a stable financial background.	–	–

Notes

1 Introduction

1 Here and elsewhere in the book, we define income poverty in the sense used by the Office for National Statistics: an income below 60 per cent of the median level (currently about £12.700 p.a. for a household of two adults and two children). This is not the only possible way of measuring income poverty, or poverty as a whole. We discuss concepts of poverty further below (see in particular note 17).

2 Timmins (2001: 23). The 'Beveridge Report' and its sequel (Beveridge 1944) are published as United Kingdom (1942).

3 See Linsley and Linsley(1993)

4 Timmins (2001: 21). Rowntree had previously conducted the pioneering study of poverty in York in 1899 (which defined a poverty line, or minimum consumption requirements line, of 21s. 6d. per week (about £8,500 per year at today's prices) and a further study in 1936. For further discussion of Rowntree's findings on poverty in the 1950s, see Hatton and Bailey (2000). The findings quoted here relate only to the city of York in which Rowntree had carried out his 1899 and 1936 enquiries, and to income poverty rather than other dimensions of deprivation; and they use an absolute poverty line rather than a relative poverty line (e.g. 60 per cent of median income) of the kind typically used by the Office of National Statistics. On a qualitative rather than a quantitative dimension, many people in 1950 still experienced what we would today call poverty. In that year, Britain still remained

> a country where many newly-wed couples still lived with their parents for lack of any other home; where tenement slums still existed, terraced houses could still shelter several families sharing a gas ring and a single lavatory and where families would still find they would have to wait up to 10 years for a council house.
>
> (Timmins 2001: 172)

5 Field and Piachaud (1971: 773).

6 However, for a return to the original concept of the poverty trap, see Chapter 6, where we argue that even the extension of the welfare state which we analyse in this book, community development financial institutions or CDFIs, has been responsible for perpetuating dependence on welfare benefits.

7 Between 1975–78 and 1990–93, the average rate of unemployment in Britain rose from 5 per cent to 9 per cent, peaking at 12 per cent in 1986.

8 For several case studies of 'postcode discrimination' and responses to it, see Chapter 4. For the geographical dimension of financial and social exclusion, see Leyshon and Thrift (1997a, 1997b); maps of financial exclusion in our survey areas are presented in Chapter 2, Figures 3a–c. In 1999, Kempson and Whyley (1999: 4) estimated the proportion of households financially excluded at 7 per cent, of which three-quarters were headed by single people rather than by a couple.

9 Including, and especially, the ultimate shock of death. In Elizabeth Gaskell's *Mary Barton*, based on Manchester in the 1830s, it is the thought that her mother 'was in a club, so that money was provided for the burial' which alone gives her a little comfort after her mother's sudden death in childbirth (Gaskell 1848/2006: 21). Funeral clubs of this kind were an important root out of which credit unions grew; and they continue to provide an important focus for the savings of poor people globally, see Collins *et al.* (2010).

10 On this theme, inspiration can be taken from the experience of many developing countries in which people much poorer than any in industrialised countries nonetheless manage to save regular small amounts if institutions – often collecting deposits on the doorstep – are available to collect savings, see Collins *et al.* (2010).

11 The record case, to our knowledge, is 'a loan shark who preyed on the sick and poor' in Birmingham,

> charging interest rates of up to 8000 per cent. [He] earned more than £800,000 from lending money at extortionate rates to vulnerable people on benefits, then threatening them when they could not pay up. He used the proceeds to buy a Porsche and a BMW and was buying a £500,000 house when he was arrested.
>
> (quoted in Frith 2005: 3)

12 See especially Brooker and Whyley (2005) but also Collard and Kempson (2005: 2).

13 Collard and Kempson (2005: 2) quote a range of 100–400 per cent; our own survey research for inner-city Glasgow, Sheffield and Derby, see Chapter 3, suggests an average of around 190 per cent with outliers well above 300 per cent.

14 The leading home credit, or doorstep-lending, company: see pp. 4–5.

15 Lawrence (2002).

16 Lawrence (2002).

17 In Britain and other industrialised countries, income poverty is typically measured, as in Figure 1.1, in relation to the national average, as the proportion of households who fall below mean or median income. Income poverty has not always been measured in this way, and it is not measured in this way in many developing countries. Seebohm Rowntree, in his surveys between 1899 and 1950, measured it in relation to the cost of a minimum consumption basket (see note 4 above); and especially in developing countries, income poverty is often measured in terms of a minimum consumption basket (such as $1 a day or $2 day; see World Bank (2000: 17, box 1.2), and subsequent *World Development Reports* from the World Bank). For a time-series picture of poverty levels variously defined at 70 per cent, 60 per cent, 50 per cent and 30 per cent of median income, the latter defined as 'severe' poverty (Institute of Fiscal Studies, see Brewer *et al.* 2010: figures 4.1 and 4.4).

All this relates to income poverty, which is the dimension of poverty on which we principally focus in this book. Others are also important, beginning with the other four 'giants' considered by Beveridge – 'squalor, ignorance, disease and idleness [unemployment]'; but in addition, the quality of social relationships is also very important, and is the theme of our Chapter 5. Many analysts measure all of these dimensions of poverty in terms of their impact on assets (such as housing quality or car ownership) as well as in terms of their impact on income flows. Finally, it is important to stress that some aspects of poverty and deprivation are not easy to measure, and relate to subjective feelings – such as *vulnerability*, or fear that income or assets will be pushed below an acceptable level in the future – thus, it is possible to feel vulnerable without being currently poor. These differing concepts of poverty and deprivation are important for policy. In Chapters 4 and 6 we argue that CDFIs can protect clients against vulnerability by seeking to build up their holdings of savings and other assets – an approach known as *asset-based welfare policy*.

18 As we recall from the previous note, this comparison is not quite legitimate, because Rowntree was using an absolute poverty definition rather than the relative poverty definition used by the Office of National Statistics.

19 The share of government in total CDFI funding in 2003 was 25 per cent (17 per cent Phoenix Fund and 8 per cent local authorities and regional development authorities), the rest being contributed by banks (21 per cent), individual depositors and investors (12 per cent), charitable trusts and foundations (7 per cent) and 'other sources' (37 per cent). By 2009 the share of all branches of government had fallen to 19 per cent, with banks now contributing 35 per cent and other sources including charitable trusts contributing 46 per cent. Source: Community Development Finance Association, *Annual Reports*, 2003 and 2009.

20 Just under 80 per cent of the estimated thirty million microfinance clients around the world are women (MIXmarket index, 2009 (http://www.themix.org)).

21 Both ASPIRE, Belfast and Wellpark Enterprise Centre, Glasgow, attempted around the millennium to enforce financial discipline within their CDFIs by requiring their clients to join solidarity groups, no member of which could receive credit if any group member was in default on their loan repayments, on the Grameen Bank model. The ASPIRE experiment was quickly abandoned following the failure of attempts to work out a suitable model for the provision of mentoring support to clients (personal communication, Niamh Goggin, March 2002). The Wellpark model was incorporated into the Scottish Microfinance Programme, financed by the Scottish government, but was abandoned as financially prohibitive in 2004. WEETU, which operates 'a holistic package of support which includes confidence building and business skills training', and thus is one of the most 'welfare-oriented' CDFIs in Britain within the spectrum from welfare-oriented to business-oriented, alone continues to provide group loans in Britain (see for example WEETU 2005). However, at the time of writing there are reports that the Grameen Bank itself is proposing to open a subsidiary in Glasgow, in partnership with Glasgow Caledonian University (see Chapter 7).

22 Some of the five Labour Party promises of 1997, although not undertaking to reduce poverty directly, were nonetheless attacks on the 'five giants', in particular the commitments to cut school class sizes and hospital waiting lists.

23 In 2000 the Blair government formally adopted the aim of reducing poverty (in the sense of the proportion of those below 60 per cent of median income) below 10 per cent. (At the time it was about 17 per cent of the population, see Figure 1.1, and it is now rising once again.)

24 France, Germany, Scandinavia and Spain were slower than the UK to provide incentives to accelerate the transition from welfare into work during the 1990s, and as a consequence their unemployment levels remained at a higher level than those prevailing in the UK; see Blanchard and Wolfers (2000)

25 Tony Blair, Foreword to United Kingdom, Social Exclusion Unit (2000: 5).

26 The application of this way of thinking rapidly produced a change in the culture of CDFIs. One of the authors first became aware of this by attending both the first conference of the CDFA in April 2000, on the campus of the University of East Anglia, Norwich, and the second, in the four-star Marriott Hotel in Birmingham the following year. In the first conference, the participants were mainly NGOs with a good few academics and civil servants, and in the lobby of the conference participants were invited to buy baskets, scented candles and cardigans made by clients of WEETU, one of the organisers of the conference. Just one year later, in the marble-panelled environment of the Marriott Hotel, much had changed. Gone were the denim jeans, the sandals, the scented candles, and many of the NGOs, and their place was taken by bankers with smart suits and mobile phones, then a novelty. Nor was it just the appearance of the conference which had changed, but its agenda. In 2000 a majority of the presentations at the conference were about ultimate objectives, such as poverty, dimensions of well-

being, gender and community cohesion; by 2001, they were about means, notably means of levering additional money into the CDFI sector.

27 For the US case see Ellen and O'Regan (2008: 845), who show that in the mid 1990s people in lower-income urban neighbourhoods in the US began to experience sustained increases in well-being for the first time since the beginning of the 1980s. In both countries, the incumbent governments (Clinton in the US and Blair in the UK) ascribed the credit to the 'active labour-market' policies being pursued in Britain and America by contrast with the more controlled policies prevailing in Europe (Blanchard and Wolfers 2000).

28 Interview with author, Easterhouse, Glasgow, 17 November 2009.

29 The publicity for personal-lending CDFIs invariably contains a comparison between the annual percentage interest rates charged by CDFIs (typically, see below, between 10 and 25 per cent) and the rates charged by doorstep lenders (often, see discussion above, well above 100 per cent).

30 The Treasury (United Kingdom, HM Treasury 2004: 44) emphasised that 'face-to-face money advice [by contrast, for example, with contact by telephone, radio or computer] is a popular medium of delivery for those on low incomes, who are most likely to be experiencing financial exclusion'. But an even bigger problem is to bring advice to those who not seek it or perceive the need for it.

31 Scotcash has seconded two senior advisers to its staff from the Glasgow Citizens' Advice Bureau, one a banker and one an accountant. Many applicants for Scotcash loans are turned down but offered advice with the intention that it will both save them money immediately (for example, advisees who are being harassed for repayment by a doorstep lender can often get a stay of execution as the result of a phone call from the Scotcash adviser to the doorstep lender; Scotcash calculates that £1.3 million has been saved for clients by this route) and also create knowledge and behaviours that make them more eligible for loans. These strategies are extensively discussed in Chapters 4 through 6.

32 From MIX index (http://www.themix.org).

2 Scope and method

1 South Wales is represented by East Lancs Moneyline, which holds a contract with local housing associations to provide community financial services for the whole of the principality.

2 John Kay's book on *Foundations of Corporate Success* (1993) uses the term *architecture* to denote both the decision-making structures of corporations and the networks of relationships which connect them to the outside world. In Chapters 3 and 4, we also use the word in this dual sense, but with modifications in order to move from the environment of private corporations to the environment of voluntary non-profit organisations.

3 The questionnaire is reproduced on the project website (http://www.poverty.group. sheffield.ac.uk).

4 This is the desirable approach in principle, and certainly better than simply observing *change over time* – as is done by publications such as *Inside Out* (Community Development Finance Association 2005, 2008, 2009) in making estimates of the number of jobs created by CDFIs – since change over time could be produced by all kinds of factors other than the CDFI. This is particularly relevant to the period 2007–09, which was a period of widespread recession across the UK.

3 Financial performance of CDFIs

1 On Grameen, BRAC and BRI, see the profiles of those institutions presented by Hulme and Mosley (1996: vol. 1, ch. 2). Grameen now has more than eight million clients.

2 As illustrated by Table 3.1, few CDFIs in industrialised countries, and none in Britain, have been able to go beyond 5,000 active clients, or one-thousandth of the number reached by BRI (Indonesia) and Grameen Bank and BRAC (Bangladesh).

3 Typically, they are non-governmental organisations, not regulated by the Financial Services Authority and therefore not licensed by that authority to accept deposits.

4 These support agencies are multiple and include regulatory agencies and other branches of central government; housing bureaux and other agencies of local government, commercial banks and credit unions, CABs, business links, advice centres and community organisations. The role of these agencies is discussed in Chapter 7.

5 For a guide to the extensive literature on business objectives see, of course, Kay (1993) but also Cyert and March (1964) and Lipczynski *et al.* (2009).

6 An Industrial and Provident Society is a financial institution with a charitable purpose, licensed to receive donations but not to take savings deposits from the public.

7 The atmosphere of the CDFA conference has, since 2001, endeavoured to get as far away as possible from academic debate, and has consisted of a blend of game show and holiday camp. Sessions held in recent years have included a karaoke contest, a one-minute debating contest between the European Microfinance Network and the CDFA and, in both 2006 and 2010, a 'fantasy World Cup', in which contestants were invited to build their dream CDFI from eleven possible components including 'strong marketing activities' 'door to door collection of payments' and 'membership of the CDFA'. No session in 2010 discussed the big problem facing the sector, namely its extreme financial fragility, although there were plenty of covert tête-à-têtes on this theme between conference members. In general there is a preoccupation with the liabilities rather than the assets side of the portfolio, and in particular with levering in money from the private sector. The titles of some of the 2010 sessions well illustrate the prevailing ethos: 'Regeneration through Innovation', 'Business Planning for CDFIs', 'Spotting the Risks Lurking in the Undergrowth' and, most symbolically of the lot, 'Show me the Money!'

8 Against the argument being put here, it should be emphasised that doorstep lenders such as National Provident, which are commercially more successful than any CDFI, also tend to eschew commercial publicity and to rely on word-of-mouth.

9 The combination of linkages (ii) and (iii) is known as *bridging social capital.* We say a great deal more about bridging social capital in Chapter 5.

10 Sometimes quite large medium: in 2000 a loan was made to Barrhead Sanitaryware, a maker of bathroom equipment with 60 employees, on the grounds that it was a 'social enterprise' by virtue of being located in a depressed area.

11 Now known as the Enterprise Guarantee Scheme (EGS).

12 'It costs us ten times the time for ten 10K loans as one 10K loan and we earn the same money back. Loans under £5K need subsidy in terms of time and aftercare and we can't get this subsidy'. Private communication, Eunice Lancaster, 10 August 2010.

13 Interview, Will Nisbet, Glasgow North Regeneration Agency, 26 November 2009.

14 Interview, Andrew Baker, chief executive, Derby Loans, 29 July 2007.

15 Derby Loans has been notably proactive in its advertising strategies – in 2005 the chief executive, Andrew Baker, spent over £2,000 placing advertisements on Arriva buses within the city. Few other CDFIs publicise themselves on this scale.

16 One of us (Mosley) must declare an interest. He has been on the board of Moneyline Yorkshire since 2004, and since 2008 on the joint board of Sheffield Credit Union, Moneyline Yorkshire and FISY.

17 At one stage in 2007–08 there was discussion of closer union between the Doncaster, Barnsley, Sheffield and Rotherham credit unions, not directly involving Moneyline. These discussions were abandoned in 2008.

18 The DWP, in allocating its latest tranche of Growth Fund grants, did express a wish for them to be disbursed through credit unions, rather than through CDFIs, in the case where a suitable credit union was available to act as a lending vehicle; but this was

only an expression of opinion, and it would have been quite possible for Growth Fund money to be disbursed, through a CDFI as for example at ELM and Derby Loans. I am most grateful for discussions on this point with Fiona Greaves, who, however, takes no responsibility for the views expressed here.

19 On this issue, see letter from United Kingdom, HM Treasury (2005).

20 The CDFA's survey *Inside Out* (Community Development Finance Association 2008) reports 17,000 cumulative loans to fifty-four institutions, giving an average per institution of 314 loans per institution.

21 Private communication, Leah Cameron, managing director, Scotcash, 14 September 2009.

22 Interview, Anne Mills and Robert Mackay, debt advisers, Scotcash office, 15 October 2009.

23 It is an external asset also. The Scotcash debt advisers are now working part-time for the Debt Advisory Service, a Scottish government service which negotiates debt 'workouts' for heavily indebted people.

24 Private communication, Leah Cameron, managing director, Scotcash, 14 September 2009.

25 A specialisation in back-office services, in particular IT, was also to become a key element in the financial architecture of the Birmingham personal-lending CDFI, Street UK (see Chapter 5).

26 Many of these contracts, however, were simply a consolidation of interim arrangements awarded on the basis of established working relationships with local authority housing departments and other sponsors, which the DWP Growth Fund formalised. The success of the working relationships, rather than of the formal bidding process with the DWP, were thus the key element in the CDFI's architecture. Interview, ELM, 26 April 2010.

27 For the difficulties encountered by two pioneer CDFI business lenders, ASPIRE and Street UK, both of them financed by the Esmee Fairbairn Foundation, see New Economics Foundation (2004), Forster *et al.* (2006) and United Kingdom, BIS (2010: 152–153).

28 Note that a charge or imputation needs to be made for credit even if the finance is obtained on grant terms, reflecting the opportunity cost or amount the money would have earned if not invested in the CDFI.

29 If in equation (3.1) $i = 5$ per cent and $a = 20$ per cent, which are five-year averages 2005–09 for the organisations listed in Table 1.2, then even if we set capitalisation costs (K) at zero, $r^* > 50$ per cent unless $p < 12$ per cent. In fact, from the same table, the average rate of default for business-lending CDFIs is 14 per cent and for consumer-lending organisations is 24 per cent, suggesting that to break even, business-lending CDFIs would need to raise their interest rates to over 50 per cent and consumer-lending CDFIs to nearly double that – well in excess of their present charges. (This is not nearly as outrageous as it sounds: doorstep lenders, as discussed in Chapter 1, are currently charging nearly 200 per cent, thus CDFIs could remain competitive with them even if charging break-even rates.)

30 If the data in Figure 3.2 are pooled they yield the following relationship between average costs and the size of the CDFI loanbook:

Costs as % of portfolio = 0837**–0.63** size of loan book (£000), obs=25, adjusted $r^2 = 0.36$ (7.17)   (3.76)

(** denotes significance at the 1 per cent level, and * denotes significance at the 5 per cent level). OLS estimation; pooled data for ELM, Scotcash, Moneyline Yorkshire and Derby Loans, 2001–09; sources as in Figure 3.2.

The implication is that with each £000 by which the value of the loan book increases, the average cost of lending falls by two-thirds of 1 per cent: thus a £50,000 increase in the loan book, on this reasoning, brings down the cost of lending (as a percentage of the portfolio) by an average of about 35 per cent.

31 However, in the ethnic-minority Black Business in Birmingham (3Bs), which terminated its CDFI operations in 2008, the default rate was more than 85 per cent, and the break-even interest rate was astronomical, far too high to even represent on Figure 3.2. 3Bs and the reasons for its demise are discussed in Chapter 5.

32 For discussion of these in the context of developing countries see Hulme and Mosley (1996: Ch. 4).

33 Except, at present for WEETU, Norwich (see Chapter 1). Plans have been announced for the Grameen Foundation to begin lending in Sighthill, north-central Glasgow, in 2011, but the organisational model by which this will be done has not been announced. Further discussion of the Grameen initiative is in Chapter 7.

34 Interview, Anita Wright, ELM, Blackburn, 26 April 2010.

35 To our knowledge this is not practised by any UK CDFI institution. It is practised by some of the regional development banks of Indonesia (see Hulme and Mosley 1996: Vol. 2, Ch. 10)

36 *Operational sustainability* is the ability of a microfinance institution to cover its current operating costs (administrative costs plus default) with income from its loan portfolio, and *financial sustainability* is its ability to cover all its costs including the payment of interest on all the capital it has to raise. See United Kingdom, BIS (2010: 152–153).

37 Some US CDFIs, however, are now approaching viability: see case studies in New Economics Foundation (2008: Ch. 3).

4 CDFI clients: impacts on individuals

1 Recent research on the history of microfinance has laid emphasis on the asset dimension of poverty, and action to counteract it by developing institutions for the mobilisation of savings, as a determinant of effective initiatives against financial exclusion in Ireland, Italy, Germany and other places in the nineteenth century (Hollis and Sweetman 1998: 1875). Recent literature of both rural and urban poverty in developing countries (for example Moser 1998, World Bank 2000 and many of the essays in Addison *et al.* 2009) has tended to prioritise the asset dimension of poverty, since access to assets determines both future income possibilities and power-relationships between individuals.

2 'Impact' is measured as change in the business's net income (2007–09) as a percentage of the change in the control group's net income over the same period.

3 Tolstoy (1873/1954: 13).

4 Often the inverse of this measure is used – the ratio of assets to debt, or risk efficacy. However what is important in not the size of debt, as how easy it is to service.

5 Interview, Ian Maxfield, managing director, Collstream Ltd, Pride Park, Derby, 16 April 2010.

6 Interview, Patricia Watson, managing director, Able2Wear, Kirkintilloch, 17 November 2009.

7 Interview, Managing Director, client DSL17, 27 April 2007.

8 DSL client, name anonymised – in liquidation. Report prepared by Stirling Toner and Co. for the First Statutory Meeting of Creditors, Crowne Plaza Hotel, Glasgow, 26 August 2008.

9 Question 74 on the questionnaire asked: 'For what purpose do you intend to use your current loan?' The three most popular responses (clients were allowed to multi-code) were: holidays (28 per cent of respondents), Christmas (25 per cent) and home repairs (21 per cent). Other popular responses were decorating (17 per cent of cases) and paying off debts (13 per cent of cases).

10 In the Joseph Rowntree Foundation sample, four out of five of all exits from poverty by individuals (over the period 1991–99) were triggered by income events and only one in five by demographic events (Kemp *et al.* 2004: 13, drawing on Jenkins and

Rigg 2001). However, for pensioner households, increases in non-benefit, non-labour income (including private pensions and savings and demographic events such as improved health) were the most important cause of exits from poverty and more important than either income from work or from benefits (Kemp *et al.* 2004: 19).

11 This is vividly illustrated by Dearden *et al.* 2010.

12 The phrase used by Dearden *et al.*, who work with a small intensive sample of fifty-seven interviewees, is 'There was little evidence of widespread saving among [low-income] participants in this research.' The importance of saving as a buffer against shocks is stressed by Kempson and Finney (2009), but in their (larger) sample 'fewer than one in five (18 per cent) of all lower-income families saved any money formally'. Our own study, which covers both informal and formal types of saving, finds that the proportion of respondents with formal savings is higher, at around 30 per cent.

13 Our concept of a *'rational' coping strategy* is adapted from the Deakin coping scale devised by Moore (2003). For the measure used here, see Table 4.4.

14 In our judgment this is because where Scotcash clients engage in community activities this increases, often quite deliberately, their transparency to the outside world; people who would be willing to default on a loan or to give up their habit of saving if they could keep that behaviour private will be much more reluctant (ashamed) to do so if that behaviour can be observed by others. Examples of this 'goldfish bowl effect', as we call it, are given in Chapter 5.

15 Recall the finding (Note 9 above) that the main reason given by personal-loan clients for borrowing is to provide consumption treats, including Christmas presents.

16 The shock simulated in our questionnaire was 'Suppose that you suddenly had a financial emergency and needed £1,000 in a hurry, what would you do?' The question was first asked as an unprompted question, and then the nineteen possible responses listed in the Appendix were reviewed, and the respondent's answer was coded on a scale from 1 (for the answer 'never') to 5 (for the answer 'always').

17 The split between the 'improver' and decliner' part of the questionnaire was much more dramatic in relation to prompts which could be seen as a invitation to analysis (such as 'identify the source of the problem', which was rejected by most of the decliners and accepted by most of the improvers) than in relation to prompts which asked whether the respondent would seek help, which tended to be accepted by both parties.

In our survey questionnaire, we asked 'If you had a financial emergency and needed £1,000 in a hurry, what do you think you would do?' and after leaving time for an unprompted response, coded the respondent's subsequent replies according to the nineteen suggested responses on the Deakin scale, which appear as question 29 of that questionnaire. We define the 'rationality' of the respondent's response pattern as the ratio of the 'rational' responses (2) 'analyse my reaction to the problem', (5) 'get more information about the situation', (6) 'identify the source of the problem' and (7) 'take control of the situation', to the 'emotional' responses (12) 'feel miserable about the situation', (13) 'keep my fingers crossed that it will go away', (14) 'pray for it to go away' and (15) 'hope for a solution to appear'. Values of this ratio above 1 suggest a predominance of rational over emotional coping mechanisms in the respondent, and values below 1 imply the reverse.

18 Interview, Rob McKay and Anne Mills, Scotcash office, 20 October 2009.

19 In question 22 of the survey questionnaire we consider ten types of social organisation (social club, Women's Institute, community group (choir or orchestra, tenants' organisation, community centre, neighbourhood watch), church, mosque or religious organisation, political party, school parent–teacher organisation, support group or welfare organisation, hobby or interest group, pensioners' club or lunch club, other groups).

20 Some 2,816 savings accounts are now held by ELM clients (860 in Blackburn, 670 in Bury, 419 in St Helens, 316 in Burnley, 231 in Grimsby and some 320 in other centres), a figure close to the estimated 3,250 active loan accounts quoted in Chapter 1.

21 In Yorkshire Moneyline the credit union is physically located within the same premises as Moneyline.

22 Interview, Sharon Willis, loan officer, East Lancs Moneyline, Blackburn, 26 April 2010.

23 Interview, Sharon Willis, loan officer, East Lancs Moneyline, Blackburn, 26 April 2010.

24 'I would never be able to afford things without a loan; I would probably find another company to use instead. [The availability of Scotcash finance] means I don't need to save as I can just borrow instead.' Respondent Scotcash121 (single parent, twenty-eight, G40, September 2009).

25 See Case Study 3.

26 Most of our interviewees responded to the idea of saving as an idea so far beyond their current possibilities as to demonstrate that the interviewer must lack imagination even to suggest the idea. A majority of our sample in Derby Loans and Sheffield Moneyline, when offered savings advice, rejected it, sometimes indignantly. Two relevant testimonies, both low-income savers and 'positive outliers' on Figure 4.5, are relevant. First, Sheffield 110 (single parent, one child, income transition £9,000 to £12,500, i.e. severe poverty to just below the poverty line; in last two months has married, partner's income is a major factor in income increase): 'Moneyline helped me when I was struggling, I feel that I'm beginning to require a reputation for dependability. It's much harder to save since I had children, but I want to do it to have driving lessons ... which will make it easier for me to get work.' Second, Derby62 (income transition £12,000 to £13,500, from just below to just above poverty line).

> The loan helped me pay off a large debt I had been struggling to pay, it gave me a breathing space. I have paid off (two doorstep loans from Provident and Shoppacheckers, on which I used to pay £63 per month in interest charges). I am still saving, but not as I used to due to increased responsibilities.

The relevant words here are 'breathing space' and 'reputation'. CDFI finance gave these clients, both of them 'instrumental savers' in the phrase of Kempson and Finney (2009) in orientation, the respite to be able to plan and build a reputation rather than simply fend off demands.

27 See Taylor (2010). It has been announced that the scheme will be piloted in the Sighthill area of north-central Glasgow by Grameen Bank staff and will be evaluated, with a focus on its health impact, by research staff of Glasgow Caledonian University. However, at the time of writing no lending operations have begun.

28 We also estimated, for our business borrower sample, equation (4.2a) in which physical capital and the risk ratio (outstanding debt as a proportion of capital assets) is added to the regression, using the same 3SLS model as in Table 4.9. For the income equation, this gave the result:

$$\text{change in income} = \frac{3,757.8}{(0.84)} - \frac{0.52}{(0.72)} \text{ borrowing from CDFI} + \frac{1.68^*}{(1.63)} \text{ change in}$$

$$\text{saving} + \frac{0.034^{**}}{1.98} \text{ value of client's capital assets} \frac{-1,123}{(0.25)} \text{ risk ratio} \frac{-4,643.0}{(0.44)} \text{ health}$$

$$\text{shocks} + \frac{1,364.9}{(0.33)} \text{ demographic shocks, } n = 43, r^2 = 0.51.$$

This could not be called an exciting result and is constrained by the small number of business clients, but at least confirms the significance and complementarity of savings and physical capital in the business client's portfolio.

29 In other cases benefits served so as not to buffer but to amplify a shock, as in the cases of many increases in labour income within our sample, which were amplified by

increases in working tax credit which exceeded the new employment-related reductions in, for example, income support and job seekers' allowance. For a general discussion of the relationship between CDFIs and benefits see Chapter 6.
30 See the anecdotes keyed by Notes 21, 22 and 23 above.
31 Sheffield Moneyline provides a 'skeleton' advice service, see p. 32.

5 CDFI clients: community-level impacts

1 The definition of social capital is much disputed. Our own is as follows:

> Social capital consists of networks of social relationships which raise productivity, typically by increasing trust and mutual cooperation *within* the network ('bonding' social capital) or *between* the network and other persons, organisations or networks which are in a position to increase its effectiveness ('bridging' social capital).

2 An exception needs to be made for the case of WEETU (Women's Education and Employment Training Union) in Norwich, which does explicitly build solidarity networks between women (Chapter 1).
3 Commentaries on the New Deal for Communities include Lawless *et al.* (2009) (and other references in *Urban Studies*). There is some evidence from Fuller and Mellor's study of Newcastle (2008) of causation in the reverse direction, namely of a failed attempt to comply with the requirements of the New Deal for Communities causing a community finance initiative, Financial Inclusion Newcastle, to fall apart.
4 The Regeneration Agencies are a Glasgow innovation, consisting of a one-stop shop for small business services in social inclusion partnership (i.e. low income) areas of the city, financed by public, private and voluntary-sector capital. We discuss them further in Chapter 7.
5 Larger firms have access to the Business Gateway (the Scottish equivalent of Business Link); but Business Gateway services, unlike Regeneration Agency services, have to be paid for after an initial consultation, and as with Business Link, there is much controversy about their effectiveness. See Chapter 4.
6 Interview with Karen Barr and Kim Duff, Barmulloch, Glasgow, 5 August 2009.
7 Washing football shirts is an important part of the enterprise's bulk business. The Catholic/Protestant divide has influence on business and social divisions in Glasgow, albeit a pale echo of those to be found in Northern Ireland. Soapy Bubbles lost a contract to wash the shirts of a football team from their Protestant coach when some shirts from a traditionally Catholic club were found in their washing machine.
8 Respondents 6, 10: survey questionnaire, questions 84–85 (business questionnaire).
9 The protest meetings are described by Jacobs *et al.* (2007: 624–626), who relate that 'in the neighbouring high-rise estate of Sighthill, [the residents'] own independent survey was pivotal in the decision to upgrade rather than demolish'. In Red Road, the residents failed to get a questionnaire survey organised, and as a consequence, 'the ability of the campaign to generate robust alternative facts about Red Road [was] compromised' (ibid.: 625). Within the local housing association, Lawson and Kearns' comparative analysis of GHA local housing organisations notes that

> the 'confident' [local housing] committees were predominantly in areas described as stable and desirable with good-quality housing, [whereas] the 'responsive' and 'powerless' committees tended to be situated in areas experiencing major regeneration, many [of which] had multi-storey flats in poor condition as the predominant housing type, combined with poor-quality environments.
>
> (Lawson and Kearns 2010: 1,459)

10 This is not pure altruism but partly reciprocity. Partly as a result of their initiatives, Karen and Kim find that they are never short of help when they need someone to look after the launderette while they are away, or as short-term voluntary labour to deal with a peak in labour demand.

11 Karen would also like to start a 'pound shop' cum fast food outlet, but competition is expected from the existing Chinese takeaway.

12 Glasgow East (formerly Glasgow Shettleston) is the constituency with the lowest per capita income level in Britain (source: *Labour Market Trends*, published by the Department of Employment (now the DWP)). On other indices, notably health, it also scores lower than any other Scottish or English neighbourhood (source: *Scottish Index of Multiple Deprivation* 2009, Scottish Government, Office of National Statistics (http://www.scotland.gov.uk/simd2006)).

13 Interview, John Gibson, 5 February 2008.

14 Interview, John Gibson, 16 November 2009.

15 See Brook (2005: 113–123), for a development of the argument that an investment in the trustworthiness of one's employees enables labour markets to work better.

16 Interview, Alan Porteous, Glasgow East Regeneration Agency, 18 November 2009.

17 *Heidelberg News* (customer magazine of Heidelberg Press), issue 251 (2004: 58).

18 Interview, Jim MacVicar, 5 February 2008.

19 Interview with Rob Mackay and Anne Mills, Scotcash office, 20 October 2009.

20 The applicability to the ethnic-minority issue will be clear.

21 Interview, Don Parker, Osmaston Information Centre, 20 August 2007.

22 In Scotcash, those who helped, within the list above, to establish 'bonding' social networks are not predominantly among the upper part of the Scotcash income distribution, all except 115 were poor (on the £12,500 p.a. definition), and twenty-five were extremely poor.

23 In Table 5.1, for those clients for which we have data, we find that it is only those with both high (>1) rational *and* social scores who establish networks.

24 For an extension of this argument to developing countries (and in particular SEWA of north-western India, a microfinance organisation which is also a registered trade union, and which has a proud history of assisting microfinance clients to resist intimidation by the police and by local government officials threatening to destroy their street-trading activities) see the World Bank's *World Development Report 2000* on poverty.

25 Trust indicator (column 2 of Table 5.2) is the average score of respondents to question 70, 'Do you have family or friends whom you would trust in the event of a serious personal problem?' on the scale:

   1 No, there is no one I would trust.
   2 There are a very few people I would trust.
   3 There are several people I would trust.

   Note that this is a measure of the respondent's *overall* level of trust – not of her trust in members of specific affinity groups such as those discussed in Table 5.1.

26 Those actions include, in our view, actions which can reduce individuals' vulnerability and thereby make them more trusting (see Lenton and Mosley 2010).

27 According to the Rowntree Foundation's study of *Communities in Recession* (Tunstall and Fenton 2009: 8) the hardest hit regions (those with jobseekers' allowance claim rates in the top 10 per cent in England) were 'in the West Midlands, North West, and Yorkshire and Humberside'.

28 Interview, Steve Walker, chief executive, ART, 22 July 2010.

29 The 3Bs brochure, 'Looking to the future: a new chapter in supporting business growth and sustainability' (2006: 4).

30 Interview, Owen McKenzie, 3Bs, 6 September 2010.

31 Interview, Owen McKenzie, 3Bs, 6 September 2010.

32 Most board members were from the public or voluntary sector and in several cases from the City Council. Only one was from a private-sector organisation (Jaguar Cars).

33 Interview, CDFI manager, 22 July 2010.

34 Interview, CDFI manager, 1 November 2010; interview, client B19, 2 October 2010.

35 A majority of Halal clients, however, have chosen not to take up the Sharia option on the grounds that it is not remunerative. See Case Study 8.

36 Interview, Nas Hussain, general manager, Birmingham Enterprise, 2 September 2010.

37 Interview, Mohammad Nazir, general manager, Halal Fund, 1 November 2010.

38 Interview, client B17, 2 September 2010.

39 Interview, client B17, 2 September 2010.

40 Halal Fund gave the example of a project to sell water-treatment plants in Pakistan and other Gulf states which was hampered by the defective English of the chief engineer participating in the project. Halal helped translate several documents vital to the securing of export contracts as a part of its service.

41 No data on Prince's Trust are presented in Table 5.4.

42 In the West Midlands in 2006, 21 per cent of Pakistanis, 22 per cent of Bangladeshis and 17 per cent of Chinese are self-employed, in relation to 12.2 per cent in the population as a whole. For other ethnic groups, the proportions are reversed – in particular, for black Africans and Caribbeans the proportions that are self-employed are 4.4 per cent and 3.7 per cent, by contrast with 8.5 per cent and 6.0 per cent for England as a whole (Advantage West Midlands 2008: Table 7; Fraser 2006: 24, Figure 2-2-1).

43 Both the Halal Fund and ART have since 2009 participated in a project to provide Saturday-morning education, with an emphasis on language education, which answers this need.

44 At the St Andrews Centre, 'every Saturday morning when there is a wedding people are doing business in the carpark'. Interview, Owen McKenzie, 3Bs, 18 June 2010.

45 Interview, client B18, Custard Factory, Birmingham, 2 October 2010.

46 A particular merit of the New Jerusalem Church has been its ability to extend its congregation and its network of business support activities, outside the Afro-Caribbean community which provides its leadership and core membership.

47 For an illustration from Manchester in the 1840s, see Chapter 1, Note 8. For a comparative review for developing countries see Geertz (1962).

48 For a case in which CDFI clients directly sought to contribute to the resolution of disputes and tensions within a neighbourhood see p. 100 (client Scotcash76). The relationship between crime, economic well-being and institutional contributions to it such as CDFIs is notably contested: see Pyle and Deadman (1994) who argue that crime rates have since the 1950s had a tendency to increase faster during recessions, and Tunstall and Fenton (2009) for discussion in the context of the current recession. It is however notable that in Bridgeton (G40), the high-deprivation region of Glasgow with the smallest CDFI presence, and its Sheffield counterpart Burngreave (S4), crime rates are among the highest in their respective cities (see Figures 3.1 and 3.5) (Townsend 2009).

49 Interview, Muhammad Yunus, 10 May 1986. Those taking the same position in relation to mentoring within UK microfinance include Street UK, Birmingham (interview, Martin Hockly, 15 November 2010).

50 This already happens with the entrepreneurs' groups established by the Glasgow East Regeneration Agency; see Case Study 5.

51 We are aware that Scotcash has gradually expanded its publicity effort, publicising itself not only in local newspapers and the GHA newspaper and housing offices but also in libraries and leisure centres and indeed in this area is an exemplar for other CDFIs. The idea here proposed is to make that publicity effort more person-to-person and to add a mutual support element to it.

6 Fiscal impacts

1 In Britain the central government contribution, between 1999 and 2003, came from

the Department of Trade and Industry's Phoenix Fund (Chapter 1), and from 2004 until 2011 from the Department of Work and Pensions' Social Exclusion Fund (popularly known as the Growth Fund).

2 Several CDFIs, (e.g. Scotcash and ELM) were able to persuade local authority housing departments to lend to this group, on the grounds that it reduce the rent arrears suffered by the housing departments.

3 There have been several assessments of WTC, notably Brewer *et al.* (2003b) which suggest that the WTC had more impact on the labour supply of single parents than of any other category of the low paid.

4 The fear of income loss consequent on losing benefits has been described as 'the biggest single obstacle to aspiring small businesses making the transition from unemployment into work' by the chief ethnic-minorities consultant to Birmingham Enterprise (interview with the author, 2 September 2010).

5 Much of the inspiration for this approach comes from the same Frank Field who co-invented the idea of a benefits poverty trap in 1972 (Chapter 1; see Field and Piachaud 1972). Field, the Labour MP for Birkenhead since 1979, has been appointed a special adviser on poverty to the (Conservative/Liberal Democrat) coalition government. Especially for the educational element in this approach, see interview by Rachel Sylvester and Alice Thomson with Frank Field, in the *Guardian*, 11 September 2010.

6 So far, this objective has only achieved by the Blackburn branch of ELM, and most UK CDFIs are well short of viability (Table 1.2).

7 Often CDFI loan advisers, with help from CAB and such-like advice agencies, help CDFI clients increase their benefit entitlements in this way, and thereby strengthen the pinning-in effect. A poster in the Scotcash office proudly explains how in 2009 clients were enabled to claim an additional £1.3 million in benefits to which they were entitled through the good offices of Scotcash's money advisers. A number of personal-lending clients expressed the view that taking a loan made it more important for them to protect their entitlement to welfare benefits.

8 The greater the beneficiary's risk aversion, the less her mobility (physical and in relation to number of children) and the less her access to gateways which might enable her to find work (such as social contacts or skills), the greater the likelihood that we will see this pinning-in effect.

9 See Chapter 3, Case Study 3. The Savings Gateway idea, now cancelled by the new coalition government, is an illustration of this kind of asset-based policy.

10 For a detailed study of the role of CDFIs in exit strategies from poverty (including some clients, such as Derby55, whose exit strategy was based almost entirely on increasing use of welfare benefits) see Chapter 4.

11 We have, however, observed, in the lower part of Table 6.5, a tendency among the consumer-lending group for the escapers from poverty to make less use of disability-related and housing-related benefits than those who remained poor.

12 In terms of the diagram of Figure 6.1, this is tantamount to saying that the right-hand end of the sloping line in that diagram, represents the rewards to work for low-income people in relation to the rewards to non-work.

13 United Kingdom, DWP (2010: para. 18, p. 5). Note that no time dimension is attached to this prediction.

7 Where next?

1 The DWP growth fund was extended for six months in May 2011 and is currently expected to terminate in November 2011 (see page 12 above).

2 Average default rates for UK CDFIs (proportion of portfolio written off) in 2009 were for just under 13 per cent, and for personal loans 28 per cent (Table 1.2). One dimension of Scotcash's achievement is that it was operating in this riskier personal loans

sector. In our view, sponsors, including and especially the DWP, can add to these incentives by withdrawing support organisations with high default rates, or at least making the maintenance of support contingent on reductions in the default rate.

3 See Hermes and Lensink (2007). The situation may change soon. The Grameen Foundation has recently signed a contract with Glasgow Caledonian University to supply microfinance in Glasgow, starting in 2011 with a pilot project in the Sighthill area just north of the city centre. The technology to be used by the project has not been determined, but it is expected that the approach will draw on experience with the Grameen Foundation's experience in New York City, which uses a group-lending model.

4 Other approaches are applied at the individual level outside Britain. In particular several developing countries, following the lead of the Indonesian regional development banks, connect pay to performance, and pay full salary only to those loan officers whose loan collection record is good. This has not yet, to our knowledge, been done in Britain, but the approach is related to the 'efficiency wage' approach applied by Scotcash, which is to pay loan officers more than the going rate as an incentive to stay with the firm and raise productivity.

5 Amongst UK CDFIs, this approach is also favoured by ELM and Street UK; see Chapter 3.

6 That is, the ELM system as it operates in the Blackburn head office.

7 Note that in Derby there is now no credit union, so partnership with a credit union (*à la* Scotcash/Yorkshire Moneyline) is not an option.

8 The numbers and proportions of personal-lending clients who received money advice from any source (CDFI, CAB, National Debtline or other debt support unit) were as follows:

- Sheffield Moneyline 17 (10 per cent of borrower sample); Derby Loans 16 (21 per cent of borrower sample); Scotcash 34 (37 per cent of borrower sample).
- All business-loan clients received mentoring or advice from one source or another and so are not listed here.
- Scotcash, therefore, has the highest density of personal-loan clients receiving advice, and also the fastest rate of exit from poverty among the personal-loan group (Table 4.6). Receipt of money advice is correlated with increases in personal savings, which helps to explain the greater likelihood of exit from poverty (Table 4.9).
- For an American study also showing that receipt of financial advice is positively associated with ability to save, see Bernheim *et al.* (1996).

9 Interview with East Lancs Moneyline staff 26 April 2010; interview with Yorkshire (Sheffield) Moneyline staff 29 November 2010.

10 In Sheffield, this debt advice is provided through a Debt Support Unit, funded by the Sheffield City Council in association with the national Financial Inclusion Fund, which acts as a referral agency for the three Citizens' Advice Bureaux already established in the city and also provides training services for debt advisers.

11 The London CDFI Fair Finance has also established an in-house money advice unit, in association with the Royal Bank of Scotland (United Kingdom, HM Treasury 2007: 33; New Philanthropy Capital 2009: 35).

12 The Scotcash money advisers are recruited from the Glasgow office of CAB. More detail of their approach is provided in Case Study 1. A particularly relevant aspect of their approach is that they are willing to negotiate directly with doorstep lenders in order to get clients' debts rescheduled, and to give clients information about how to increase their entitlements to benefits; they then build on the confidence achieved through such coups in order to persuade clients to consider actions that might previously have been considered infeasible, such as making savings deposits or searching for work.. Note also that in Scotcash money advice is used as a consolation prize for those judged to be unbankable – which enables the institution to screen clients rigorously and thereby maintain the quality of its portfolio (see Chapter 3).

13 See data at Note 8 above.

14 Sheffield Moneyline does operate a skeleton money advice service in partnership with HBOS, but it cannot be compared with the Scotcash money advice service because it is an experimental service, providing advice only to groups such as offenders and students with special needs, which can only reach a very few clients, not a money advice service available to all. It was hoped to install a Debt Support Unit money advice worker (see Note 9 above) in 2010 within the Moneyline/Sheffield Credit Union office, but this idea was aborted late in the year as a consequence of government expenditure cuts.

15 For a good survey of the US microfinance scene, see New Economics Foundation (2008: 41–53).

16 In the summer of 2008, before the credit crunch became really severe, the New Economics Foundation's survey of opinion amongst business CDFIs recorded that 'the most vivid disappointment among respondents is the lack of engagement of the banks' (New Economics Foundation 2008: 37).

17 Partnerships are of course possible with other forms of financial institution, such as credit unions; however, to state the obvious, these do not have the financial strength of commercial banks, and indeed in bad times this weakness may prove a liability and not an asset to the partner CDFI. The partnership between Sheffield Moneyline and the Sheffield Credit Union (of which one of the authors is a director: this view is a strictly personal one) provides a good illustration of this point. Since 2006, all DWP Growth Fund financing and all staff resources have been allocated to the Credit Union rather than to Moneyline, with the objective of protecting the dominant organisation: none of the partnership's eight loan officers/credit controllers have responsibility purely for Moneyline operations and, as a consequence, Moneyline has had a tendency to be forced to the back of the queue for key services (such as recovery of overdue loans).

18 For the cases of the Sri Lanka Federation of Thrift and Cooperative Societies and the Bank Rakyat Indonesia unit desa scheme, both of which were radically redesigned in the 1980s in the wake of the global financial crisis of that time, see Hulme and Mosley (1996: Ch. 9).

Bibliography

Adam, S., C. Emmerson, C. Frayne and A. Goodman (2006) 'Early quantitative evidence on the impact of the Pathways to Work programme', Institute of Fiscal Studies (IFS) occasional paper, online, available at: http://www.ifs.org.uk/publications/3639.

Addison, T., D. Hulme and R. Kanbur (2009) *Poverty dynamics: interdisciplinary perspectives*, Oxford: Oxford University Press.

Advantage West Midlands (2008) *The West Midlands: a demographic profile*, Birmingham: Advantage West Midlands Regional Development Authority. Online, available at: http://www.advantagewm.co.uk.

Advantage West Midlands (2010) 'Banking on "break out": ethnic minority businesses and their access to finance', MEECOE (Minority Ethnic Enterprise Centre of Expertise) Briefing, Issue 5.

Affleck, A. and M. Mellor (2006) 'Community development finance: a neo-market solution to social exclusion?' *Journal of Social Policy*, 35, 303–319.

Anderson, D. and Farida Khambata (1985) 'Financing small-scale industry and agriculture in developing countries: the merits and limitations of "commercial" policies', *Economic Development and Cultural Change*, 33, 373–395.

Andranovich, G., A. Modarres and G. Riposa (2005) 'Community banking and economic development: lessons from Los Angeles', *Community Development Journal*, 42, 194–205.

Armendariz de Aghion, B. and J. Morduch (2005) *The economics of microfinance*, Cambridge, MA: MIT Press.

Askonas, P. and A. Stewart (2000) *Social inclusion: possibilities and tensions*, London: Palgrave Macmillan.

Balmer, N., P. Pleasence, A. Buck and H.C. Walker (2005) 'Worried sick: the experience of debt problems and their relationship with health, illness and disability', *Social Policy and Society*, 5, 39–51.

Bernheim, B., D.M. Garrett and D. Maki (1997) 'Education and saving; the long-term effects of high school financial curriculum mandates', *Journal of Public Economics*, 80, 435–466.

Besley, T., S. Coate and G. Loury (1993) 'The economics of rotating savings and credit associations', *American Economic Review*, 83, 792–810.

Biosca, O., P. Lenton and P. Mosley (2010) 'Microfinance non-financial services: a key for poverty alleviation?' unpublished paper, University of Sheffield.

Blanchard, Olivier and Justin Wolfers (2000) 'The role of shocks and institutions in the rise of European unemployment', *Economic Journal*, 116, 1–33.

Brewer, Mike (2010) 'Cuts to welfare spending, take 2', Powerpoints. London: Institute for Fiscal Studies, online, available at: http://www.ifs.org/budgets/sr2010/welfare.pdf.

Brewer, Mike, Tom Clark and Matthew Wakefield (2002) 'Five years of social security reform in the UK', IFS Working Paper 02/12, online, available at: http://www.ifs. org/wps/wp0212.pdf.

Brewer, M., T. Clark and A. Goodman (2003a) 'Child poverty in Britain and the United States', *Economic Journal*, 113, 240–257.

Brewer, M., D. Phillips and L. Sibieta (2010) 'What has happened to "severe poverty" under Labour?', Election Briefing Note No. 3, online, available at: http://www.ifs.org. uk.

Brewer, M., A. Duncan, A. Shephard and M.J. Suarez (2003b) 'Did Working Families' Tax Credit work? Analysing the impact of in-work support on labour supply and programme participation', IFS Working Paper, online, available at: http://www.ifs.org/publications/2546.

Brewer, M., A. Goodman, A. Muriel and L. Sibieta (2007) 'Poverty and inequality in Britain: 2007', IFS Briefing Note 73, London: Institute for Fiscal Studies.

Brewer, M., A. Muriel, D. Phillips and L. Sibieta (2009) 'Poverty and inequality in Britain: 2009', IFS Commentary C109, London: Institute for Fiscal Studies.

Brook, Keith (2005) 'Labour market participation: the influence of social capital', *Labour Market Trends*, Office for National Statistics, March, 113–123.

Brooker, Steve and Claire Whyley (2005) *Locked in, kept out: the extent of competition within the UK home credit industry*, York: Joseph Rowntree Foundation.

Burchardt, T. (2005) 'Selective inclusion: asylum seekers and other marginalised groups', in J. Hills and K. Stewart (eds) *A more equal society? New Labour, poverty, inequality and exclusion*, Bristol: Policy Press.

Burchardt, T., J. Le Grand and D. Piachaud (2002) 'Degrees of exclusion: developing a dynamic, multidimensional measure', in J. Hills, J. Le Grand and D. Piachaud (eds) *Understanding social exclusion*, Oxford: Oxford University Press.

Burgess, S. and C. Propper (2002) 'The dynamics of poverty in Britain', in J. Hills, J. Le Grand and D. Piachaud (eds) *Understanding social exclusion*, Oxford: Oxford University Press.

Cameron, A. (2005) 'Geographies of welfare and exclusion: initial report', *Progress in Human Geography*, 29, 194–203.

Cangiano, Alessio (2010) *Mapping of race and poverty in Birmingham*, Oxford: Barrow Cadbury Trust and ESRC Centre on Migration, Policy and Society.

Canova, Luigina, Anna Maria Manganelli Rattazzi and Paul Webley (2005) 'The hierarchical structure of saving motives', *Journal of Economic Psychology*, 26, 21–34.

Cantillon, S. and B. Nolan (2001) 'Poverty within households: measuring gender differences using nonmonetary indicators', *Feminist Economics*, 7, 5–23.

Carr, James H. and Zhong Yi Tong (2002) *Replicating microfinance in the United States*, Baltimore, MD: Johns Hopkins University Press.

Carver, Charles S., Michael F. Scheier and Jagdish Weintraub (1989) 'Assessing coping strategies: a theoretically based approach', *Journal of Personality and Social Psychology*, 56, 267–283.

Casley, D. and D.A. Lury (1983) *Evaluation methods for rural development projects and programmes*, Washington, DC: World Bank.

Community Development Finance Association (CDFA) (2003, 2005, 2008, 2009) *Inside out: the state of community development finance*. Since 2008, online, available at: http://www.cdfa.org.uk.

Collard, S. and E. Kempson (2005) *Affordable credit: the way forward*, York: Joseph Rowntree Foundation.

Collins, D., J. Morduch, S. Rutherford and O. Ruthven (2010) *Portfolios of the poor: how the world's poor live on $2 a day*, Princeton, NJ: Princeton University Press.

Crawford, Claire, Lorraine Dearden, Alice Mesnard, Jonathan Shaw, Barbara Sianesi and Peter Unwin (2008) 'Ethnic parity in JobCentre Plus programmes and mainstream services: main report', Institute for Fiscal Sudies working paper, online, available at: http://www.ifs.org.uk/publications/4203.

Crook, J. and S. Hochguertel (2006) 'Household debt and credit constraints: comparative microevidence from four OECD countries', unpublished paper presented at Seminar on Debt and Personal Finance, Reading University, 9 June.

Cull, R., A. Demirguc-Kunt and J. Morduch (2007) 'Financial performance and outreach: a global analysis of leading microbanks', *Economic Journal*, 117, 107–134.

Cyert, R. and J.G. March (1964) *A behavioural theory of the firm*, Englewood Cliffs, NJ: Prentice-Hall.

Deakins, D., J.G. Hussain and M. Ram (1995) 'Ethnic entrepreneurs and commercial banks: untapped potential', *Regional Studies*, 29, 95–100.

Dearden, C., J. Goode, G. Whitfield and L. Cox (2010) *Credit and debt in low-income families*, York: Joseph Rowntree Foundation, online, available at: http://www.jrf.org.uk.

Dercon, S. (2006) 'Vulnerability: a survey of the literature', Chapter in World Bank, Proceedings of the World Bank Annual Conference on Development Economics – Europe (ABCDE-Europe), Amsterdam, 2005. Published as special issue of *World Bank Economic Review*.

Dickens, R. and D. Ellwood (2001) 'Welfare to work: poverty in Britain and the US', *New Economy*, 8, 98–103

Dickens, R. and D. Ellwood (2003) 'Child poverty in Britain and the United States', *Economic Journal*, 113, 219–240.

Dollar, D. and A. Kraay (2002) 'Growth is good for the poor', *Journal of Economic Growth*, 7, 195–225.

Ellen, Ingrid Gould and Katherine O'Regan (2008) 'Reversal of fortunes? Lower-income urban neighbourhoods in the US in the 1990s', *Urban Studies*, 45, 845–869.

Emmerson, Carl and Matthew Wakefield (2001) 'The Saving Gateway and the Child Trust Fund: is asset-based welfare "well fair"?' IFS Commentary 85, London: Institute for Fiscal Studies.

Evans, M. and L. Williams (2009) *A generation of change, a lifetime of difference? Social policy in Britain since 1979*, Bristol: Policy Press. Summary of findings at Joseph Rowntree Foundation, online, available at: http://www.jrf.org.uk.

Experian plc (2009) 'Mapping the demand for, and supply of, third sector affordable credit: research for the third sector credit Working Group of the Financial Inclusion Taskforce', online, available at: http://www.hm-treasury.gov.uk/d/research.pdf.

Field, Frank and David Piachaud (1971) article in *New Statesman*, 3 December 1971, pp. 772–773.

Finney, A. and Elaine Kempson (2009) 'Regression analysis of the unbanked, using the 2006–07 Family Resources Survey', unpublished paper, Personal Finance Research Centre, University of Bristol.

Forrest, Ray and Ade Kearns (2001) 'Social cohesion, social capital and the neighbourhood', *Urban Studies*, 38, 2125–2143.

Forster, Sarah, Ellen Lederman, John Mayshak and Tanya Mercer (2006) *Aspire: microloans for business: operational and funding lessons for the future of microfinance in the UK*, London: Esmee Fairbairn Foundation.

Fraser S. (2006) 'Finance for small and medium-sized enterprises: comparisons of ethnic minority and white-owned business: a report on the 2005 Survey of SME finances ethnic minority booster survey', University of Warwick: Warwick Business School.

Frith, Maxine (2005) 'Loan shark who charged 8000% interest rate jailed for four years', *Independent*, 27 July, 3.

Fuller, Duncan and Mary Mellor (2008) 'Banking for the poor: addressing the needs of financially excluded communities in Newcastle upon Tyne', *Urban Studies*, 45, 1505–1524.

Gaile, L. and J. Foster (1996) *Review of methodological approaches to the study of the impact of microenterprise credit programs*, Washington, DC: Management Systems International.

Gaskell, Elizabeth (1848/2006) *Mary Barton* (originally published by Edward Chapman, 1848), Oxford: World's Classics, 2006.

Geertz, C. (1962) 'The rotating savings and credit association: a "middle rung" in development', *Economic Development and Cultural Change*, 10, 241–263.

Gilbert, E. (2005) 'Common cents: situating money in time and place', *Economy and Society*, 34, 357–388.

Gordon, D., R. Levitas, C. Pantazis, D. Patsios, S. Payne, P. Townsend, L. Adelman, K. Ashworth, S. Middleton, J. Bradshaw and J. Willliams (2000) *Poverty and social exclusion in Britain*, York: Joseph Rowntree Foundation.

Goth, Peter, Donal McKillop and Charles Ferguson (2006) *Building better credit unions*, Bristol: Policy Press, and York: Joseph Rowntree Foundation.

Gough, J., A. Eisenschitz and A. McCulloch (2006) *Spaces of social exclusion*, London: Routledge.

Guo, B., J. Huang, M. Sherraden and L. Zou (2008) 'Dual incentives and dual asset building: policy implications of the Hutubi rural social security loan programme in China', *Journal of Social Policy*, 37, 453–470.

Haggard, S. and R. Kaufman (2008) *Development, democracy and welfare states: Latin America, East Asia and Eastern Europe*, Princeton, NJ: Princeton University Press.

Hamid, S.A., J. Roberts and P. Mosley (2011) 'Evaluating the health effects of micro health insurance placement: evidence from Bangladesh', *World Development*, forthcoming.

Hatton, T. and R. Bailey (2000) 'Seebohm Rowntree and the postwar poverty puzzle', *Economic History Review*, 53, 517–543.

Henderson, D. and F. Khambata (1985) 'Financing small scale industry and agriculture in developing countries: the merits and limitations of "commercial" policies', *Economic Development and Cultural Change*, 33, 349–373.

Hermes, N. (2007) 'The empirics of microfinance: what do we know?' *Economic Journal*, 117, 1–11.

Hermes, N. and R. Lensink (2007) 'Introduction: the economics of microfinance: what do we know?' *Economic Journal*, 117, 1–11.

Hills, J. and K. Stewart (2005a) *A more equal society? New Labour, poverty, inequality and exclusion*, Bristol: Policy Press.

Hills, J. and K. Stewart (2005b) 'A tide turned but mountains yet to climb?' in J. Hills and K. Stewart (eds) *A more equal society? New Labour, poverty, inequality and exclusion*, Bristol: Policy Press.

Hills, J., J. Le Grand and D. Piachaud (eds) (2002) *Understanding social exclusion*, Oxford: Oxford University Press.

Hirschman, A.O. (1963) *Development projects observed*, Cambridge, MA: Harvard University Press.

Hollis, A. and A. Sweetman (1998) 'Microcredit: what can we learn from the past?' *World Development*, 28, 79–98.

Hudson, J., G.-J. Huang and S. Kuhner (2008) 'Between ideas, institutions and interests: analysing third way welfare reform programmes in Germany and the United Kingdom', *Journal of Social Policy*, 37, 207–230.

Hulme, D. (2000) 'Impact assessment methodologies for microfinance: theory, experience and better practice', *World Development*, 28, 79–98.

Hulme, D. and P. Mosley (1996) *Finance against poverty*, 2 vols, London: Routledge.

Hussain, J. and P. Mosley (2010) 'CDFIs and the determinants of microbusiness survival among UK ethnic minorities', unpublished working paper, Birmingham City University and University of Sheffield.

Jacobs, Jane, Stephen Cairns and Ignaz Strebel (2007) ' "A tall storey…, but, a fact just the same": the Red Road high-rise as a black box', *Urban Studies*, 44, 609–629.

Jayo, Barbara, Anabel Gonzalez and Casey Conzett (2010) *Overview of the microcredit sector in the European Union*, Paris: European Microfinance Network, and Madrid: Fundacion Nantik Lum.

Jenkins, S.P. (2000) 'Modelling household income dynamics', *Journal of Population Economics*, 13, 529–567.

Jenkins, S.P. and J.A. Rigg (2001) 'The dynamics of poverty in Britain', Department for Work and Pensions Research Report 157, Leeds: Corporate Document Services.

Johnston, R., J. Forrest and M. Poulsen (2002) 'Are there ethnic enclaves/ghettos in English cities?' *Urban Studies*, 39, 591–618.

Jones, M. and R. Lowe (2002) *From Beveridge to Blair: the first fifty years of Britain's welfare state, 1948–1998*, Manchester: Manchester University Press.

Joseph Rowntree Foundation (2006) 'Monitoring poverty and social exclusion in the UK', Joseph Rowntree Foundation, December, online, available at: http://www.jrf.org.uk/KNOWLEDGE/findings/socialpolicy/1979.asp.

Joseph Rowntree Foundation (2009) 'Communities in recession: the impact on deprived neighbourhoods', unpublished report, online, available at: http://www.jrf.org.uk/media-centre/communities-in-recession.

Joyce, Robert, Alastair Muriel, David Phillips and Luke Sibieta (2010) 'Poverty and inequality in UK 2010', Commentary C116, London: Institute for Fiscal Studies.

Karlan, D. and M. Valdivia (2010) 'Teaching entrepreneurship: impact of business training on microfinance clients and institutions', unpublished working paper, Yale University.

Karlsson, Niklas, P. Dellgran, B. Klingander and T. Gaerling (2004) 'Household consumption: influences of aspiration level, social comparison and money management', *Journal of Economic Psychology*, 25, 753–769.

Kay, John (1993) *Foundations of corporate success*, Oxford: Oxford University Press.

Kearns, Ade, Kenneth Gibb and Daniel Mackay (2000) 'Area deprivation in Scotland: a new assessment', *Urban Studies*, 37, 1535–1559.

Kemp, Peter, Jonathan Bradshaw, Paul Dornan, Naomi Finch and Emese Mayhew (2004) *Routes out of poverty: a research review*, York: Joseph Rowntree Foundation, online, available at: http://www.jrf.org.uk.

Kempson, Elaine (1996) 'Life on a low income: an overview of research on budgeting, debt and credit among the financially excluded', unpublished paper, University of Bristol.

Kempson, E. and A. Finney (2009) 'Saving in lower-income households: a review of the evidence', Personal Finance Research Centre, University of Bristol, online, available at: http://www.hm-treasury.gov.uk/d/fitf_saving_in_lower_income_households_fullreport.pdf.

Kempson, E. and C. Whyley (1999) *Kept out or opted out? Understanding and combating financial exclusion*, Bristol: Policy Press.

Kempson, E., Anna Ellison, Claire Whyley and P. Jones (2009) 'Is a not-for-profit home credit business feasible?' report to Joseph Rowntree Foundation, online, available at: http://www.jrf.org.uk.

Khandker, Shahidur (1998) *Fighting poverty with microcredit: experience in Bangladesh*, Washington, DC: Oxford University Press for World Bank.

King, S. and A. Tomkins (eds) (2003) *The poor in England 1770–1850: an economy of makeshifts*, Manchester: Manchester University Press.

Knack, S. and P. Keefer (1997) 'Is there an economic return to social capital?' *Quarterly Journal of Economics*, 112, 1251–1288.

Kolodinsky, J., C. Stewart and A. Bullard (2006) 'Measuring economic and social impacts of membership in a community development financial institution', *Journal of Family and Economic Issues*, 27, 27–47.

Lawless, P., M. Foden, I. Wilson and C. Beatty (2009) 'Understanding area-based regeneration: the New Deal for Communities programme in England', *Urban Studies*, 47, 257–275.

Lawrence, Felicity (2002) 'The agony of living with debt on your doorstep', *Guardian*, 2 November, online, available at: http://guardian.co.uk/print/0,,4558540-103690,00.html.

Lawson, L. and A. Kearns (2010) '"Community empowerment" in the context of the Glasgow housing stock transfer', *Urban Studies*, 47, 1459–1478.

Lea, S., P. Webley and C. Walker (1995) 'Psychological factors in consumer debt: money management, economic socialisation and credit use', *Journal of Economic Psychology*, 16, 681–701.

Lenton, P. and P. Mosley (2008) 'Debt and health', unpublished working paper, University of Sheffield.

Lenton, P. and P. Mosley (2010) 'Financial exit routes from the poverty trap', unpublished paper, University of Sheffield.

Lepianka, D., W. van Oorschot and J. Gelissen (2009) 'Popular explanations of poverty: a critical discussion of empirical research', *Journal of Social Policy*, 38, 421–438.

Levitas, R. (2006) 'The concept and measurement of social exclusion', in C. Pantazis, D. Gordon and R. Levitas (eds) *Poverty and social exclusion in Britain: the millennium survey*, Bristol: Policy Press.

Leyshon, A. and N. Thrift (1997a) 'Geographies of financial exclusion: financial abandonment in Britain and the United States', in A. Leyshon and N. Thrift (eds) *Money/ space: geographies of monetary transformation*, London: Routledge.

Leyshon, A. and N. Thrift (1997b) *Money/space: geographies of monetary transformation*, London: Routledge.

Leyshon, A., P. Signoretta, D. Knights, C. Alferoff and D. Burton (2006) 'Walking with moneylenders: the ecology of the UK home-collected credit industry', *Urban Studies*, 43, 161–186.

Linsley, C.A. and C.L. Linsley (1993) 'Booth, Rowntree and Llewelyn Smith: a reassessment of interwar poverty', *Economic History Review*, 46, 88–104.

Lipczynski, J., J. Wilson and J. Goddard (2009) *Industrial organisation*, 3rd edn, Harlow: Pearson Education.

Lister, R. (2001) 'Doing good by stealth: the politics of poverty and inequality under New Labour', *New Economy*, 8, 65–70.

Lister, R. (2004) *Poverty*, Cambridge: Polity Press (Key Concepts Series).

Lloyd, E. (2006) 'Children, poverty and social exclusion', in C. Pantazis, D. Gordon and R. Levitas (eds) *Poverty and social exclusion in Britain: the millennium survey*, Bristol: Policy Press.

Lloyd-Sherlock, P. (2008) '"Doing a bit more for the poor?" Social assistance in Latin America', *Journal of Social Policy*, 37, 621–639.

Lupton, R. and A. Power (2002) 'Social exclusion and neighbourhoods', in J. Hills, J. Le Grand and D. Piachaud (eds) *Understanding social exclusion*, Oxford: Oxford University Press.

McEwan, Cheryl, Jane Pollard and Nick Henry (2005) 'The "global" in the city economy: multicultural economic development in Birmingham', *International Journal of Urban and Regional Research*, 29, 916–933.

McKay, S. and S. Collard (2006) 'Debt and financial exclusion', in C. Pantazis, D. Gordon and R. Levitas (eds) *Poverty and social exclusion in Britain: the millennium survey*, Bristol: Policy Press.

McKernan, S.-M. (2002) 'The impact of microcredit programs on self-employment profits: do noncredit program aspects matter?' *Review of Economics and Statistics*, 84, 93–115.

McKnight, A. (2002) 'Low-paid work: drip-feeding the poor', in J. Hills, J. Le Grand and D. Piachaud (eds) *Understanding social exclusion*, Oxford: Oxford University Press.

Magadi, M. (2010) 'Risk factors for severe child poverty in the UK', *Journal of Social Policy*, 39, 297–316.

Magee, W., E. Fong and R. Wilkes (2007) 'Neighbourhood ethnic concentration and discrimination', *Journal of Social Policy*, 37, 37–61.

Maltby, Jo (2009) 'Savings mobilisation by and for nineteenth-century women', unpublished paper, Business School, University of York.

Milbourne, Linda (2009) 'Remodelling the third sector: advancing collaboration or competition in community-based initiatives?' *Journal of Social Policy*, 38, 277–297.

Mitchell, James, Kostas Mouratidis and Martin Weale, 2009? 'Poverty and debt', unpublished report, National Institute of Economic and Social Research, online, available at: http://www.niesr.ac.uk/pubs/dps/dp261.pdf. Summary from Joseph Rowntree Foundation, online, available at: http://www.jrf.org.uk.

Moore, Kathleen (2003) 'The Deakin coping scale: strategies for the management of demands', *Australian Journal of Advanced Nursing*, 21, 13–19.

Mooya, Manya and C. Cloete (2007) 'Informal urban property markets and poverty alleviation: a conceptual framework', *Urban Studies*, 44, 147–165.

Morduch, Jonathan (1999) 'The role of subsidies in microfinance: evidence from the Grameen Bank', *Journal of Development Economics*, 60, 229–248.

Morduch, Jonathon and Haley, Barbara (2002) *Analysis of the Effects of Microfinance on Poverty Reduction*, New York University: NYU Wagner Working Paper 104.

Moser, Caroline (1998) 'The asset vulnerability framework: reassessing urban poverty reduction strategies', *World Development*, 26, 1–19.

Mosley, Paul and Elizabeth Dowler (2003) *Poverty and social inclusion in north and south*, London: Routledge.

Mosley, Paul and Lucy Steel (2004) 'Microfinance, the labour market and social inclusion', *Social Policy and Administration*, 38, 721–743.

New Economics Foundation (2008) 'Reconsidering UK community development finance', New Economics Foundation, 3 Jonathan Street, London SE11 5NH, online, available at: http://www.neweconomics.org.

New Philanthropy Capital (2009) 'Short changed: financial exclusion: a guide for donors and funders', New Philanthropy Capital, 3 Downstream, London SE1 9BG, online, available at: http://www.philanthropycapital.org.uk.

Oc, T. and S. Tiesdell (1999) 'Supporting ethnic minority business: a review of business support for ethnic minorities in city challenge areas', *Urban Studies*, 36, 1723–1745.

Orwell, George (1936) *The road to Wigan Pier*, Left Book Club edition, London: Gollancz.

Palmer, H. and P. Conaty (2002) *Profiting from poverty: why debt is big business in Britain*, London: New Economics Foundation.

Pantazis, C. (2001) 'Introduction', in C. Pantazis and D. Gordon (eds) *Tackling inequalities: where are we now and what can be done?* Bristol: Policy Press.

Pantazis, C. and E. Ruspini (2006) 'Gender, poverty and social exclusion', in C. Pantazis, D. Gordon and R. Levitas (eds) *Poverty and social exclusion in Britain: the millennium survey*, Bristol: Policy Press.

Pantazis, C., D. Gordon and R. Levitas (eds) (2006) *Poverty and social exclusion in Britain: the millennium survey*, Bristol: Policy Press.

Parekh, A., T. MacInnes and P. Kenway (2010) *Monitoring poverty and social exclusion 2010*, York: Joseph Rowntree Foundation, online, available at: http://www.jrf.org.uk.

Piachaud, D. and H. Sutherland (2002) 'Child Poverty', in J. Hills, J. Le Grand and D. Piachaud (eds) *Understanding social exclusion*, Oxford: Oxford University Press.

Pleasance, P., A. Buck, N.J. Balmer and K. Williams (2007) 'A helping hand: the impact of debt advice centres on people's lives', University of Warwick Legal Services Research Centre.

Pollard, J. (2004) 'From industrial district to "urban village"? Manufacturing, money and consumption in Birmingham's Jewellery Quarter', *Urban Studies*, 41, 173–193.

Pretes, M. (2002) 'Microequity and microfinance', *World Development*, 30, 1341–1355.

Putnam, R. (1993) *Making democracy work: civic traditions in modern Italy*, Princeton, NJ: Princeton University Press.

Pyle, D.J. and D.F. Deadman (1994) 'Crime and the business cycle in post-war Britain', *British Journal of Criminology*, 34, 339–357.

Rae, A. (2009) 'Isolated entities or integrated neighbourhoods? An alternative view of the measurement of deprivation', *Urban Studies*, 46, 1859–1878.

Reserve Bank of India (1954) *All-India Rural Credit Survey.* Vol. 1, *The Survey Report* (part 1, 'Rural families'; part 2, 'Credit agencies'), Vol. 2, *The General Report*, Vol. 3, *The Technical Report*, Bombay: Reserve Bank of India.

Robinson, D. (2005) 'The search for community cohesion: key themes and dominant concepts of the public policy agenda', *Urban Studies*, 42, 1411–1427.

Rogaly, B., T. Fisher and E. Mayo (1999) *Poverty, social exclusion and microfinance in Britain*, Oxford: Oxfam, in association with the New Economics Foundation.

Rowlingson, K. (2006) ' "Living poor to die rich"? or "spending the kids' inheritance"? Attitudes to assets and inheritance in later life', *Journal of Social Policy*, 35, 175–192.

Salway, Sarah, Lucinda Platt, Punita Chowbey, Kaveri Harriss and Elizabeth Bayliss (2007) *Long-term ill-health, poverty and ethnicity*, Bristol: Policy Press. Summary online, available at: http://www.jrf.org.uk.

Scotcash (2008) 'Annual report and financial accounts: 4 October 2006 – 31 March 2008', Glasgow: Scotcash, 55 Bell St., Glasgow G1.

Sefton, T. and H. Sutherland (2005) 'Inequality and poverty under new Labour', in J. Hills and K. Stewart (eds) *A more equal society? New Labour, poverty, inequality and exclusion*, Bristol: Policy Press.

Sen, A.K. (1982) *Poverty and famines*, Oxford: Oxford University Press

Sen, A.K. and J. Dreze (1989) *Hunger and public action*, Oxford: Clarendon Press.

Shaw, Eleanor, Sara Carter, Wing Lam and Fiona Wilson (2005) 'Social capital and accessing finance: the relevance of networks', unpublished paper to 28th National Conference of Institute for Small Business and Entrepreneurship.

Shelter (2007) 'Shelter homepage', online, available at: http://england.shelter.org.uk/home/index.cfm.

Sherraden, Michael (1991) *Assets and the poor: a new American welfare policy*, New York: M.E. Sharpe.

Sinclair, Vaughn G. and Kenneth A. Wallston (2004) 'The development and psychometric evaluation of the brief resilient coping scale', *Assessment*, 11, 94–101.

Smallbone, D., M. Ram, D. Deakins and R. Alcock (2003) 'Access to finance by ethnic minority small businesses in the UK', *International Small Business Journal*, 21, 291–314.

Smith, S.S. (2000) 'Mobilising social resources: race, ethnic and gender differences in social capital and persisting wage inequalities', *Sociological Quarterly*, 41, 509–537.

Steel, C. Lucy (1999) 'Bridging gaps: a study of microfinance', MPhil thesis, University of Glasgow.

Stone, Brice and Rosalinda Vazquez Maury (2006) 'Indicators of personal financial debt using a multi-disciplinary behavioural model', *Journal of Economic Psychology*, 27, 543–556.

Taylor, Jerome (2010) 'Coming here, the man who lends cash to people banks won't touch', *Independent*, 10 June.

Taylor, Marilyn, Mandy Wilson, Derrick Purdue and Pete Wilde (2007a) *Changing neighbourhoods: lessons from the Joseph Rowntree Foundation (JRF) Neighbourhood Programme*, Bristol: Policy Press.

Taylor, Marilyn, Mandy Wilson, Derrick Purdue and Pete Wilde (2007b) *Changing neighbourhoods: the impact of 'light touch' support in 20 communities*, York: Joseph Rowntree Foundation, online, available at: http://www.jrf.org.uk.

Taylor-Gooby, P. ed. (2001) *Risk, trust and welfare*, Basingstoke: Palgrave Macmillan.

Taylor-Gooby, P., T. Larsen and J. Kananen (2004) 'Market means and welfare ends: the UK welfare state experiment', *Journal of Social Policy*, 33, 573–592.

Timmins, N. (2001) *The five giants: a biography of the welfare state*, London: Harper-Collins.

Tolstoy, L. (1873/1954) *Anna Karenina*, Harmondsworth: Penguin.

Tomlinson, M., R. Walker and G. Williams (2008) 'Measuring poverty in Britain as a multi-dimensional concept, 1991 to 2003', *Journal of Social Policy*, 37, 597–620.

Townsend, Mark (2009) 'Gun culture sweeps through Sheffield estates as postcode gangs do battle', *Observer*, 19 July.

Tunstall, R. with J. Fenton (2009) *Communities in recession: the impact on deprived neighbourhoods*, York: Joseph Rowntree Foundation, online, available at: http://www.jrf.org.uk.

United Kingdom (1942) 'Social insurance and allied services', report by Sir William Beveridge, Cmnd 6404, London: Her Majesty's Stationery Office.

United Kingdom, Department for Business, Innovation and Skills (BIS) (2010) 'Evaluation of community development finance institutions', London: BIS, Cabinet Office (Office of the Third Sector) and GHK Consulting Ltd.

United Kingdom, Department of Trade and Industry, Small Business Service (2004) 'An evaluation of Phoenix Fund support for community development finance institutions:

final report for the small business service', GHK Consulting, 526 Fulham Road, London SW6 5NR.

United Kingdom, Department for Work and Pensions (DWP) (2010) 'Universal credit: welfare that works', White Paper (Cm 7957), London: Her Majesty's Stationery Office.

United Kingdom, HM Treasury (1999) 'Enterprise and social exclusion: national strategy for neighbourhood renewal: Policy Action Team 3'. London: Her Majesty's Stationery Office.

United Kingdom, HM Treasury (2001) 'Savings and assets for all', online, available at: http://www.hm-treasury.gov.uk/pdf/2001/savings_assets_2604.pdf.

United Kingdom, HM Treasury (2004) *Promoting financial inclusion: report of the financial inclusion task force*, London: HM Treasury, online, available at: http://www.hmtreasury.gov.uk/d/pbr04_profininc_complete_394.pdf.

United Kingdom, HM Treasury (2005) 'Credit union interest rate consultation', open letter by Financial Inclusion Taskforce, June, online, available at: http://financial.inclusion.taskforce@hm-treasury.gov.uk.

United Kingdom, HM Treasury (2007) 'Financial inclusion action plan 2008–11', London: Her Majesty's Stationery Office.

United Kingdom, HM Treasury (2010) 'Mainstreaming financial inclusion: dealing with financial distress: access to debt advice', online, available at: http://www.hm_treasury.gov.uk/d/fit_access_to_debt_advice.pdf.

United Kingdom, Office of the Deputy Prime Minister (2004) *Action on debt: why it matters and what you can do*, London: Stationery Office.

United Kingdom, Social Exclusion Unit (2000) *National strategy for neighbourhood renewal: a framework for consultation*, London: Social Exclusion Unit.

Van der Heijden, Eline, J. Nelissen, J. Potters and H. Verbon (1998) 'The poverty game and the pension game: the role of reciprocity', *Journal of Economic Psychology*, 19, 5–41.

Walker, Catherine (1996) 'Financial management, coping and debt in households under financial strain', *Journal of Economic Psychology*, 17, 789–807.

Watson, Duncan (2000) 'In search of the poor', *Journal of Economic Psychology*, 21, 495–515.

WEETU (Women's Employment Enterprise and Training Unit) (2005) 'WEETU: a social return on investment analysis', Norwich, 28 November, online, available at: http://www.weetu.org.

Whiteley, Paul (2000) 'Economic growth and social capital', *Political Studies*, 48, 443–466.

Woolcock, Michael (1998) 'Social capital and economic development: toward a theoretical synthesis and policy framework', *Theory and Society*, 27, 151–208.

Woolcock, Michael (1999) 'Learning from failures in microfinance', *American Journal of Economics and Sociology*, 58, 17–42.

Woolcock, Michael and Deepa Narayan (2000) 'Social capital: implications for development theory, research and policy', *World Bank Research Observer*, 15, 225–249.

World Bank (2000) *World Development Report 2000: attacking poverty*, Washington, DC: World Bank.

Index

References to material in the endnotes are in *italics*

2004 financial inclusion initiative 12, 136
3Bs *see* Black Business in Birmingham
  (3Bs)

administrative costs, of CDFIs 38–44
Advantage West Midlands 30, 115, 117,
  119
advice: to accompany loans 72, 76, 84, 87,
  150–1, 156; by church organisations
  100; to non-loan clients of CDFIs 33,
  105, 154, 156, 158–61, *196*; *see also*
  Citizens' Advice Bureaux (CABs); debt
  advice; mentoring; money advice
Afro Business Network 101
Afro-Caribbeans, as entrepreneurs 101,
  104, 108–9, 115, 117, 126–7
alcoholism 11, 73, 100
annual percentage rates (APRs) *see* interest
  rates
'architecture' of CDFIs: in figurative sense
  17, 25–6, 28, 31, 35–7, 42, 46, 53, 56,
  62, 155, *189*; in literal sense 34; *see also*
  distinctive capabilities; innovation;
  reputation; social capital
arrears, of CDFIs 13, 26, 32–3, 35, 38–46,
  117, 122, 154, *196*
Arrow Fund (West Midlands) 120–1
ART *see* Aston Reinvestment Trust (ART)
ASPIRE, Northern Ireland CDFI 6, 8, 79,
  93–4, 159, *186, 189*
assets 27–48, 69, 87, 153; 'asset-based'
  welfare policies 87, 132, 134–6;
  'relational assets' 69; *see also* physical
  capital; social capital
Aston Reinvestment Trust (ART), West
  Midlands CDFI 8, 38, 51, 101, 114–15,
  120, 127, 157, 159, 166, *194*

attitudes, of CDFI clients 54–5, 72–3, 81;
  see also coping strategies
attrition 19, 23

'baby bonds' *see* child tax credit
Baker, Andrew 30, *188*
Bangladeshis 121
banks: lending behaviour in low-income
  areas 2; relations with CDFIs 4, 139;
  Chapter 7 *passim*; relations with small
  enterprise clients 62; *see also* Barclays;
  HBOS; Royal Bank of Scotland
Bank Rakyat Indonesia (BRI) *187, 198*
Barclays Bank xiii, 31
Barmulloch Community Council
  (Glasgow) 94–7
Barr, Karen xv, 94–7
Belfast 10
benefits *see* welfare benefits
Beveridge, Sir William 1; 'five giants', 1,
  9, 47; report on *Social Insurance and
  Allied Services* (1942) 1, *184*; *see also*
  welfare state
Birmingham 17–18, 20, 49, 99, 108,
  111–28
Birmingham City Council 117
Birmingham Enterprise 115, 119, *196*
Blackburn 44, *197*
Black Business in Birmingham (3Bs),
  Birmingham CDFI 42, 51, 99, 117–19,
  159, 166, *190, 194*; *see also* Community
  Roots
Black Country Reinvestment Society
  (BCRS), West Midlands CDFI 38, 101,
  120–1, 127, 157, 159
Blair, Tony *186*
Bolivia 44

BRAC (Bangladesh Rural Advancement
    Committee) 24
Brown, Gordon 9, 135–6
buckfast tonic wine 11
burial societies *185*
Business Link 75, 166, 193
business loans, by CDFIs 9–10, 13, 31, 35,
    48–9, 51–2, 57–62, 66–71, 92–101,
    112–13, 137–8, 142, 149; *see also* 3Bs;
    ART; BCRS; Derby Loans; DSL;
    SENTA

Cameron, Leah xiv, 189
capitalisation costs, of CDFIs 38
carer's allowance 141, 144
charities 26, 39; *see also* voluntary
    organisations
child benefit 134, 144
child poverty 89, 136
Child Poverty Action Group 141
Child Tax Credit 134–6, 144
Christmas presents 69, 137, *190*
chronic poverty 2; *see also* poverty trap
churches, role in promoting community
    cohesion: Catholics and Protestants, in
    Northern Ireland 93–4; Catholics, in
    Glasgow 97–100, *193*; Muslim
    communities, in Birmingham and
    elsewhere 111–28; Pentacostalist
    churches, in Birmingham and elsewhere
    99, 127
Citizens' Advice Bureaux (CAB) 33, 75,
    78, 102–3
collateral 3, 7, 41–2, 154
community: adopted as buzzword by 1997
    Labour government 89; community
    cohesion, measures to promote, Chapter
    5 *passim*; involvement 73; *see also*
    social organisations; social capital
community associations 58
Community Development Finance
    Association (CDFA): data on CDFIs 14,
    187, 189; ethos 27, *186, 188*; 'Fantasy
    World Cup' 188; holiday-camp
    atmosphere *188*
Community Development Finance
    Institutions (CDFIs): data on 14; defined
    6; 'distinctive capabilities' (architecture,
    reputation and capacity for innovation)
    25, 27; historical origins 6–7, *190*;
    impact on health 63–6; impact on
    income 66–71; impact on public welfare
    spending, Chapter 6 *passim*; impact on
    small business development 57–62;

overall impact 10; Chapters 4–6 *passim*;
    publicity 35–7; *see also* business loans;
    microfinance; personal loans
Community Investment Tax Relief 89
Community Roots, Birmingham training
    organisation 99, 101, 108–9, 117–19
consumer loans, by CDFIs *see* personal
    loans
control groups 17–19, 48, 64
coping strategies 52, 54–7, 64, 72–3, 81,
    84, 112–13, *191*; *see also* debt,
    management of
costs, of CDFIs 13–14, 38–46
Council Tax Credit 144
Coventry and Warwickshire Reinvestment
    Trust 121
credit control 39, 41–4, 117, 154
'credit plus' 91
credit unions: defined 3; interest rates 3;
    historical origins 3, *185, 190*;
    relationships with CDFIs 29, 35–7,
    70–139; in Derby 29; in Glasgow 33,
    73, 96, 100, 109; in Northern Ireland 93;
    in Sheffield *see* Sheffield Credit Union;
    Sheffield Moneyline
crime 54, 95–7, *195*; *see also* vandalism
crises 52–7, 59–62, 98–9; *see also* shocks;
    coping strategies
'cycle of deprivation' *see* poverty trap

Deakin scale 64, *191*; *see also* coping
    strategies
debt: debt to assets ratio 56–8; difficulty of
    repaying out of benefits 4; increase
    during 1980s 2; link to poverty trap 12;
    Chapter 4 *passim* 105; management of
    58, 91; *see also* debt advice; risk
    efficacy
debt advice 33–4, 72, 76, 84, 87, 106–9,
    158–61, *189, 197*
default 53–4
delinquency *see* arrears
demographic shocks 81, 84, 87, 150–1
Department for Work and Pensions (DWP)
    35–7, 40, 42, 46; as sponsor of credit
    unions 12, 27–8, 31, *189*; Pathways to
    Work programme 135; *see also* Growth
    Fund; HM Treasury
deprivation, measurement of 22–4, 114,
    150, 194; *see also* poverty
Derby 12, 17–18, 59; *see also* Derby
    Loans
Derby Loans (after 2009; known as
    Midlands Community Finance) 12, 20,

24, 30–1, 35–6, 40–2, 45–6, 49–51, 53, 59, 63–6, 75, 88, 102–5, 109, 121, 127, 156, 158, 160
disability living allowance 140–1, 144
disabled people 60–1, 100, 108–9
discrimination, ethnic 115; *see also* racism
'distinctive capabilities' of business and voluntary organisations 25–8, 36–7, 46; *see also* architecture; innovation; Kay, John; reputation
divorce 53
domestic violence 34
Doncaster Business Advice Centre (DONBAC) 8
'doorstep lenders' 4–5, 11, 47, 62, 76–7, 105, 107–13, 125, 153, 160, 178, 181, *192*; interest rates 4–5; loan terms 5; *see also* home credit
DSL (Developing Strathclyde Ltd.), Scottish CDFI 6, 8, 11, 20, 28–9, 33, 36, 38, 42, 45, 49–51, 53, 62, 67–8, 75, 94–9, 157, 159
Duff, Kim xv, 94–7

Easterhouse, Glasgow suburb 11, 97–9, 141
East Lancashire Moneyline (ELM) 12, 17, 20, 28, 34–5, 37, 39–46, 74–5, 78, 129, 154, 156, 158–61
East Midlands Development Authority (EMDA) 30
economies of scale 39–44, 46; *see also* outreach; costs
education 47–8, 56, 97–9, 112–13, 150, 195; *see also* advice; mentoring; technical support; training
Employment and Support Allowance (ESA) 135
empowerment 47, 107, 110
entrepreneurship, by CDFIs 35–7, 59–62; social entrepreneurship by CDFI members 94–128; *see also* innovation; small business

Fair Finance Consortium (West Midlands) 120–1
Fair Finance, London CDFI *197*
Families' and Children's Survey 66
Field, Frank 2, 15, *184, 196*
financial exclusion 69, 91, 138
financial performance of CDFIs 13–14, 26, 33; Chapter 3 *passim*; *see also* arrears; costs; revenues; viability
Financial Inclusion South Yorkshire 31

Financial Services Authority 3, 26, 139, *188*
funeral clubs *see* burial societies

Gaskell, Elizabeth *185*
Gibson, John xv
Glasgow 11–12, 17–18, 21, 28, 74, 94–9, *187*; *see also* DSL; local economic development companies (LEDCs); Scotcash
Glasgow Caledonian University *157, 186, 192, 197*
Glasgow City Council 33, 62, 88, 158–9
Glasgow Housing Association (GHA) 33, 94–7, 158, 160, 193, 195
Goggin, Niamh xiv, *186*; *see also* ASPIRE
Government (UK central): role in establishing CDFIs 33; *see also* Department for Work and Pensions; Treasury
Grameen Bank 13, 24, 39, 79, 85, 125, 128, 155, *186–7, 190, 192, 197*; *see also* Yunus, Muhammad
Grameen Foundation 190, 197
Greaves, Fiona xiv, *189*
group lending *see* solidarity groups
'Growth Fund' 12, 31–2, 36–7, *188–9, 196, 198*; *see also* Department for Work and Pensions (DWP); HM Treasury

Halal Fund 114, 119–24, 156, *195*
Handsworth, Birmingham 111
HBOS (Halifax Bank of Scotland) 102, 156, 159, 161, 198
Health 47, 54, 60, 63–6, 87; as determinant of small business performance 53, 60; shocks to health 76, 84, 87; *see also* health-seeking behaviour
health-seeking behaviour 47, 63
Hirschman, Albert 162
holidays 69, *190*
home credit 4; *see also* doorstep lenders
housing benefit 140, 144
housing finance 11, 34; *see also* mortgages
housing tenure 48, 106, 108–9, 111
Hughes, Jane xiv
Hulme, David 21
human capital 47, 54, 97–9, 162; *see also* education; health; training
Hussain, Javed xv

incapacity benefit 141, 144
incentives 34–7, 46; *see also* architecture of CDFIs; innovation

income, personal 47–8, 51, 83;
    'equivalised' income defined 49
income support 138, 141, 144
Index of Multiple Deprivation 83, 150–1
Indonesia *190, 197; see also* Bank Rakyat
    Indonesia
Indians, in Birmingham 111–28; *see also*
    Sikh gurdwara
information technology 34, 54–5, *189*
innovation, in CDFIs 25–6, 28, 36–7, 46
insurance 41, 54; of house contents 33
interest rates: annual percentage rates
    (APR) 38, 45; 'break-even' 38–41, *189*;
    charged by CDFIs 32–3, 35; charged by
    'doorstep lenders' 4; charged by loan
    sharks 3–4, *185*
Italy 107, 110

Jackson, Helen xiii
Jobseekers' Allowance 133, 138, 140–1,
    144
Joseph Rowntree Foundation 70, 80, 90,
    190, 194

Kay, John 17, 25, *187*
Kurdish community, in Derby and
    Birmingham 104, 127, *195*

labour markets 24, 70, 76–7, 81, 97–9
Lancaster, Eunice xiv, 29, *188*
'lifestyle businesses' 50, 118, 152
livelihoods 52; *see also* well-being
loan delinquency *see* arrears
loan sharks 3–4, 34, 47, 84–5, 107, *185*
local economic development companies
    (LEDCs; now Regeneration Agencies),
    Glasgow 29, 94–7, 157, *193*

Mackay, Rob xiv, *189, 194*
Macpherson, Sharon xiii
MacVicar, Jim xv
malnutrition 63–5
Manchester 3, *185, 195*
mentoring 56–7, 72, 108–9, 119–24, 155
microfinance 7, 154; historical antecedents
    of *190*; in Britain *see* community
    development finance institutions
    (CDFIs); in developing countries 13, 39,
    41, *186*; in other European countries
    131, *190*; in US 44, *187, 190; see also*
    Bank Rakyat Indonesia; BRAC; SEWA
Midlands Community Finance *see* Derby
    Loans
mobile phones 42, 59

money advice 31, *188, 192*
Moneyline Yorkshire *see* Sheffield
    Moneyline
mortgages 34

National Health Service 1
National Provident, home credit company
    4–5, 35, 72, 78–9, 100, 102–3, 112–13,
    175, 182, *188, 192*
neighbourhoods 90, 107; *see also*
    community; Joseph Rowntree
    Foundation; social capital
Newcastle upon Tyne 4
New Deal for Communities 91, *193*
New Deal (Labour Party 1997–2010) 9,
    133–4, 139
New Jerusalem Church (Birmingham) 99,
    114, 127, 166, *195; see also* churches,
    pentecostalist
Nigeria 101, 104
noisy neighbours 100
non-profit organisations 26; *see also*
    charities; voluntary organisations
Normanton, Derby neighbourhood 30,
    104, 141
Northern Ireland 93–4

Office for National Statistics (ONS) 64,
    184
Open University 103, 109
Osmaston Information Centre (Derby)
    105, 110, 129
outreach, of CDFIs 25, 46
overdues *see* arrears

Pakistani community, in Derby and
    Birmingham 103–4, 111–28, *195*
Parent-teacher associations 73
Parker, Don xv
partnerships 53–4
pawnbrokers 3
peer-monitoring 7, 106
personal guarantees 42
personal loans (often referred to as
    'consumer loans') by CDFIs 11, 13,
    31–5, 48–9, 63–71, 101–13, 137–8, 142,
    145, 157, 162
Phoenix Fund, government fund for
    business CDFIs 10, 30, 89, 117, 136,
    140, *186*
Piachaud, David 2, 15
Pollock, Nicola xiii
'postcode discrimination' 94, *184; see also*
    financial exclusion

poverty: definition of 1, 47; food poverty 63; incidence by locality *194*; in developing countries 13, 39, 41; in relation to uptake of welfare benefits 146–9; time pattern (1960s to present) 5–6; transitions out of poverty 56–7, 64, 69–89; *see also* deprivation; financial exclusion; poverty line; poverty trap; vulnerability

poverty line 2, 48, 52–3, 64, 69; *see also* Rowntree, Seebohm; Beveridge, (Lord) William; World Bank

'poverty trap' 2, 15, 50–1; strategies for escaping from 71–89; *see also* Field, Frank

Powell, Sallie xiv

Prince's Trust 120–1

probit estimation, of escape from poverty 81

'progressive lending' 154

public goods 87, 158

publicity, by CDFIs *see* CDFIs; entrepreneurship

Putnam, Robert 85, 89–91, 106–10, 128

qualitative methods 48

quasi-experiments 19

racism 96, 111–27; *see also* ethnic minorities

rationality, of coping strategies 64, *191*

recession, in UK 2007–9, 13, 48, 66, 104, 118, 153, 160

redistribution 89

Red Road flats, Glasgow 94–7, *193–4*

Regeneration Agencies (Glasgow) *see* local economic development companies (LEDCs)

Regional Development Authorities (RDAs) 13, 30, 32, 46, 153; *see also* Advantage West Midlands; East Midlands Development Authority (EMDA)

religion *see* churches

reputation, of CDFIs 25, 27, 46, 73, 183, *192*

risk 52–7, 63, 66, 108–9

rotating savings and credit associations (roscas) 103, 105–6, 109, 124–5

Rowntree, B *see* bohm *186*, 1899 poverty survey *184*, 1936 poverty survey *184*, 1950 poverty survey 1, *184*

Royal Bank of Scotland (RBS) 27, 33, 156, 158–9, 161

St Wilfrid's Day Care Centre (Sheffield) 103, 180

Salford Moneyline 27, 29, 159

sampling 19, 22–4

savings 35, 37, 64, 76, 85, 150–1, 154, 156, 158–61, 182, 192; as correlate of exit from poverty 71–89; by CDFI clients 25, 75–7; by credit unions 3; concept of saving used in our survey 83; in developing countries 25, *185*; in relation to viability of CDFIs 44; Savings Gateway 136, 140, 155, 162, *196*

savings mobilisation 33

Scotcash 12, 20, 30, 32–5, 37, 39–42, 45, 49–50, 63–8, 100, 102, 109, 128–9, 154, 156, 158–61, *191*, *194*, *196–7*

selection bias 81

self-employment 57–62, 64, 132, 139, *195*; *see also* labour market

Sen, A.K. 69, 135

SEWA (Ahmedabad, India) *194*

Sharia loans 115, 118, *195*

Sheffield 4, 17–19

Sheffield City Council 32

Sheffield Credit Union 31–2, 74–5, 128, *188*, *198*; *see also* Sheffield Moneyline

Sheffield Enterprise Agency (SENTA), former Yorkshire CDFI 8

Sheffield Moneyline 31–2, 35, 40–2, 45, 49–50, 63–8, 74–5, 88, 102, 109, 128, 158, *188*, *197–8*; *see also* Shelton, Alec xiv

shocks 52–7, 59–62, 64, 72, 81, 87, 98–9, *191*; *see also* crises; coping strategies

Shorebank, US CDFI 160

Sikh gurdwara, Birmingham 114–15, 124

small businesses 10, 50–2, 56, 94–104, 114, 129; *see also* microenterprises; CDFI business loans

Small Firms Loan Guarantee (SFLG) scheme, operated by UK Department of Trade and Industry 29, 38, 41, 94

smoking 63–5

social capital 26, 55, 72–3, 76–7, 80, 84–5, 106, 128, 149, 153, 162; among ethnic minorities 115–28; 'bad' 91–2; 'bonding' 26, 90–1, 104, 108–9, 126–7; 'bridging' 33, 90–1, 94, 101, 104–9, 120, 126–7; creation of within communities 92–128; our definition 193; *see also* architecture (of CDFIs); community cohesion

social care 99, 108–9, 127
'social Darwinism' 89
social enterprises 11, 14, 97, *188*
Social Exclusion Unit, established by UK
    government in 1997 9, 89
Social Fund (government small-loan fund)
    160
social networks *see* social capital
social organisations *191*; *see also* social
    capital
solidarity groups 41–2, 79; *see also*
    microfinance
solvency, of CDFIs 38
South Coast Moneyline (Portsmouth) 27,
    38, 40, 42, 159–60
Sparkbrook, Birmingham 111, 124–5,
    129–30
spin-offs, from CDFI clients to others 24
sponsorship, of CDFIs 44–5
Sri Lanka (Federation of Thrift and Co-op
    Societies) *198*
state *see* government
strategic assets *see* distinctive capabilities
Street UK 121, 128, 159, *189*; *see also*
    Salford Moneyline
'sub-prime financial organisations':
    defined 3; *see also* doorstep lenders;
    home credit; loan sharks; pawnbrokers
subsidy 15, 88; *see also* financial
    performance; viability
subsidy dependence index 44–5; *see also*
    viability
Sure Start 9, 75
survival, of firms 52, 57–62
sustainability, financial *see* viability

tax credits 34; Chapter 6 passim; *see also*
    Child Tax Credit; Working (Families')
    Tax Credit
technical support, for CDFIs 56–7,
    119–24, 155
Thatcher, Margaret 2, 89
Tolstoy, Leo 53
training 97–9, 108–9, 178
(Her Majesty's) Treasury 9–10, *187*, *189*
trust 90, 106–13, *194*; *see also* social
    capital

Udenze, Paul xiv
unemployment 5–6, 47, 119, 132, 137,
    139, *184*
Universal Credit 152, 160
urban poverty, mapping of 17–18; *see also*
    deprivation; poverty

vandalism 54
viability (financial sustainability) of CDFIs
    13–14, 38–45, *190*
vodka 11
voluntary organisations Chapter 5 *passim*
    194; *see also* Barmulloch Community
    Council; Osmaston Information Centre;
    St Wilfrid's Day Centre (Sheffield)
vulnerability 47, 94–7, *185*

Waddell, Linsay xiv
Walker, Steve xiv
Watson, Patricia xv, 57–8, 60–1
websites 54–5; *see also* information
    technology
welfare benefits 11, 48, 64, 81, 105, 153;
    Chapter 6 *passim*; impact of CDFIs on
    137–52; *see also* welfare state
welfare state 7, 11, *184*; Beveridge's report
    on 1, *184*; impact of CDFIs on 137–52
well-being 47; *see also* income; assets;
    health; education; empowerment;
    vulnerability
Wellpark Enterprise Centre, Glasgow 6, 8,
    186
Women, as clients of microfinance
    institutions and CDFIs 7, *185*
Women's Employment, Enterprise and
    Training Unit (WEETU), East Anglian
    CDFI 8–9, *186*, *190*, *193*
Working (Families') Tax Credit 9, 133–4,
    140–1, 143–6, 150–2, *196*
World Bank: 'dollar-a-day' poverty
    measure *185*; World Development
    Report 2000 90
worry 66

Yorkshire Moneyline *see* Sheffield
    Moneyline
Yunus, Muhammad 7